To mike

Thank you,

Danielle
Kennedy

Advance Praise for
Selling
The Danielle Kennedy Way
by Danielle Kennedy

"If you have the desire to reach your full potential in sales, you'll find the value of the material in this book to be incalculable. It's a "must-read" for anyone committed to a career in selling. Danny has the unique ability to teach in such a way that you don't realize how much you're learning because you enjoy it so much."

> **Tom Hopkins, CPAE**
> **World Renowned Sales Trainer**
> **Author of: *How To Master The Art of Selling***

"No one can sell, like Danielle! I'm sold on this book ... you will be, too."

> **Dr. Denis Waitley, author**
> ***The Psychology of Winning***

"It's loaded with tons of fresh selling tips and best of all—it's User Friendly. All I can say is, I sure hope none of my competitors read it."

> **Stew Leonard**
> **Stew Leonard's, The World's Largest Dairy Store**

"Danielle Kennedy has written a sales book from the heart. I know her common sense approach to instinctive salesmanship works, because she and I have been successfully practicing these principles all our lives. Her down to earth approach is a breath of fresh air in an era when sales "How To" books are sometimes overwritten and technocratic."

> **Judi Sheppard Missett**
> **Founder, CEO**
> **Jazzercise, Inc.**

"*Selling: The Danielle Kennedy Way* is not another one of those bromide-filled theoretical sales books; it doesn't instruct you to parrot back some pat, artificial-sounding manipulative ploys. Danielle Kennedy shows all sales professionals how to tap their most valuable assets: personal intuition and instinct. Don't fall for any of those hackneyed, trite collections of slick tricks—put Kennedy's authentic, reality-based strategies to work and unleash your own true personal powers. Your customers will love you for it. The book will help you feel much better about your selling, will make your customers want to talk with you, and yes, will make you a great deal of money."

> **George R. Walther, CPAE**
> **Author of *Phone Power* and *Power Talking***

"One of today's most notable salespersons and lecturers, Danielle Kennedy has hit the mark again with this book. This step-by-step guide to selling gives the most inexperienced salesperson the tools, and more importantly, the confidence to sell like a seasoned pro."

"A talented sales speaker, Danielle Kennedy has put her vast selling experience and skill into one easy-to-read book. The few dollars and hours invested in this book are sure to bring years of success and profit."

"Danielle Kennedy reveals her array of pragmatic selling approaches and everyday practices that will lead even the most inexperienced salesperson straight to the bank."

Jimmy Calano, CEO
CareerTrack

"Everyone wants the 'Midas Touch'—you have it now in your hands. *Selling: The Danielle Kennedy Way* will be the single most important and effective way to quick-start your selling career, enhance your existing selling career and make your selling career mushroom to dimensions you haven't even conceived of! This is the salespersons' Bible—read it, write in it and don't loan it out."

Judith Briles, author of
The Confidence Factor and Woman To Woman
Media Personality/Talk Show Host

"This book is a unique and wonderful contribution to the art of professional selling. Danielle Kennedy has brought together a remarkable blend of practical insights and skills combined with a sensitive knowledge of personal emotions and character. Every sales professional should have this book as a part of their permanent reading libraries."

Brian Tracy, CPAE
Brian Tracy Learning Systems
Author of: "Psychology of Achievement"

"Brimming with common sense, this book is like a dinner conversation with an experienced mentor with fresh vision for selling. Danielle is a marvelous individual and a proven sales person who has not only had to develop her sales techniques and practice them, but has had to live with the consequences of her decisions over the past twenty years. One terrific lady and book!"

Kathryn G. Thompson
Chairman/CEO
Kathryn G. Thompson Development Company

"Health and fitness is our life's work and passion. We "sell" our message every day and we use the philosophies of Danielle Kennedy when we do it. Her book is the *best* on selling!"

Kathie and Peter Davis
Co-Founders of International Dance and
Exercise Association and American Council
on Exercise

"It looks like America's Mother of Sales Development may have written the mother of all sales books. *Selling: The Danielle Kennedy Way* is a very readable, extremely entertaining guide for anyone who is or wants to be in sales. It's packed with specific, useful ideas for everyone from the beginner to the seasoned pro. From the platform or the printed page, Danielle Kennedy's greatest gift is her genuineness. You'll laugh as you learn. Don't pass this one up."

Michael LeBoeuf
Author of: *How To Win Customers and Keep Them for Life*

"Danielle Kennedy has written a most *readable* book—highly informative with a personal touch. Her own voice comes through in a book that is articulate, clear, and entertaining. She makes selling an interesting subject for everyone."

Noel Riley Fitch
Author of: *Sylvia Beach and the Lost Generation:
A History of Literary Paris in the Twenties and Thirties*

"Danielle Kennedy has written a book we can use *right now* at Discovery Toys. Her philosophy and methods of selling are some of the most original and creative ideas of this century."

Lane Nemeth, President
Discovery Toys

"I didn't intend to buy this book; I was looking for a half-price cat calendar. But, the young sales woman I met was so enthusiastic, so helpful and so professional about recommending *Selling: The Danielle Kennedy Way* that I left the store with ten copies. It was only after reading the book that I realized she'd used Ms. Kennedy's techniques to sell me those books!"

"Fun, well constructed and full of the art and heart of selling. (And, she's written a pretty good book, too)."

"This excellent book is written by a woman who is intelligent, funny, attractive, wealthy, and a splendid teacher. I hate her."

"A superb book on how to sell without hocking your soul and making a pact with the devil. This is an approach to sales that can increase your income without decreasing your self respect. It probably won't do that well."

"I've seen hundreds of speakers come and go; and, I think, Danielle was one of them."

"Danielle's remarkably successful approach is full of warmth, joy and success for both the buyer and the seller."

"She knows how to avoid sacrificing family, friends, love and laughter in order to be successful. And in this book, she shares not only the secrets to her professional success, but to her personal happiness as well. Read it so you don't have to weep."

> **C. W. Metcalf**
> **Author of the Video & Audio Series**
> **"Humor, Risk & Change"™**
> **Educator, Performer, Lecturer, Management**
> **Consultant, Shoe Salesman**

"Danielle, your book is a winner! Anyone who reads Danielle Kennedy's book, internalizes the skills shared and starts selling the Danielle Kennedy way, will gain enormous rewards. I have admired Danielle Kennedy's incredible energy level and great speaking skills for many years. Now it is my pleasure to applaud this tremendous book."

> **Don Hutson, CPAE**
> **Author of:** *High Performance Selling*
> **Co-Author of:** *Insights Into Excellence*
> **Cavett Award Winner**

"Selling today is about taking care of customers, building long-term relationships, and a major commitment to service. Danielle Kennedy shows anyone in sales exactly how to sell by becoming a true partner with their clients."

> **Barry J. Farber**
> **President**
> **Farber Training Systems, Inc.**
> **Co-Author of:** *Breakthrough Selling: Customer Building*
> *Strategies From the Best in the Business*

"There is in Danielle Kennedy's writing an energy, a passion, that freights her message every bit as persuasively as the message itself. If she's selling, I'm sold."

> **Digby Wolfe**
> **USC Professor,**
> **Multiple Emmy Award Nominee & Winner**

"Danielle Kennedy has elevated the business of selling to a blend of art and science. Like the most gifted artists, she learned early on to trust her inner voice, with self-confidence and success as the natural extensions of instinct, intuition and education. Equal parts engaging anecdotes and sage how-to advice, *Selling* is a witty, incisive and useful primer on striking a balance in one's life as well as in one's work. The down-to-earth lessons taught here—creative approaches to problem-solving, effective communication—are as practical as they are inspiring."

Alex Szekely, President
Golden Door and Rancho La Puerta
Fitness Resorts, Inc.

"All salesmen, whether they are new in the profession or veterans, at times will go through a "slump." This book should get any salesman out of the "slump" and back on the road to success."

Chandler B. Barton
Chairman and Chief Executive Officer
Coldwell Banker

"Danielle is truly a legend in her own time. Her story will capture your attention. She is a role model for me and many other Superstar Sales Professionals. Make her your role model!"

Tom Winninger, CPAE, CSP
President, National Speakers Association

"Danielle Kennedy is one of the most dynamic women I know. Her success in selling emanates from her own experiences in self-motivation, in communication, and in self-confidence. She is a highly respected international speaker and writer who has turned her own successes into messages that offer hope and optimism for thousands. Reading her book is a must for everyone in today's workplace."

Catherine Dunn, BVM, Ph.D.
President, Clarke College
Dubuque, Iowa

"If Danielle Kennedy sez it, you can print it. It'll work. Read this volume and experience new paradigms."

Ty Boyd, CPAE
Author of: *Visions: From the Leaders of Today*
For the Leaders of Tomorrow

"Danielle's honest and intuitive approach to selling is refreshingly apparent on these pages. She is a teacher ... and to anyone in the field of sales, this book should become required reading."

Flavia Weedn
Artist, Writer, Designer

"Danny's book is a reminder of how natural we were when we first started selling. It is so easy to get caught up in 'the business' and forget how important it is to be passionate once again for our products."

Shirley Pepys
President
Noel Joanna, Inc.

"There is no other sales trainer with more credibility, practicality and likability than Danielle Kennedy. If you are committed to a more productive future you must read this book. I attended Danielle Kennedy's first talk, and have been learning from her ever since. It is impossible to listen or to read Danielle's practical and proven ideas and not be more successful."

Patricia Fripp, CSP, CPAE
Author of: *Get What You Want*

"When I want to learn about selling and learn it right, I want the teacher to be someone who has done it and done it *big time!* But at the same time, I want that teacher to show me how to build a loyal clientele that will keep me in the selling business for years to come. In this book, Danielle Kennedy *more* than fulfills these requirements. It's a winner! Hands down."

Danny Cox, CPAE
Professional Speaker/Trainer

"A veritable encyclopedia of selling how-to's. Danielle has assembled state of the art selling know how and laced it with original and fresh approaches. It will pull you out of any slump and catapult you on the road to success."

Jane and Bob Handly
Authors of: "Why Women Worry"
"Getting Unstuck"
"Beyond Fear"
"Anxiety and Panic Attacks, Their Cause and Cure"

"Danielle Kennedy epitomizes someone who started with natural talent and then, with dedication and determination, made the talent blossom into something glorious and permanent and inspiring to millions of people. The "permanent" may be the biggest challenge for any achiever . . . success recedes so quickly . . . but Danielle keeps *honing* her talent, finding different ways for it to be realized and I expect that will be true of her when she is 90."

> **Pat McCormick**
> **Four Time Olympic Gold Medalist**
> **Athlete Olympic Consulting**

"This is a great book for anyone who wants to learn a lot of selling savvy. I recommend it wholeheartedly."

> **Nido R. Qubein, CPAE**
> **Chairman of Creative Services, Inc.**
> **High Point, NC**

"This book has powerful messages expressed with the divinity of simplicity. The substance is entertaining and illustrated with convincing stories."

> **Cavett Robert, CPAE**
> **Founder of National Speakers Association**
> **Sixty years as one of America's top sales trainers**

"Danielle Kennedy is one of the most successful sales motivators in the nation. For years, I've heard audiences rave about the value of her speeches and ideas. Her message says 'hard work, think smart and show that you care.'"

> **Jim Cathcart, CSP, CPAE**
> **Author of:** *Relationship Selling*

"This is a fascinating, highly readable study on the selling process. I've always felt that good manners, a thorough knowledge of the product or service and a commitment to truth will beat slick strategies every time.

I wish that the book had been available when I started in the selling business *sixty* years ago. It would have saved me a lot of time!"

> **Bill Gove, CPAE**
> **1st President of the National Speakers Association**
> **Recipient Golden Gavel Award—1991**

"Danielle is one of the most outstanding speakers I have ever heard. She combines energy and enthusiasm with workable ideas for increased sales. Her leadership skills will empower you to achieve even greater success."

Rita Davenport, CSP
Lecturer and Author of "Making Time–Making Money"

"This book will triple the selling success of anyone who acts on Danielle's powerful program. Her own life provides undisputed evidence that these dynamic principles work in the real world of selling. *Selling: The Danielle Kennedy Way* is a must read!"

Glenna Salsbury, CSP, CPAE
Salsbury Enterprises
Professional Speaker & Consultant

"The thing that sets this great book apart from most sales books is that it is written by a highly successful, practicing salesperson who has earned the right to give advice to her peers. There is no theory here. Any salesperson who doesn't read this book is underprivileged."

D. John Hammond
President
American Motivational Association

"*Selling: The Danielle Kennedy Way* is *the* sales book of the 90's."

John Dolan, Attorney at Law
Author of *Negotiate Like the Pros*

SELLING
The Danielle Kennedy Way

Danielle Kennedy

PRENTICE HALL
Englewood Cliffs, New Jersey 07632

Prentice-Hall International (UK) Limited, *London*
Prentice-Hall of Australia Pty. Limited, *Sydney*
Prentice-Hall Canada, Inc., *Toronto*
Prentice-Hall Hispanoamericana, S.A., *Mexico*
Prentice-Hall of India Private Limited, *New Delhi*
Prentice-Hall of Japan, Inc., *Tokyo*
Simon & Schuster of Asia Pte. Ltd., *Singapore*
Editora Prentice-Hall do Brasil, Ltda., *Rio de Janeiro*

© 1991 *by*

PRENTICE-HALL, Inc.

Englewood Cliffs, NJ

10 9 8 7 6 5 4 3 2 1

Library of Congress Cataloging-in-Publication Data

Kennedy, Danielle.
  Selling—the Danielle Kennedy way / by Danielle Kennedy.
    p.   cm.

  Includes index.
  ISBN 0-13-803727-2
  1. Real estate business.   2. —Real estate agents.   I. Title.
HD1375.K396   1991
333.33'068'8—dc20   91-22045
                                                                      CIP

ISBN 0-13-803727-2

PRENTICE HALL
Business Information & Publishing Division
Englewood Cliffs, NJ 07632
Simon & Schuster. A Paramount Communications Company

To Grampa Dan

"Vision is the art of seeing things invisible."

Jonathan Swift

Introduction

Who would have guessed when I was 27 years old, flat broke, and expecting my fifth child, that I would launch a legendary sales career? It all started in my kitchen. I had a 25-food cord on my telephone. This allowed me to talk to a prospect, feed a baby a bottle of milk, and walk over to the stove to stir the spaghetti. My first goal was to be able to buy food. I remember walking into the grocery store with two or three children and holding a half empty change purse, praying I could stretch the money to pay for the groceries.

I hated those moments in my life. I dreamed of buying a 22 cubic foot freezer, filling it to the brim, and never having to be humiliated in a grocery store again. After 11 months in sales, I owned a well-stocked freezer.

For the next 10 years, I door-knocked and cold-called my way to financial freedom, rising to the top 1% of all salespeople in my 500,000 member industry. The kitchen pantry shelves were lined with gigantic trophies and framed sales awards along with all the food my growing family could eat.

I consistently sold 100 homes a year and kept that record up until I opened my own multi-office brokerage firm in the mid-1970s. As a business owner, I recruited and developed a 100-person sales force which eventually held the number one market share position in our city.

My track record in sales propelled me into a third career—the lecture circuit. Everyone wanted to know how a woman with five children and no formal training was able to sell in the millions. They started calling me an expert and a major publisher asked me to write a book on the subject.

I could hardly keep up with the demands of speaking engagements, selling, raising a family, and running a business. In 1980, I decided to concentrate on becoming a master sales educator and selling my methodology. I sold my sales company, started Danielle Kennedy Productions and began travelling full time across North America, Canada, and Australia.

Five thousand salespeople began to listen to my message each month. I received glowing progress reports from these students, telling me that my methods changed their production dramatically. Many of them started earning in excess of a half a million dollars a year.

I developed educational materials, including an extensive video and audio library of how tos, workbooks, and time planning systems. My company's impressive annual earnings prove that salespeople repeatedly buy my products because they get results. Are you impressed with my credentials so far? I hope so, because no matter what product, service, idea, or talent you represent, I want you to be impressed enough to buy this book, which is divided into four valuable parts: **Personal Power, Business Development, Appointments,** and **Service.** Inside its pages you will see how I have interacted with people in a very clear, down-to-earth, and powerful, but non-manipulative, style. My "closing the sale" dialogues have been developed over my lifetime and they are based on human emotion, benefits, and facts, not pressure and guilt. You will find them refreshing and easy to transfer to your own personal set of selling principles and practices.

Nothing compares to the unique way I develop business. I promise I can chase your "call-reluctance" away with some of the most creative and attention-getting telephone and in-person dialogues that you have ever heard. My "phone home" conversations can turn any stranger into a helper.

Are you having problems making regular calls in your territory? The "Progressive Network Step-up Program" in Chapter Four will get you working your territory the smart way, double both your income and pleasure, and give the competition insomnia.

Do you know how to sell your ideas in writing? I can develop a personal promotion crusade for you.

Do you wish you could interview customers as skillfully as Larry King or Connie Chung? I can and I will be glad to show you how.

Are you struggling to bail out of a sales slump? My "Twelve Step Recovery Program" will get some money back in your bank account fast.

Are you disgusted with yourself because you waste time? My "Vision Planning" program guarantees to assist you with personal self-control and time management.

I have never treated selling like a game and customers as players. The sound of words like "ploy" and "technique" make me feel uncomfortable. Selling is an art. When we do it right the communication becomes very creative. The customer's needs are always changing, which challenges us to formulate new solutions for them. When we work from the highest part of our intelligence to the bottom of our heart, our customers begin to trust our judgment.

Selling is also scientific. You have to study yourself and others closely in order to know what methods work. Over the years, I came to realize that some things that looked easy could be very difficult to master. The naturalness and ease that a dancer, writer, scientist, or entrepreneur demonstrates to the world come from trial and error, awkward experiments and movements, and painstaking efforts. Part of the science of selling is keeping a written journal of progress. As we write and reflect, we learn how to separate ourselves from our customers and their problems. This detachment gives us a sense of inner freedom that allows us to present more options to them based on their needs rather than our own self-serving motives.

In Chapter One, I give you a simple formula to create a sales journal which you can convert into a treasury of money-making concepts and dialogues.

The simple act of selling requires a committed and disciplined lifestyle. It demands that you study and analyze the ever-changing marketplace; work hard and long hours prospecting and interviewing worthy candidates for your product and service; ask courageously, but courteously, to close the sale and follow up on every aspect of that agreement; stay healthy and balanced as a human being. Not one of these can be forgotten or eliminated. If it is, selling becomes unnatural and extremely uncomfortable and the rewards are few.

My love for the selling life borders on the fanatic. I think our country is built on the selling skills of talented individuals who developed their "sell-to-survive instinct" into a state-of-the-art form of communication. I call that method "natural selling" and I teach thousands of salespeople how to become wealthy putting its principles into practice.

This book is a "how-to-sell memoir" that I promise will serve you well. It will not only develop your selling sense and skills, but increase those natural highs that only this profession bestows on those who serve their customers passionately. Now, turn the page and let's get started.

Danielle Kennedy

Acknowledgments

The simple "thank you" doesn't cover it, but here goes:

My mentor and teacher—Noel Riley Fitch, professor of advanced non-fiction at the University of Southern California. I hate your red pencil but I love you.

My writing cronies at USC in the Masters In Professional Writing Program—Ann Seaman, Gwyn Erwin, Jack Jaacks, DeDe Shuff. I treasure your friendships and enormous talents.

My friend Viki King—You showed me how to write from the heart.

Tom Hopkins—Thanks for your continued faith in my abilities.

Nadine Trammell, my "fifth" daughter who saved my life with her typing talents on the last mile home.

Dixie Robilio—A woman for all seasons. What would I do without you?

Jennifer Shanahan, you put the icing on the cake.

My editor at Prentice Hall—Ellen Schneid Coleman—You know how to read my mind, and I often need an interpreter.

Mama Rose—All things are possible for me, because of you.

The Big Kids—You understand how weird I get when I am writing. Thanks for laughing at me and making me laugh too. The Little Big Kid, Kathleen—Thanks for asking for hugs every fifteen minutes.

Captain Mike—Your insights, highly-developed sell-sense, love, and support made this book a reality.

Contents

PERMISSIONS

Chapter 1:
> Wynn Davis, *The Best of Success,* Great Quotations, Inc., Lombard, IL, 1988, page 219 (Arthur Schopenhauer).

Chapter 2:
> Wynn Davis, *The Best of Success,* Great Quotations, Inc., Lombard, IL, 1988, page 325 (Joseph Murphy).

Chapter 4:
> Woody Allen, as quoted in *Speaker's Library of Business Stories, Anecdotes and Humor;* Joe Griffith; Prentice Hall, Englewood Cliffs, NJ, 1990, page 339.

Chapter 5:
> Diana Hacker, *A Writer's Reference,* St. Martin's Press, Inc., 1989, page 22. Reprinted by permission of St. Martin's Press.

Chapter 7:
> Wynn Davis, *The Best of Success,* Great Quotations, Inc., Lombard, IL, 1988, page 82 (Raymond Holliwell).

Chapter 9:
> Father Theodore Hesburgh, *God, Country, Notre Dame,* Doubleday, 1990, page 302.

Chapter 11:
> Wynn Davis, *The Best of Success,* Great Quotations, Inc., Lombard, IL, 1988, page 106 (Orison Swett Marden).

Chapter 12:
> "Mother to Son" From SELECTED POEMS by Langston Hughes, Copyright 1926 by Alfred A. Knopf, Inc. and renewed 1954 by Langston Hughes. Reprinted by permission of the publisher.

Part One

TAP YOUR PERSONAL POWER

1 The Power Base of Natural Selling: Instinct, Intuition, and Education

---

"We forfeit three-fourths of ourselves in order to be like other people."

ARTHUR SCHOPENHAUER

Selling is in my genes. I have no medical proof, but it makes sense to me because of my heritage. My grandparents (on both sides of the family) came on a boat to America over 100 years ago from Naples, Italy, and County Cork, Ireland, to seek opportunity—jobs, homes, spouses, and a new way of life. If this wasn't prospecting in a strange new territory, what is? With very little education they made their dreams of living in this country come true. This courageous legacy was passed down to my parents and now to me.

DEVELOP YOUR CRITICAL SELL-TO-SURVIVE INSTINCT

There are numerous definitions of the word "selling," but my favorite is from the *Random House Dictionary*, "to cause or persuade to accept." My grandparents persuaded people to accept them in order to find work, shelter, and food. Without formal sales training, they convinced people they could work and be of service. They followed their raw "sell to survive" instincts in order to get what they needed.

My "sell to survive" instinct has come in handy, both on and off the job. A few years ago, I was lecturing in another country and, in my usual fashion, I rushed back to the airport five minutes after I finished. When I arrived, I was told that the airlines went on strike and my ticket home was no longer valid.

The first thing I did was prospect all over the airport to see if there was anybody flying out who could give me a ride. The terminal was deserted and I was just about to give up hope when suddenly, a band of people showed up carrying suitcases and heading for the gate. I followed them and eavesdropped on their conversation.

"As soon as we get there, I am playing Black Jack."

"Not me. I love Keno."

My instincts told me the time was right to start selling myself. I walked up to a friendly-looking woman and said, "Where are you going?"

"Las Vegas."

My heart leaped, but I remained calm and asked, "What's happening there?"

"Our association is going down to see the MGM 500."

I thought to myself, "Here is my ride." Once I get to Las Vegas, I can figure out how to get to Orange County, California.

I looked at her and said, "I have a terrible problem. I just gave a lecture here and have a return ticket to my home in California, but the ticket is no longer valid because of the strike. My husband and eight children are waiting for me. If I could fly to Las Vegas with your group, I could pay for the ticket by mail once I get home."

"We would love to have you join us, but I think all the seats have been reserved. If someone cancels, maybe you can take their place. But you will just have to stand here by the gate and wait to see who doesn't show up."

I watched over 200 people board the chartered "Fun Flight" to Las Vegas. I almost gave up hope, but then the organizer came up to me and announced, "You can go on the plane. One person canceled at the last minute."

We arrived in Las Vegas around midnight and I thanked the friendliest people I have ever met for the lift. I called my family, reported my newest location and told them I would most likely be stuck in Las Vegas until the next day.

Around one o'clock in the morning, I saw a plane come out of nowhere in the sky. The plane landed on the same runway as my Las Vegas charter. Two men stepped out and when they walked into the waiting area, I found out they were from Orange County. The pilot had been hired to fly the other guy to Las Vegas.

I overheard him say he had to fly back immediately, but he was so tired he was hoping he could stay awake.

That is when I jumped in and sold the pilot on the idea of my keeping him awake by singing, telling stories, or just staying quiet all the way home. He picked storytelling and I kept his plane filled with hot air all the way home.

At three o'clock in the morning we landed at Orange County's private terminal. It had only been 24 hours since I saw my husband, but it seemed more like 24 years. How does a woman with no money leave a foreign country that is having an airline strike and return home in plenty of time to drive her children to school the next day?

Where I come from, it is called the "sell to survive" instinct.

According to my mom, I have been using this instinct for years. She claims my behavior as early as age two proves it.

"Before I could get into the kitchen to start a pot, you were hollering out the window inviting our neighbor Mrs. Salisbury to come over 'for a cup of coffee and bring some donuts.' Your dad and I were amazed at your simple but candid approach."

I got plenty of encouragement to keep selling both at home and in school. My teachers, the Catholic nuns, were great sales coaches. I can remember how excited I got in grade school when they announced the newspaper subscription drive. The principal kicked off the contest with a pep talk that matched the likes of the late Vince Lombardi.

In high school, the good sisters got me knocking on doors selling cookies and candy bars to raise money for the building fund. I will never forget the most dangerous door I ever approached. One day I was scoping the neighborhood getting ready to prospect when I noticed a home that appeared to be the nicest looking one on the block. I had a hunch that whoever lived inside could probably afford a few of my candy bars. I decided to follow my instincts and see if I was right.

The entrance to the home was very intimidating. An iron gate closed off the driveway and front door from the street. There was a voice box and intercom button next to the gate, so I pushed it. A raspy sounding voice with an Italian accent blasted over the speaker:

"Whose-a-there?"

"Barrett's my name. Danielle Barrett. I'm here on behalf of the good nuns up the street at Trinity High School who *desperately* need money right away to build more classrooms. Buy a candy bar and you will help the cause. What do you think?"

"Kid, I don't have-a-time to think, but come here a minute."

The next thing I know the electronic gate opened up, so I just walked up the driveway. He was pacing in the doorway looking like Marlon Brando, wearing a long silk robe and a scowl on his face.

"How much?"

"A buck a bar," I replied, trying to match his rough and ready style.

Then he pulled a wad of cash out from his left pocket and shoved a single bill into my eyeball. I reached up, grabbed it and took a double take. It was fifty dollars.

I was so flabbergasted I couldn't close my mouth.

His closing remarks were,

"Keepa the change and . . . keepa the bars."

I tried to say "thank you" but he slammed the door in my face. I kept humming, "When the moon hits your eye like a big pizza pie" all the way home. Later I found out that I had sold 50 undelivered candy bars to one of the most prominent gangsters in the city. I had no idea when he personally answered the door that he normally had the bodyguard greet callers, but the help had the day off.

I just happened to catch the godfather himself.

The Crooked Candy Bar Escapade taught me one of my first lessons in effective natural selling:

BELIEVE IN YOUR OWN UNIQUE AND DISTINCTIVE VOICE

The hunch itself, that little voice inside me that figured out I should call on the Mafia man in the first place, is known as intuition. Intuition is defined as "a direct perception of truth or fact independent of any reasoning process."

As children we let intuition guide us, but once we grow up we begin to doubt our friendly inner advisor. My dear friend Flavia Weedn, a great writer, painter, and philosopher, told me about the personal struggles she faced believing in herself during the early months of her career:

> The greatest obstacle I had to overcome was to rid myself of overwhelming feelings of inferiority concerning my work in the beginning. I remember well my initial feelings at that first art show when I saw all the professionals around me. I kept taking the paintings in and out of the trunk of my car before I finally set up. At the end of the day, one artist whose work I admired said to me, "Flavia, I hope you keep painting—your work has a kind of magic because it sings. And that's the ingredient most artists strive for." During the thirty years since that statement, I have worked with many schooled technicians who are very well skilled and yet whose work has no magic. It's been lost somewhere or overshadowed by what they have been taught.
>
> So, for me, being self-taught was a tremendous advantage. I developed my own style and because I was unafraid to let myself be vulnerable, my work had imagination and feeling. I thank God I had courage enough to take a risk in the beginning, and am reminded of what might have happened if I hadn't taken my paintings out of my car that day, by a quote from Oliver Wendell Holmes: "Alas for those who never sing, but die with their music still in them."

Like Flavia, I received no formal training when I first went into the sales field. There is no substitute for the kind of educational experience that begins with a good training program. However, to be considered "well-trained" is very different from becoming "well educated."

LEGENDARY NATURALS NEVER GRADUATE

The word "education" is derived from the Greek word "educare" and it means "to change from within." As a teacher, I wish to be regarded as an *educator* not a *trainer* because I know the effects of education are everlasting.

Sales Training	Sales Education
Formal programs that are designed to teach people how to react and respond.	Formal and informal opportunities that teach people how to think in order to determine needs.
Sometimes encourages manipulation, intimidation, strategies, techniques, ploys in order to close the sale.	Encourages right-brain activity. Creative problem solving, in-depth study, and honest communication.
Sometimes based on salesperson's dazzling personality.	Based on the salesperson's character.

You will be challenged throughout this book to commit yourself to a life-long education. If good training programs can enhance that education, then by all means get involved. Remember, never choose a program that suppresses your original thinking.

CREATE YOUR OWN CURRICULUM ... WRITING YOUR PERSONAL SALES JOURNAL

When I was 18, I had a summer job selling at a local furniture store. A young couple came in and were looking for a couch, table, chairs, and some lamps. They were getting married soon and had saved some money for furniture for their first apartment.

I was naturally interested in the same things they were. I knew every piece of furniture on the showroom floor. I was planning to get married soon myself, so I had my eye on some things. I took them around the store just like I owned the place. We sat down and tested the comfort of couches. We imagined making a romantic dinner for two at a particular dinette set. They were totally captivated and hung on every word I said. Quite frankly, I was amazing myself.

I was so good I should have taken notes on everything I said. Don't we amaze ourselves sometimes? Do you ever record what you say after a great day with a customer? Most salespeople never get in the habit and then two or three weeks later they are doing a presentation and they sound terrible. They forgot all the brilliant things they did two weeks earlier. They go home at night and toss and turn in bed thinking of all the things they should have said.

Once I got into real estate sales I was forced to examine what was working for me. I had no guidance and every time I worked with a new customer I learned something brilliant or embarrassing. I then began keeping a journal. Part of the reason I did this was because I was already in the habit of writing things down that I was learning; but I was using little pieces of scratch paper and they were strewn all over my desk, car, kitchen, and bedroom. I needed one place I could put all this information so I wouldn't lose it.

I began leaving my journal on the desk at my office from time to time. Other members of the staff would always ask me what new tid-bit I had entered in the journal. The next thing I knew it became the office study guide. When someone was stuck with a negotiation problem they would ask me how I would handle such a situation. Did I have a winning script written down about such a problem? Could they use it on their next appointment? Five years later I converted that journal into a book entitled *Breakaway.*

It was self-published and it did so well that the second edition was picked up by Prentice-Hall and is now in its third edition. It has sold over half a million copies and is titled today, *How To List And Sell Real Estate In The 90s.* That's a good example of "natural selling."

Here are some important ground rules to establish as you begin to formulate your own personal curriculum of selling with the use of a sales journal.

1. Ask yourself: What type of journal is practical for me? A small pocket book? A notebook size binder that fits in my briefcase? Will I carry it with me or just leave it at the office or at home to make entries during quiet times of reflection? Do I need two journals—one for office and one for home or the car? Can I use a small pocket tape recorder and get the same results?

2. Follow your flashes. That means when you have a flash of brilliance either when you are with customers, driving in the car, or during the middle of the night, force yourself to write down your thought. I don't mind who is around anymore—I stop and write. Many times while I am lecturing, I might say to the audience, "Hold on a minute. Did I say that? That was pure genius. Excuse me while I take some quick notes."

3. Be brief in your notetaking. You have to learn to paraphrase, use buzz words, and outline. Let's use my candy bar story as an example. The spur-of-the-moment script that took the customer off guard was: "What do you think?" I used that right after I explained the purpose of selling the candy bars. That question is a valuable one that can be transferred to many future prospecting calls. It catches people off guard, seems to elicit a response, and is definitely worth

noting. The journal entry reads: "Use the 'what do you think?' script on foot and phone. Pause and remain silent after you ask the question."

Take the time to write these valuable gems in your journal. You might want to get more detailed as time goes by. You can buy tabs for your notebook and divide the scripts into such categories as marketing concepts, time planning tips, and so on. You might want to divide your journal into the same four parts as this book—Personal Power, Business Development, Appointments, and Service.

Additional suggestions:

1. Within 12 hours after you consummate a sale, take time to write in your journal. Reflect on the entire process between you and the customer(s) and try to pinpoint and write down the constructive lessons, dialogues, and concepts learned.

2. Share your journals at sales meetings. Brainstorm with colleagues. Don't be secretive about it. As you learn, pass it on. If everybody is sharing, the air of excitement in your department or company will be refreshing. In addition, profits will skyrocket. When I owned my own business, the time between 9:00 A.M. and 10:00 A.M. every Wednesday was set aside for those who wanted to come into my office and share war stories. We even called it "war story hour." Both new and experienced salespeople would bring in their journals and share both their victories and defeats. Often the bleakest of circumstances ended up bestowing a brilliant future script on the most disheartened salesperson.

3. Write clearly. There is nothing worse than not being able to read your own pearls of wisdom.

A FRESH AND NATURAL APPROACH TO SALES SCRIPTING

A sales journal contains dialogues between you and the prospect. I call these conversations "natural scripting" because these words transform themselves into money-making scripts for the salesperson. A basic training program teaches students to memorize previously proven, effective standard scripts to ensure confidence when they prospect for leads, handle objections, and close the sale. All proven and effective sales talk was once spur-of-the-moment brilliance. That is why it is important to study the two basic sales talks every natural is proficient in using in the sales process: *The Prepared Dialogue* and *The Impromptu Dialogue*. Study impromptu dialogue first because all prepared scripting started out as effective impromptu conversations with the customer.

SIX PAINLESS POINTERS FOR IMPROVING YOUR IMPROVISATION

All prepared dialogue starts out as impromptu conversation with the customer. These are spur-of-the-moment talks when you have little chance to prepare. Intuition guides the improvisational moment. This can be dangerous for the new salesperson if he or she does not have sufficient knowledge about the subject. Then improvising becomes the big bluff and customers sense you are blowing smoke.

If you are new to the sales world and do not have the confidence to speak extemporaneously, learn the dozens of prepared scripts contained in this book to get you started in talking to the prospect. Soon you will find yourself delivering your own impromptu discourses to the customer. Here are some guidelines to follow when you get enough experience, knowledge, and courage under your belt to venture out into the world of improv:

1. Choose a product or service you can become committed to and passionate about selling. This motivates you to study all about it and the more knowledge you possess, the less afraid you will be to open your mouth without the security of a memorized presentation.

Recently a sales student challenged my improv abilities at a seminar in front of 300 participants. She said: "I have only been selling my product for three years, but I have racked up quite a track record. I have excellent references and endorsement letters, but I am at a point of frustration. I find myself in competition at this point with the 'high rollers,' the legends of my industry. What do I say to the customer when they challenge me with, 'Why should I talk to you when I am already doing business with (or have the opportunity to do business with) the best your industry has to offer?'"

Do we all give up because there is no prepared dialogue for that problem? This example shows the importance of becoming educated and not just trained, so you can learn to think fast on your feet. I asked her: "Are you comfortable with the knowledge base you have concerning your product?"

"Yes, I feel I know more than the legend does, have more energy, and could do a better job."

I asked her why she felt that way.

"Because I am not number one yet and I want to be. I want to become a legend and gain that kind of respect and income. I believe my desire to become the best drives me to go beyond the type of service even a 'legend' is prepared to deliver to the customer. I don't have one ounce of complacency inside of me."

Her motivation was intense. When she commented that she was not number one yet, I got the first clue for the impromptu dialogue I was about to present to her.

I suggested she try something like this: "Mr. Customer, I can offer you the same thing that others who are labelled 'second best' offer their customers: service way beyond the call of duty: energy, attention, and first class service. I am motivated and our company is snapping at the heels of the company holding the #1 position right now. We have a lot to gain and so do you."

I went a step further. "There is no trace of complacency in my style of doing business. Don't get me wrong. I have great respect for the company (person) you are doing business with (or may do business with), but I have studied my product and all the competing products extensively. Because of this knowledge and deep commitment, I know that I can offer you unparalleled service.

"You owe it to yourself and your company to hear my presentation before you make a final decision to stick with your present service (or select that product or service). The biggest mistake a customer can make is to assume they are making the right decision without clearly understanding their other options. May I have the opportunity to present them to you?"

My impromptu dialogue now became her prepared script for the next confrontation with her customer.

2. Ask an intelligent question in order to get your bearings and more information before you respond to the customer's objection. Do not ramble, apologize, or act surprised. Remember, you wouldn't be asked a question unless the buyer was interested in your product and considered you somewhat of an expert.

3. Look for a theme that you can build on. Remember the salesperson said she wanted to be number one? That triggered the Avis/Hertz image in my mind and I built the dialogue from that image and theme.

4. There are three parts to every prepared speech: Introduction, Body, and Conclusion. Follow this format when you speak extemporaneously. Remember to stick to each point and back it up with specifics.

5. Tap your mental storehouse. Look to the past dialogues you have used in prepared presentations to assist you. Look to the present and future to support your statements, too. As you see articles in papers or magazines that support your product or service, clip them and keep files. These files act as a backup for creating prepared and

impromptu dialogue. In addition, when you cite current statistics, you sound convincing.

6. Quit while you are ahead. When you speak from an impromptu position, a little bit goes a long way. Some people go on and on because they feel they are not making headway with the customer. Do not try to bluff your way through anything. Impromptu speaking must come from a solid base of knowledge.

GUIDELINES FOR ORIGINAL READY-TO-USE DIALOGUES

Prepared dialogue usually originates from listening to customers' needs. Over the years I have developed scripts through self-correction, listening to customers, other salespeople, and my own surprising moments of brilliance. I took notes in my journal along the way so I could pass this communication on to you.

Once you start using these ready-to-use dialogues, you will find yourself improving upon my scripts and delivering a combination of your own original work as well as mine. I look forward to becoming your partner in this creative adventure with your future customers.

Here are some guidelines to remember:

- Decide whether you should memorize these passages word for word or paraphrase them. When you paraphrase, you can write outlines of each dialogue in your journal instead of copying them word for word.
- Prepared scripts are based on reasons to call the prospect, such as current changes and updates in the marketplace and surveys, as well as general information about your product or service.
- Research and get some background information before you use either type of dialogue. Ask yourself the following questions:
  — What do they intend to use your product for?
  — What department of the company should this call be directed to?
  — Are they using something similar now?
  — Why are they changing distributors or services?
  — Is this the first time such a product or service is being considered?
  — Is this a lead from a mutual friend? If you have that information

ahead of time you can leverage your way in the door with a mentor's name.

— Is cost a factor?

— Do you know if the customer's tempo is casual or formal?

Send for any brochures or other aids that will give you background information before you make the initial call.

LET GO AND TRUST THE NATURAL PROCESS

Once you start becoming skilled at both types of dialoguing, learn to trust the natural process. Process is synonymous with words like "passage," "set of changes," and "transformation." Natural process is very difficult to accept, but I have always looked to children as role models to inspire me. Every time I watch a child learn how to walk, I am reminded of the slow but consistent power of letting the natural process do its job.

Watch a feisty little baby creep around, grab the side of a table, pull himself up, and then proudly let go and attempt to take a few steps. Then the big fall comes after he trips over his own feet and bangs his head. However, a child's resiliency and built-in positive attitude is amazing. Yes, babies cry, but only for a few seconds and then they are off and running again. Do we ever hear the one-year-old complain to the parents: "If I do not learn to walk in the next 30 days, will you carry me for the rest of my life?"

Natural salespeople rebound like the child does, believing that any obstacle they face during the course of their careers is only a temporary setback.

Some trained salespeople do not understand the value of process. They think they can speed up the process and force the customer to buy their product. My husband Mike and I experienced the insensitivity of such an individual several years ago when we went out shopping for a second car. We were ready to spend our money because we knew exactly what we wanted—low mileage, low price—just a basic car with no frills. This was a second car that our house full of teenagers would be driving as well.

I called several dealerships, asking about the specific car we wanted and the list price. One particular salesperson I talked to got me pretty excited.

"This car usually goes for $5,300, but if you come in today, I can get it for you for a lot less." Being half-Irish and half-cheap, I jumped on his offer.

After convincing Mike that this dealer had exactly what we wanted, including the color, he agreed to check things out. We ended up taking a few of our sons along. The "I can get it for you less" salesman was willing and waiting to take us all for a test drive. My son Joe was egging us on. He did not know about my negotiating philosophy that recommends families work as a united front to get the best deal for themselves.

"Great, Mom. This is the car for our family. Wow, did you hear what he said? 50 MILES TO THE GALLON!"

Let's face it, this kid would have been thrilled to ride a camel, if he knew that was his last way to get around town. We finally said to the salesman: "You mentioned over the phone we could get it for less than $5,300. How much less?"

The salesperson replied in a somewhat aggravated tone, "Well, are you going to buy the car today?"

We said: "Well, that depends on what the price is and the figures you give us."

Again he says, "Are you going to buy the car today or not?"

I was getting upset. Standing in the foreground were two or three other rude individuals just sort of staring at our family.

Finally, Mike said, "Can we sit down in your office and see how this works out financially?"

The guy took us into his closing booth and worked out a sheet full of numbers at the full price of $5,300. "These are the figures without tax, licensing, radio, etc."

I said, "How much can we get off of this price, as you suggested on the phone?"

"I don't know. I will have to ask my boss."

When the salesman left the room our son brought up a good point: "When he was asking us if we could buy the car today, we should have asked him if he had the authority to sell us the car today."

A few minutes later, the salesman came back and asked us how we were going to be paying for the car. We told him if the price was right, we might pay cash.

The man left again and when he returned, acted very put out and said, "There is just no way we can sell you this car under $5,300." We never met the guy in the back room smoking the cigar and calling the signals. We were so mad we just got up and went home.

Trying to speed up the natural selling process through force never works. Salespeople who do not trust process are working from fear. It is very easy to detect the difference between the behavior of the outstanding Natural and the obnoxious salesperson who thinks he can manipulate circumstances that require time, a patient attitude, and good problem solving-skills.

Obnoxious	Outstanding
Tries to create the illusion of need and premature urgency.	Tries to determine needs.
The Goal: The commission.	The Goal: The customer's future business.
Usually resents people. Tries to act "interesting."	A "people" person. Is genuinely interested.
Thinks selling is a game.	Knows selling is an art and science.
Uses verbal traps.	Uses problem-solving skills.
Scarcity principle: Imagines there is not enough to go around.	Knows hard work pays and there is plenty of business to go around.
Win/lose philosophy.	Win/win philosophy.
Sneaky with customers/peers.	Open, confronting and honest.
Walks in unprepared.	Does homework before.
Impatient and seeking instant gratification.	Knows the benefits of delayed gratification.
Neglects business development circle, therefore overly attached to outcomes.	Strong business developer, therefore detached but concerned about outcomes.

Remind yourself how quickly you can cross the line between outstanding and obnoxious behavior when you begin to work against natural process.

Once you begin to trust yourself, record your newest dialogues, and move with natural process, you will need a formula to creatively solve your customers' problems. If you find yourself struggling with a situation that is in a stuck position with no forward momentum, practice the following methods of solving customer problems.

MY CUSTOM-DESIGNED SOLUTION SELLING METHODS

The inner-solution selling method is a dynamic way to use instinct and intuition to help guide you when you need a new creative approach for working out problems with your customers. I devised a problem-solving formula that you can start using immediately.

I must emphasize that these good ideas often come when you are totally relaxed—in dreams at night, dozing on an airplane, or jogging down the beach. The mind likes to get creative when there is no tension or pressure. That is why you must have your journal handy, or at least paper and pen, so you can transcribe your own internal solutions.

Here's an example of how my inner-solution selling method worked in my own life.

One time, I was thinking about ways to help salespeople during times of economic downturns. I wanted to develop a three-day educational experience full of creative solutions and positive synergism that was beyond comparison. I thought my timing was right because I had developed my credibility as a teacher, but I was concerned about low ticket sales because business was off in many markets.

Clients that hired me reported that over the years they had been tracking those salespeople who were buying my materials; they discovered my students were their top team players under all market conditions.

When I become passionate about a project, it begins to monopolize my thoughts. So, one Sunday afternoon while I was taking a nap on a flight to Toronto, I woke up suddenly with an idea. I needed to grab my journal and start writing immediately. I found myself writing a formula that has now become my inner-solution selling method. This method is made up of four parts—Problem, Cause, Effect, and Cure.

This is what I wrote in my journal:

> *PROBLEM:* Salespeople (stocks, real estate, computers, retail, and so on) panic and refuse to spend money on educational opportunities that will stimulate both their brains and productivity at a time when they need it the most.
>
> *CAUSE:* They follow the "quicksand crowd" and listen to negative rumors from peers and newspaper stories during a downturn or change in the market. They believe their own bad press.
>
> *EFFECT:* Major decrease in productivity due to discouraged salespeople giving in to pressure, and exaggerated reports from outsiders who know very little about their business.
>
> *CURE:* As a respected master teacher, I will create a quality three-day learning experience that protects them from future roller coastering in their careers. This clinic will emphasize focus, heavy business development, and the building of mental toughness. They will learn how to practice new habits and exercise willpower. Then I must convince them to budget their time and money so they can attend. They will learn to restrict their spending on addictive pleasures that kill the pain of their predicament and immobilize them from taking a hands-on approach to their problems.

Over the next several months, I developed my sales dialogues for my telephone staff, as well as my personal appearance presentations based on my four-part formula.

After clearly defining the problem, cause, effect, and cure on paper, I wrote my prepared presentation, including the closing dialogue. I decided to pretend I was going on a job interview and was being considered as one of the candidates to fill the position of master sales coach for a certain organization. I created a strong argument for my qualifications based on the following four points:

1. Credibility—A lifetime of experience that covers all experience levels and market cycles. This assures the student that their master teacher travels in thin air, way above the crowd, and can deal with all types of problems and solutions for customers.

2. Quality—The entire three-day event will be first class: the resort and accommodations, my curriculum, and my invited legends-in-sales panel that will assist me. Also, the program will be limited to a set number of students in order to encourage group interaction.

3. Commitment—The teacher is committed to making this program available at affordable prices and will commit to a money back guarantee if the student is not completely satisfied.

4. Communication—This teacher has a track record for giving the student the "aha" experience. She will bring testimonials along for the audience to read. She will ask certain "fans" who are attending to stand up and report some of the results they experienced after reading my book, hearing a tape, or attending a seminar.

That Sunday afternoon nap paved the way for a very creative solution to my problem of promoting the clinic. I went out on several presentations during the next two months, selling hundreds of tickets based on my written inner-solution selling formula, PCEC. After my telemarketing staff heard the first presentation, they got on the phones, duplicated my dialogues, and closed more ticket sales.

The inner-solution sales method works, but it takes courage to implement the messages our intuition so generously gives. The problem, cause, effect, and cure formula shapes and organizes the information your instincts and intuition supply for you.

Use your personal power to enhance your growth through instinct, intuition, and education. In the next chapter, you will learn how to clear your pathway and remove all your self-imposed barriers so you carry out your unique natural plan.

2

A Natural Plan: How to Restore Vision and Vitality in Your Daily Selling Agenda

"We go where our vision is."

JOSEPH MURPHY

Making time count involves two important words—Wisdom and Energy. The natural plan proposed in this chapter comes from the wisdom I acquired from some very tough life experiences. The energy I possess is the result of the disciplined fitness plan I now follow every day of my life. Do not let my current credentials fool you—I was a slow starter.

I married when I was 19 and had five children by the time I was 27. Circumstances forced me to get a job when I was six months pregnant with my fifth child. The decision to get into sales was a smart one, but it was hard work with no shortcuts along the way. Though the career and the children weathered the struggles, the marriage was overburdened with emotional pain, heartache, and financial stress.

These circumstances changed my viewpoint about the concept of "time" dramatically. By 1979 I was in the throes of a divorce, something unheard of in our very Catholic family. In the midst of becoming a single parent, more traumatic events occurred: my father died; three weeks later my grandfather died; six months later my best friend, a 36-year-old wife, mother, and fellow saleswoman committed suicide.

When I first came up for air after these four shocks in my life, I was numb and acted like a robot going through the motions of being a mother and a saleswoman. I was a good actress and had the ability to hide my deep anger. I channelled all my energies into my career and my children, showing the world I could make it on my own.

One day during an especially low period, I got a call from a prospective client asking me to appraise her home. Her husband was a successful doctor in the community and she had dedicated her adult life to him and their four children. She symbolized everything I wanted out of life.

When I arrived at her home she was very upset. With tears streaming down her face she poured her heart out:

"My husband has just informed me he wants a divorce. I guess he's bored. Our children are all grown. I have no job skills. As a matter of fact, I have never balanced my own checkbook. I have to sell this home and move to a condominium. I feel as helpless as an unwed teenage mother about to go out into the big bad world."

Isn't it funny how one person's bad news becomes another person's consolation? After hearing my customer's problem, I began to take another look at the life I was living. That night, I was granted the first of many "ahas," those little injections of wisdom that come from life when we keep our heart open to receive them.

In the days and weeks ahead I entered, maybe for the first time in my life, the precious present moment. Seeing that woman's helplessness made my responsibilities seem less of a burden and more of a motivation. Every new customer made me feel so appreciative. I am very grateful that I had some setbacks early in my adult life because I got rid of my "expectant attitude" about my career, my family, and my life in general.

Every candidate who wants to master the art of natural selling must live by the above "non-expectant" principle which is the foundation of the natural plan. It is based on possessing a happy and healthy attitude, a strong body (which I cover in Chapter 12), the three circle concept which gives you the exact formula for consistently increasing your sales profits, and keeping an eye on what is important.

THE AMAZINGLY SIMPLE THREE CIRCLE CONCEPT

When I owned my own company and headed a sales force of about 123 salespeople, I hired a management consultant by the name of Richard Cosner who gave me some wonderful insights about where salespeople must focus their efforts on a consistent basis.

One day we were sitting in the conference room talking about the typical problems salespeople contend with regularly: paperwork and follow-up, spending either not enough or too much time on appointments with customers, sales slumps, and the sudden lack of new prospects.

Rich asked me to go get three colored pencils—red, green, and blue—and a blank piece of paper. He directed me to draw the following illustration with each of the colored pencils and to name each circle: The red circle represented *Business Development:* The blue circle represented *Appointments:* The green circle represented *Service.* (See Figure 2-1).

The Three Circle Concept:

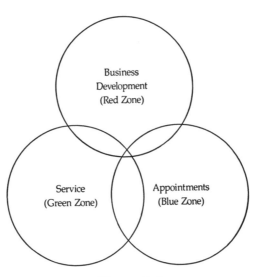

Business
Development
(Red Zone)

Service
(Green Zone)

Appointments
(Blue Zone)

Figure 2-1

BUSINESS DEVELOPMENT ... OPPORTUNITY KNOCKS

In keeping with the "non-expectant" philosophy, I must point out various pursuits which do not constitute real business development:

- Leads that are doled out by management that merely require follow-up to make the sale;
- The paid-for advertising on television, radio, print, and billboards that prompts customers to call or come in to a store or business with no effort on the part of the salesperson on the receiving end.
- Any business that is given to the salesperson just because they happened to be on duty, or have their hand out when management is giving away leads.

These gifts are not considered part of the business development effort. They belong in the appointment or service circle depending on what needs to be done to handle the prospect. There is a big difference between the trained order-taker and the natural salesperson. The natural practices self-generated client-capture. Business development is good gossip—the constructive kind. I call it spreading good rumors about myself, my product, and my company. I develop business any chance I get.

For instance, one time after I finished lecturing in Minneapolis I shared a cab back to the airport with a woman who attended an international convention of mid-wives. I gave her my business card and told her I lecture at conventions. I asked her who was in charge of hiring next year's speakers. She wrote down the convention chairman. I asked her if the mid-wives would be interested in learning about more ways to build their practice. She indicated they would. I suggested the title "Danielle Delivers too." We laughed and she said she would call the program chairman and tell her to look for my press kit in the mail.

Any communication that a salesperson generates that results in a future appointment is categorized under business development. Activities include:

- Telephone prospecting off a targeted list to arrange appointments.
- Making face-to-face calls in order to arrange appointments to demonstrate or present.
- Written correspondence to prospects that whets their appetite for your wares.
- Contacts with past customers or accounts, mentors, centers of influence.
- Spur-of-the-moment conversations that lead to future business.

Sales slumps occur because we stop business developing. In Chapter 12 I will show you how therapeutic it is to business develop yourself right out of the slump.

TURN APPOINTMENTS INTO SALES

Appointments are meetings with the customers—both in person or on the telephone, that explain and describe the benefits of your product, idea, or service. Business development gets your toe in the door and a solid appointment keeps it there.

You can conduct an appointment almost anywhere. If you are just getting started and lack a sophisticated setting to present your wares, do not let that be an excuse not to go after the business. I was told when I got in sales I needed to drive around in a big fancy car in order to impress my customers on the appointment. I drove a red Volkswagen squareback the first three years until I could afford a better car. I demonstrated to senior executives from Kodak, Procter and Gamble, B. P. John Furniture, Dial Soap, and A T & T, in the only car I could afford to drive.

I have conducted appointments:

— In the customer's car or my car.

— At the customer's home or in my home.

— Restaurants

— Airplanes, trains, buses, boats

— Hospital maternity wards

— Any business office

— On telephones located on street corners, airports, airplanes, cars

— Golf courses, swimming pools, ski slopes, dance floors

— Shopping centers, grocery stores, and malls

— Ballet studios, Little League, and football fields

I have been out on appointments just days after my children were born. The senior vice presidents of a national firm met me in their corporate headquarters two weeks after my last child was born. My baby daughter Kathleen and I were the only females in the room. I was asked to write and present a sales and marketing campaign to senior management that I could present to their sales forces all over the country. While Kathleen slept comfortably in a porta-crib over in the corner of the board room, I sold the brass on my newest approach for their salespeople to increase their market share.

It took two more months of presentations before the program was unanimously approved. I signed a contract for a 10-city tour to deliver the goods to their national sales team. First class accommodations for Kathleen were also included.

Sometimes it takes numerous appointments before the sale is consummated. It may take a computer salesperson a combination of 10 in-person and phone visits over a 24-month period. Each appointment involves doing homework and extensive preparation. Natural salespeople sell their expertise, not their time. Each successive appointment diminishes road blocks and builds a climax of excitement about the product with the customer.

THE SATISFIED CUSTOMER

Service is positive customer communication after the sale. Did the customer get what he paid for? Is the customer happy? Will they do business with you in the future? Will they refer other prospects to you and your company? Service includes personal contact both in person and by phone—letters, notes, postcards, greeting cards, and other forms of written client follow-up; flowers and gifts; and elaborate yearly promotions when the budget provides.

The system you implement is the key factor in keeping the customer happy after the sale. Without a regular call-back system, methods of remembrance, and continual reminders to customers that you want their business for life, you will never attain the 100% referral business every natural enjoys. The three circle concept has become a formula that I have lived by and passed on to thousands of salespeople everywhere. Become aware of the circle where you spend most of your time. Remember that when you spend more time and effort in the business development area, you increase your number of appointments and chances that you will have more customers to serve long term.

CLEAN UP THE PAST AND UNLEASH YOUR CREATIVITY

Legend tells us that Chinese fathers used to have an interesting custom. They would tie a rope from the ceiling to the floor at the beginning of the day and strike a match and set it on fire. By the end of the day the rope was in ashes. Those ashes were there to remind their children that the past was dead.

My dad did not burn ropes in our living room but he delivered the same message to me when I was growing up. I made it a point never to whine or bring up the past in front of him. If he heard me do so, he yelled out unsolicited advice to me.

"Hey kid, do I hear you moaning about something that is over and done with? A dead issue? Yesterday's newspaper? Sounds like it's time for you to be excused and go somewhere to give yourself a 'mental enema'."

When I entered sales I soon discovered that it was mandatory to burn the past every day in order to survive. I remembered dad's advice and I began giving myself mental enemas early in my selling career. Try it right now as you read this.

> For the next 30 seconds put this book down, sit in a comfortable chair, get very relaxed, and close your eyes. Sit in your own darkness and try not to think about anything. Imagine you are clearing your head. Press an imaginary CLEAR button just above the bridge of your nose. BEGIN. STOP.

How did you do? When I first tried this, my mind was speeding at 100 miles per hour. Thoughts were jumping from one problem or circumstance to another. If you had a difficult time clearing your head, the next time you try this have a brand new box of crayons in your hand. Close your eyes and lift the opened box to your nose. This will remind you of happier times when you were a kid. Sometimes I use a bag full of freshly cut green grass so I can feel like it is spring again; the way I felt when I was a student, anticipating summer vacation.

Athletes have tremendous powers of concentration, and salespeople should copy their habits and philosophy on focus. My son Kevin was an amateur gymnast for years and he helped me become more directed in my work. Kevin told me that if he lost concentration doing a difficult routine he could get physically, as well as mentally, injured.

"Let's say I just finish my floor routine. The judges marks pop up and I read my score: '7.5'. I sincerely thought I did better than that and was expecting an 8.5 or 9.0 on the scorecard. But now I have to move forward to the next event on the high bar. If I don't burn this out of my mind, just clear the thought completely, I will be at risk physically when I engage on to the high bar." I asked Kevin how he was able to shake the past disappointment out of his head so quickly.

"I use my imagination and music. As long as we have our imaginations, we can strike back at ourselves when we become our own worst enemy. If I have my Walkman handy, I turn on music that uplifts me and then I refuse to let one negative thought creep into my thought patterns. I make a conscious effort to stop my mind when I feel it moving in. I might physically pick up a piece of chalk and play with it to give myself something to do while I begin to imagine myself freely moving on the high bar at the next event."

How does all this pertain to your selling career? Imagine that it is five o'clock on a weekday afternoon and you are just about ready to leave the office when you get a call that a very big sale you have been working on for 10 months is definitely going to fall through. There was a budget cut and the executive vice president refused to sign off on the documents that would approve your bonanza sale. This is a big disappointment to you because you already had the money allocated in your personal life.

You can hardly get up the next morning to begin the process of business development all over again. Yesterday's loss is weighing you down both physically and emotionally. When you arrive at the reception desk in your office, a client who was referred to you is sitting in the waiting room and the last thing you want to do is talk to some new prospect that may end up burning off the same way as yesterday's disappointment.

You tell yourself to get rid of this prospect as quickly as possible so you can go sit at your desk and stare into a coffee cup. But business development is a numbers game and in spite of how you feel that day because of a recent loss, an exciting opportunity may be just around the corner. Here is one time where we cannot listen to the little voice inside that says: "Hide. Stay home." That is not the voice of a developed sales intuition. This is the inner enemy we all have that rears its ugly head when we are completely disgusted with ourselves.

If I find myself suffering a loss, I work on getting into the next present moment by:

- Listening to uplifting tapes (a favorite: "Song Sung Blue" by Neil Diamond).

- Taking time for a mental enema. I concentrate on deep breathing when I do this. I have learned to slow down my own heart rate.
- Seeking the companionship of a family member or friend who always does a good job of listening.
- Going to a Steve Martin movie and belly laughing.
- Doing something physical. Cleaning out closets, washing cars, gardening, and dancing are very healing.

A NEW PERSPECTIVE—VISION PLANNING AND THE COLOR SPECTRUM

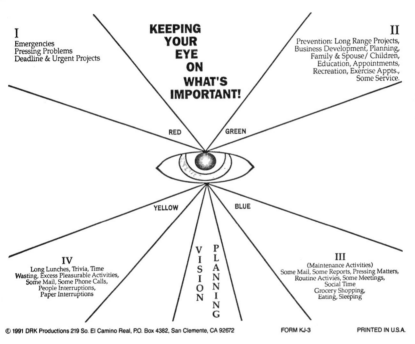

I
Emergencies
Pressing Problems
Deadline & Urgent Projects

KEEPING YOUR EYE ON WHAT'S IMPORTANT!

II
Prevention: Long Range Projects,
Business Development, Planning,
Family & Spouse/ Children,
Education, Appointments,
Recreation, Exercise Appts.,
Some Service.

RED   GREEN

YELLOW   BLUE

IV
Long Lunches, Trivia, Time
Wasting, Excess Pleasurable Activities,
Some Mail, Some Phone Calls,
People Interruptions,
Paper Interruptions

VISION PLANNING

III
(Maintenance Activities)
Some Mail, Some Reports, Pressing Matters,
Routine Activies, Some Meetings,
Social Time
Grocery Shopping,
Eating, Sleeping

© 1991 DRK Productions 219 So. El Camino Real, P.O. Box 4382, San Clemente, CA 92672   FORM KJ-3   PRINTED IN U.S.A.

Figure 2-2

A visionary focuses his or her attention on the daily activities that will produce contentment and satisfaction on a long term basis. My inner trainer helped me create this "eye" one day while I was napping. I was trying to think of a way to explain how I select certain activities on a daily, weekly, monthly, and yearly basis that result in satisfying living conditions for my family and myself. I reflected back to the times in my life when I could not see what was important. I wasted precious moments talking on the phone in idle conversation or gossip instead of enjoying my children, avoided business development because its start-up is always distasteful to me, or played with papers at my desk pretending I was busy.

The difficult part was to admit that I was blind to my own weaknesses. Every time I did something cowardly, like stay on the phone and gossip, I felt terrible anxiety and guilt. These feelings started becoming so uncomfortable, I finally gave up the bad habit. I really believe we have to stop our daily addictions by following the example of the Twelve-Step Recovery Program from Alcoholics Anonymous. Through prayer, willpower, and total commitment, they have shown us all a way to conquer any type of addiction.

Notice in the illustration on page 25 (Figure 2-2) that there are four color spectrums radiating from the eye to help give you insight into how you spend your time. The best zone is the green zone where creativity reigns. Business development, long range-projects, creative time with family and friends, or exercise keep you "green and growing" while the red and yellow areas turn you "ripe and rotten." Necessity dictates we spend part of every day in the blue zone in order to maintain required routines such as returning phone calls, answering correspondence, attending meetings, and grocery shopping.

The yellow zone is thwarted by interruptions from people and paper. By the end of the day we feel frazzled and undone because nothing we started out to do was completed. We all detest unfinished cycles and looking at lists with no lines drawn through the items. This is the predicament of the salesperson living in the cowardly yellow sphere.

The red zone is strictly emergencies, accidents, and unpredictables. The salesperson who finds himself in the red usually hates to confront problems. Such salespeople wait until everything is ready to fall apart, then at the last minute they madly rush in to put out a few fires. Stay in the red long enough and you will find yourself in the intensive care unit of selling and living.

You must use your willpower and avoid:

1. Getting sidetracked and falling out of the green and blue spectrums.
2. The red and yellow danger zones by attacking minor problems before they become major emergencies. It is an ongoing process that must be tackled daily.

STAYING IN THE GREEN

Staying in the green is your biggest challenge in selling because you have to remain flexible but disciplined. For instance, a friend of mine called and wanted to discuss something very important to her. Her friendship is as meaningful to me as spending time with a customer. She wanted to meet for lunch at noon but during that particular week I was using the lunch hour to run. Exercise falls into my green zone, and when I do not get the time to work it into my schedule I suffer and so does everyone around me.

I agreed to meet her but asked if we could choose a restaurant in the harbor where I could run. I did not want to say why because I was afraid she would feel like she was interrupting my day. I waited to tell her my plan until I saw her at the restaurant. She was in a business suit and I was in running sweats.

Once we sat down I explained that I usually do not eat before I run, but I wanted to meet with her and still keep my commitment to myself. This was just fine with her.

Before I started practicing vision planning, I hadn't learned when to be flexible and compromising. I would have dropped my exercise plan for that day and resented the fact that I did or I would not have taken the time to be with my friend.

How do you make good decisions each day? The answer has to do with what you consider important. Is socializing with a friend over lunch more important than taking an invigorating walk? Is hanging around the office with the quicksand crowd and the rumor controllers more important to you than getting out in your territory to do some business development? People always end up doing what they consider important, and it becomes apparent in their lifestyle.

TWENTY-ONE WAYS TO MORE PAY AND PLAY DAYS

Follow these 21 tips and you will find yourself in the habit of spending most of your life in the green zone:

1. Investigate your weaknesses. About 10 years ago, I was curious about myself, so I went on a personal investigation. I wanted to know why I always felt rushed and frustrated on a daily basis. I had knots in my stomach and I continually felt under the gun. Some kind of imaginary marathon was going on in my life, and I felt like I could never get to the finish line. For three days, I decided to record my daily activities briefly in a journal. After I reviewed my findings,

this account raised my awareness level and made the time I wasted each day stick out like a sore thumb. I was mad enough to start changing bad habits. Start investigating your life and use these simple guidelines:

— Use a small notebook or pocket tape recorder to report your activities.
— Three days is the maximum reporting time.
— No judgments. Just write what happens.
— Report: How many minutes a day you are—
  • On the telephone
  • Commuting
  • Doing detail and paper work
  • Parenting
  • Creatively problem solving
  • Business developing
  • On appointments
  • Servicing
  • Eating, dressing, exercising, sleeping, alone time, housekeeping (cooking, cleaning, grocery shopping)
  • Socializing
  • In meetings
— Read your findings at the end of the three days.
— What is the worst habit or time wasting activity you are involved in right now?
— Work on eliminating that habit for the next 21 days.

I do not have to do a formal three-day investigation anymore. Since I took the time to examine my ways, my awareness level has gone up and my instincts tell me when an unproductive habit must be broken. Last year I decreased my coffee intake because it was becoming too much of a ritual. I was interrupting myself too often to make coffee or go to visit a coffee garden. The worst part was what the coffee was doing to my nerve endings. I normally travel at a pretty good speed, but with coffee I was going too fast and then crashing and burning. It also increased my appetite so it was time to put my cup down and say no. When we truly desire to transform ourselves, the process never ends but the new transformation brings more inner peace and contentment.

2. Implement advance planning. Salespeople who are raising a family must plan ahead to accomplish their long range parenting and vocational responsibilities. Every September I ask my children for their school calendar, sports schedules, and extracurricular activity dates. A copy is given to my secretary and she does the best she can to schedule my life around those events during the next nine months. This puts part of the responsibility on the family members because they must bring me their schedules well in advance.

3. Plan one week in advance. Business development, appointments, service, meal plans, scheduled company meetings, reports due, children's car pools, lessons, and child-care options are carefully written down seven days in advance. I refer to the month and year-at-a-glance each week to make sure I haven't forgotten anything.

   Since I began doing this, Mondays are no longer panic-attack start-ups for the week. I know what is ahead and I can see how I can play my cards. I do my planning on Sunday night when the house is very quiet and my husband and I discuss the mechanics of the week.

4. Follow the cycle of action. There are three parts to every cycle of action: A beginning, middle, and end. All of us love to finish what we start and when we don't, our energy level and our self-esteem drop. Be careful how much you write down. You could end up hating yourself if you are not able to draw lines through all of the activities listed.

5. Review your daily action list and calendar before you go to sleep each night. When I complete my updated list before bedtime, I fall asleep faster.

6. Beware of the morning after. I refuse to look at my time planner when I first wake up in the morning. I like to wait until I can get myself in a position of attack when I have 15 uninterrupted minutes to myself.

   Attacking the day means: Take the list in your planner and begin making changes—add or subtract appointments, plan business development, and confirm personal commitments based on the current situation.

7. Use an action list to eliminate too many pieces of paper. I used to scribble on my calendar and leave a trail of little pieces of scratch paper around to remind me of things—such as prospective customers' phone numbers. I have cut back on the scratch pad addiction since I began using my action list. (See Figure 2-3.)

Daily Action List

PRIORITY Number / Color		ACCOMPLISHED ☑
☐	_____	☐
☐	_____	☐
☐	_____	☐
☐	_____	☐
☐	_____	☐
☐	_____	☐
☐	_____	☐
☐	_____	☐
☐	_____	☐
☐	_____	☐

Figure 2-3

8. Buy a planner you intend to use. Hundreds of salespeople tell me they have collected time planners for years but never used one. They find them too bulky, too small, or too complicated. Choose one you will use but keep it light and simple. I designed a special time planner for my sales students and you can write to me for a free brochure about it. Before you buy any planner ask yourself the following questions:

- If you are a female, ask yourself: Do you want to carry a purse and a planner at the same time?
- Can you find one that works for both functions?
- Will my planner fit inside my attaché case?
- How much do I want to spend?
- Would I prefer buying a new planner each year or use one that just requires refills?
- Do I want my planner to function as a prospect/client file too?
- Am I neat or messy? If I like to scribble all over the page, my calendar and squares should be big.

9. Wake up early. If you share your time between sales, spouse, and kids, wake up one hour earlier than the rest of the family to avoid an early morning crisis. By the time the rest of the house is moving out of bed, you are "in the present moment."

10. Delegate, don't dictate. It is very important to delegate those parts of our job that we can do with our eyes closed. (Servicing some customers can be done with secretarial assistance.) Then you will have the time to devote to the most important circle of influence— business development.

11. Use the word "commitment" frequently. "I would love to meet you but I have a commitment." This is never a lie because even if you intend to sit and talk to yourself after you hang up the phone, that counts.

12. Give personal/family commitments just as much priority as professional ones. Remember the green zone means you are living a whole life that includes those you love. Sometimes when you are in sales the family has to wait and sometimes the business has to wait. Use your intuition to decide which is the priority at a given time.

    If you are always weighing the scales to make sure you are on an even keel, the family will respect you for the times that you walked away from the unexpected prospect in order to keep a commitment at a recital or Little League game. Then you will have fewer explanations to give when you have to work long hours when you are on the trail of a hot prospect. Families, especially children, have memories like elephants. Respect those in your personal life as much as your colleagues.

13. Remember that the telephone is a message machine and a communication tool to develop business. Here are some ways to eliminate time wasted on the phone:

    — The call back system: If you are in and out of your office all day like most salespeople working a territory, you are probably playing call tag with people and missing some important calls. Buy a cellular phone and a fax machine if you can. Tell your secretary the specific time that you will be back in the office. This information is then passed on to the caller.

      I return calls right before lunch time and late in the afternoon. Most people get right to the point immediately before lunch and quitting time.

    — Get right to the point at the beginning of each new telephone conversation. Start out by saying: "Hi Ed, I was wondering if you could fax me this report." This approach avoids a lengthy conversation.

    — End all conversations quickly and with gratitude. "I don't need any more information right now. Thanks for the input. I appreciate the time spent." This softens the close because even people in a hurry do not like to cut off a conversation rudely.

Sometimes people won't let you hang up. Try the "commitment" word. If they still keep talking just start clicking your phone like crazy and say: "Something is wrong with this crazy phone, I better say goodbye before we get cut off." Click. It is not a lie. Something really is wrong with the phone—the person on the other end. This method should only be used with extremely insensitive people who do not understand that others are actually living life while they just seem to want to talk about it.

14. Confirm all appointments. Before you walk out of the door of your office or home, be sure everything is still right on schedule, especially when you are about to call on a strange customer for the first time. I learned this from my obstetrician. Remember I have spent 54 months of my life pregnant. This is quite a bit of waiting in a doctor's office. Confirm all your professional and personal appointments. Keep the phone number next to the scheduled appointment in your calendar or on the day's action list form.

15. Beware of sales meetings. If you lead the meeting, be sure you use an agenda, give one to each participant and follow its plan. Deliver the most valuable information first in case any of the sales staff have to leave and go out on an appointment. If you are a salesperson who is forced to attend too many meetings that take you away from the three circles, have a meeting with the sales manager and try to figure out a way to have fewer, but more organized and meaningful meetings.

16. Consolidate minor issues later in the day. When your energy starts to wane, do less important work. Business development should happen in the peak hours for you and the customer when everyone is bright and in a good mood.

     Returning phone calls, answering letters, and normal desk clearing is recommended. Feel good because you did the important work earlier when you felt up to it.

17. Drop out for drop-ins. When someone sits down in your office and makes himself right at home, do not join him. Remain standing. Be polite and say: "I wish I could chat right now but I have a commitment."

     If you cannot get them out of your office, go ahead and tell them you "gotta run." Then leave. Find a private office down the hall, a coffee shop, or even go home if it is quiet there so you can get some planned work done. Remember to state your intentions politely.

Too many people use the drop-in as an excuse to procrastinate. Remember, if something is really important to you, nobody can stand in your way.

18. Keep moving with the important mail. When the mail comes both at home and the office, follow a regular routine. I look at each piece while I am moving back to my desk or house and make it a point to pass a trash can or wastebasket on the route. I then throw all junk mail right into the trash without missing a beat. The junk mail never makes it to my desk. The only mail that keeps moving with me is the mail that requires a response (a bill, a letter, or an order form). If the mail requires a response immediately, I go right to the phone and do it. Otherwise, paper stacks up.

19. Forget long lunches. I have watched salespeople in my office kid themselves about making sufficient time to business develop. They go out to lunch at 11:30 telling everyone they will be back in an hour to continue their business development. Then they go out and have a large lunch. They still are not back in the office by one-thirty.

20. Make the most of your office in the sky. If I know I will be out of town on a particular week, I save all the reading material and correspondence in my files for the flight. If I am flying on two connecting flights, I won't eat the second meal and then I work straight through to my destination. I prepare sales presentations, speeches, chapters of my book, and pay bills and answer letters. This discipline frees up many hours for family time at home.

21. Use off hours to your advantage. Most of us natural salespeople do not do anything the normal way. I personally go to banks when nobody else does. I hit the grocery stores at odd hours, except when I was a salesperson, then I would go during the busiest times with my name tag on. I killed two birds with one stone—increasing the food and the customer supply.

Why stand in a bank line at three o'clock Friday afternoons if you don't have to? I refuse to take myself out of the green spectrum and into the other color zones on a beautiful Saturday afternoon by going grocery shopping when I could be spending time with a family member or jogging. The same principle applies to commuting. If you can go earlier or later, please do it.

If you are starting to see a new vision and are ready to get organized, let's begin part two of this book: Business Development. In the next chapter you are going to learn to love the telephone as you read a wealth of easy-to-follow dialogues that have emerged over the years from personal instinct and intuition.

Part Two

YOUR SUCCESS STARTS WITH
BUSINESS DEVELOPMENT

3 The Art of Making Big Money on the Telephone—à la Natural!

"We are what we repeatedly do."

ARISTOTLE

Do you know how to make love (not war) to a telephone? Every Natural that I know does. If you have not become passionately involved with a telephone so far in your sales career, you better start.

My husband is a master on the telephone. He calls it "dialing for dollars." He's been hard at it since he was 18 years old. Over the years I have listened to him blurt out the most original communication.

"Don't get excited, I won't try to sell you a *thing,* only a *woman* and her name is Danielle Kennedy," says the man who now promotes me and books me into conventions for speaking engagements. All recipients of his friendly, natural manner think he's "a doll."

THE "PHONE HOME" TELEPHONE VOICE

The Phone Home telephone conversation style has the "Don't I know you?" or "Gee, you sound so familiar" ring to it. The ability to be personal developed over time. I credit most of this flair to my father and my down-to-earth Midwestern background. I grew up with the Irish and Italians in a Chicago neighborhood. These people could start a conversation with anyone. Either they knew you, thought they knew you, or knew someone who did know you.

"Aren't you related to the Pope?"

"No, but my mother was."

"I thought so. I went to school with your mother's sister Ann. You resemble that side of the family."

"How many kids does your Aunt Ann have now?"

"Six."

"What a piker. I have eight. Tell your aunt I heard her old boyfriend Frank Ryan started selling auto insurance right out of high school, and now he's listed as one of the 500 richest men in America."

By the time I was an adult working in sales, I had picked up a slight case of "call reluctance." I was not alone. I noticed that some colleagues became self-conscious and embarrassed to use the phone eagerly. We are the same people who, as teenagers, used the telephone around the clock to troll for dates. What happened along the way? FEAR set in. *F*alse *E*vidence *A*ppearing *R*eal. It happens when we receive some form of rejection. The salesperson who goes into a cold sweat prospecting by the telephone got rejected, burned, or wounded and took it so personally that it stifled the old easy-going style of creating conversation and building rapport that came to her so naturally as a teenager. It can happen to the best of us, but just remember, down deep inside is the friendly persuader.

Before we start creating some fresh and natural phone scripts that will get you business developing, work the following program from start to finish and put yourself in the "phone-home" mode of speaking.

SIX EASY STEPS THAT GET YOU BACK ON THE TELEPHONE FAST

Step #1: Select a private location and use a tape recorder, a mirror, your journal full of both incoming and outgoing phone scripts, pen, and a legal-size pad. Then, select an outgoing phone dialogue in this chapter. Watch yourself in a mirror. Is your neck relaxed? Are your facial expressions rigid? Our exterior reflects our inner self. So if you look like you are in knots, your voice may also sound strained. Now push the record button on your tape recorder and pretend you are talking to a new prospect. After you do that, play back the tape and listen to your conversation. Ask yourself how you could improve your delivery. If your voice seems unnatural and the dialogue seems contrived, do not despair. As you practice, your delivery will improve.

Step #2: Create familiarity and reassurance all around you. I used family photos, framed testimonial letters, and motivational quotes like "Do It Now" to put me in the mood. Before you begin, play music that excites your spirit of play. I love Michael Jackson's *Bad* album. The opening bars of the song "The Way You Make Me Feel" prepare me to talk to any stranger.

Step #3: Use your imagination. Pretend you are a prospective customer and you are calling a bookstore to see if they have a specific book in stock. If it helps, record how you sound and get the "feel" of your inquiring phone voice.

The inquiry call is good practice because the theme of the conversation is "Can you help me?" or "I need some information." Try to transfer that same intention when you use the phone to contact future customers.

Step #4: Watch your tone of voice. Never try to come across like a big shot or act like you are trying to impress someone. The tone should be warm, but businesslike, curious, and straight to the point.

Step #5: Make your goal a fast 50 in 150—that is, 50 calls in 150 minutes. This allows you about three minutes per call. My rule in prospecting is fast action. Never give the people the impression you have time to chat. You are on a mission. Get right to the point and move on to the next number.

Step #6: Take 5 after 15. After 15 calls, take a five-minute break—stretch, take a bite of an apple, sip a drink, turn on a tune, and pat yourself on the back because you are making it happen. Then grab the phone for 15 more calls.

After you complete your phone work for the day, fill out the phone report form (see Figure 3-1). This gives you the same sense of satisfaction that drawing a line through an item on your "to do" list does. We all love to complete the commitments we make.

Did you surprise yourself when you were banging out those calls with some fancy new words or dialogues? Stop cold in your tracks after you hang up from a brilliant call and try to recapture the words you used in your journal. You may prefer to keep the tape recorder going to hear yourself while you make your 50 calls.

HOW TO BANK INCOMING CALLS

A customer's incoming call should always be enthusiastically received. The salesperson's voice should be distinct, well modulated, and upbeat. We can never be too friendly when people call for help. With outgoing calls we have to adjust our volume and tone to suit the customer's mood because we may be catching them off guard. The policy on all incoming calls should be generous enthusiasm and over-preparation. This means:

- You have knowledge of inventory on the tip of your tongue or have a cheat sheet in front of you updating what you need to know.
- Put everything in one place. I once used a tea cart with wheels. It contained a message book, pens, pads, script book, journal, advertising record that included a clipping of the day's ad in it, and other materials all salespeople need at their finger tips so they do not put

Phone Report Form

NAME _____ WEEK OF _____

	Monday	Tuesday	Wednesday	Thursday	Friday
Dials	today's goal ☐	today's goal ☐	today's goal ☐	today's goal ☐	today's goal ☐
Connects					
Sales	today's goal ☐	today's goal ☐	today's goal ☐	today's goal ☐	today's goal ☐
Send Info					
Returned Calls					

Figure 3-1

the customer in a position of being on hold. Every salesperson may easily wheel the cart to his or her desk.

- If it is a complaint call, remember the customer is always right. During the complaint call say things like, "I want to understand the problem. Please tell me more." Reassure the customer you are still friendly. Apologize and don't pass the buck.

I have called major department stores to find out if they have an item I need. The salesperson puts me on hold for five minutes and then returns to the phone with this message:

"I have six people standing at the counter and you expect me to go see if we have any more size 6s left in that color?"

I do not care how many people were standing in line. The salesperson could have immediately said:

"Can I take your name and number? I am awfully sorry but I am all alone in this department and there are six people waiting to pay for merchandise. I promise I will return the call within 30 minutes. Oh, and thanks for thinking of our store for your needs."

I watched one of the giants of retail selling just about go out of business several years ago because its sales staff was lacking in sales savvy. Along came the Nordstrom family from the Pacific Northwest who decided there was a big need for natural selling in the retail business. By educating their sales staff and teaching them how to be kind and generous to all customers, Nordstrom has successfully given the competition a run for their money and forced them to adopt sales programs.

Incoming Call Dialogues

(Customize these scripts for your product or service)

"Thanks for calling Extravagant Interiors (Company, Club, Boutique, Salon, Store, Service).

"Yes. Can you tell me your business hours?"

Note: Look in the mirror and smile while you take this call.

"Certainly. We are open every day from 9 A.M. to 10 P.M. except on Saturdays and Sundays. We close at 6 P.M. on both of those days."

"Thank you."

"And THANK YOU for thinking of Extravagant Interiors. We hope you drop by soon. We have a great sale on leather couches going on right now."

The Five-Minute Opener

This is an introductory script for salespeople or receptionists handling ad calls for both small and large businesses.

"Thanks for calling Stew's Appliances. How can I help you?"

"I am calling regarding your ad in the paper. Is the washer and dryer sale still going on? I noticed the ad last Sunday and didn't have a chance to call sooner."

"Let me ask you a quick question (don't pause). Will you be where you are now for the next five minutes?"

"I guess I can be."

"Great. May I have the *privilege* of knowing your name and number so I can call you right back after I check with the boss on the status of those appliances and the current sale prices?"

"Okay, but hurry up. I'm Jack Jaacks at 555-2121."

"I promise I will be back with you momentarily."

This dialogue is a great way to get a name and phone number. Note the word "privilege." It softens the request, but does the job.

"Will you be where you are now for the next five minutes?" throws the caller off guard. I picked that up from my family and friends. Someone would call and ask me that and arouse my curiosity. I always responded with a maybe or yes because I got the feeling that if I said no, I would miss something.

Stop right now, find a mirror, and try this. Get your tape recorder and record the above dialogue two times—once with a smile on your face and once without a smile. Now play back both readings. You will *hear* the same expressions you *saw* in the mirror. Remember: "Smile and the world smiles with you."

Here's another classy opener:

"Thanks for calling The Fit Fling. How may we serve you?" (Instead of 'How may I serve you' you may prefer to identify yourself.)

"Does your club offer weight machines?"

"We do offer muscle conditioning. Our muscle conditioning classes achieve astounding results for our students. We do provide free weights, but keep in mind working with other forms of resistance can provide that same toned, sculptured look that large-scale machinery does. What goals are you trying to achieve?"

"Well, I don't think women with big bulky muscles look that attractive. I thought I would use weight machines to develop more muscle than I have at this point."

"Most women like the long, lean muscle, like dancers have. We offer a "Sweat and Stretch" class today at 5:30. There is a lot of resistance work in that class and the students get a good workout as well as defined, graceful muscle development. Can you stop in and be my guest for one free class?"

This incoming call will turn into an appointment. This would not have been a possibility if the salesperson lacked the knowledge of anatomy, the services her club offers, and the art of impromptu speaking.

Naturals treat all incoming calls with kindness, respect, and an inner excitement that says, "This could be the start of something big."

Incorporate these suggestions into all your business's incoming calls.

- Always watch for an opening to promote your product or prequalify. "How did you hear about us?" is a question you should attempt to insert in the opening dialogue whenever possible. Then record that information on a daily incoming call sheet.
- Show a sense of humor. A voice with a smile is terrific, but one that is almost on the verge of fun is even better. The caller will respond accordingly.
- End on a high note. Naturals go out singing such melodies as:

"Thanks for talking to me."
"Don't forget to stop in."
"We'll take good care of you."
"Look forward to your visit."
"Don't miss our great sale. Only two more days left."
"Remember to ask for me when you come in. My name is Claudia. I have red hair and people say I look like a grown-up Annie. My day off is Wednesday." (Be sure to tell the caller your day off. Then you cannot complain that you lost the sale because your contact came in when you were not around.)
"You won't be sorry if you give us a chance to serve you."

TWENTY-ONE OUTRAGEOUS OUTGOING CALLS

These are proactive calls. These dialogues demand more than a kind and generous reaction or response. The dialogues must catch the attention of someone, and maybe take him completely off-guard. Everything inside of each of us resists the caller who interrupts our day. The utmost attention and preparation must be paid to the development of the cold call. These are the calls that dramatically increase both personal and company profits. Be sure all systems are go before you begin your 50 calls for the day:

—All materials in one place.

—Are the calling times you have selected appropriate?

When I telephoned prospects, I only called people before or after meal hours. Research your market and discover the best times for phone work.

If I were a banker I would not cold call small businesses at peak hours to talk about my excellent banking service. I would call the owner just to set up a good time to take him to lunch and then go from there.

- Be prepared to move off of the prepared dialogue into impromptu performance if the conversation calls for it.
- Use the 3 W Formula at the opening of each call: *W*ho I Am; *W*hat I am; *W*hy I am calling.
- Listen carefully. Know when to be quiet.
- Keep it simple. Complicated technique can cloud a simple selling message.
- Phone the prospect FAST.

Do not be tempted to do a presentation over the phone. Tell the prospect who wants to hang on that you can set up an appointment and do a more thorough job in person.

The Detective Call

We waste a great deal of time talking to the wrong people about our services. This telephone script helps you get in the door with the right people from the beginning.

An insurance salesperson made a thorough presentation to a senior vice president of a company over lunch. At the end of the expensive lunch, the VP said, "This all sounds wonderful, but I don't have the power to call the shots on this one, George. You need to get with our company treasurer, Ted Tightwad."

This situation may not have been a complete waste of time if this executive was included in the final decision. But if he is not a decision maker, why take him out to lunch in the first place? Beware of those who enjoy free lunches just for fun. If you are on straight commission and new to the world of selling, you could find yourself broke overnight.

To avoid an unnecessary appointment, first use common sense and try to pinpoint who would be involved in that kind of decision within the company structure. Remember, sometimes company CEOs are strictly figureheads and they will recommend that you talk to someone in their senior staff. Many companies require that the company accountant or treasurer approve all new products or services. You can save time by enlisting the aid of secretaries, personnel offices, switchboard operators, and receptionists to discover how the call should be directed. Here are a couple of good detective scripts:

(1) "Hi, Hilda. I am Danielle Kennedy with Stay Alive Insurance Company. Our corporate benefits are unmatched. I was under the impression that someone on your staff wanted details on my product. Can you direct me to who makes these types of decisions?"

She may say: "We don't do anything over the phone. Your best bet is to send your brochure or portfolio. We will review the material and go from there."

"Who should I mail this material to?"

Now you know exactly who needs to see your material. After you mail her your information, a follow-up call for an appointment is the next step.

(2) "Hi, Ms. Smith. I am not sure I am talking to the right person but perhaps you can help me. Who is in charge of making decisions regarding corporate insurance programs?"

You will get a definite name from one of these scripts. Remember to use the "The Phone Home, Gee-You-Sound Familiar" voice.

The Guard-At-The-Gate Call

One particularly frustrating morning I remembered thinking secretaries were like bodyguards. I was sitting at my desk thinking, "How do I get past the guard at the gate?" Then I said to myself, I bet most people are rude to secretaries. They want to talk to the boss and this middle man or woman gets in the way. Yet I knew that secretaries have more pull with the boss than most people realize. So, the next time I called a VP, I tried "the guard at the gate" dialogue.

"Good morning, Stuffed Shirt, Inc. May I help you?"

I replied: "Can you tell me the first name of Mr. Jones' secretary?"

"Certainly. That's Sheila Shun. May I connect you?"

"Please."

"Hi, Sheila. I am calling *long-distance.* (Whenever you make a toll call say this.) I know you are just as busy as I am, but I need to ask you a favor. I was told (use a mentor's name when appropriate) Mr. Jones needs some information from me regarding———. When is the best time of the day to give him a call back and speak with him directly about the research I completed for him?"

Sometimes I am unexpectedly surprised with:

"Danielle, I think I see him coming out of his office right now. Let's see if I can put you through to him."

Other responses are also positive:

"Thanks for being so considerate, Danielle. Things are very hectic around here. Can you call back about 4:00 P.M?"

The Survey Call

Direct sales people should use the following script when attempting to penetrate a new area. You can style it to your own needs.

"Hello, I am Danielle Kennedy, your local "phony fingernail salesperson" (Avon rep, A-1 Insurance agent, Banker, Realtor, Printer). I am surveying my town (or area) to see whom you presently are doing business with and if you are happy with their service. Do you have a favorite finger nailer and are you pleased with how things are working out?"

This script is a numbers call. You will get many turndowns so keep in mind the 100 to 1 rule. It takes 100 calls to get 1 yes or a maybe. Handle the turn-downs lightly and keep calling fast.

If they are happy with their representative:

"Thanks for talking to me. If you ever consider making a change, I hope you will remember me. I really work hard for my customers."

If you get a positive response or hear even the slightest flirtation, try to set up an appointment.

"Hey, I am always looking for a better deal. I like my sales representative, but who knows (kind of kidding around)—what have you got to offer?"

I reply with: "It's tough to beat my prices or service. My only problem is I have a commitment in just a few minutes and I couldn't do my service justice over the phone. The best thing to do is let me set up an appointment with you, NO OBLIGATION of course, so you can find out your other options. Are you available this evening—say around 7:30?"

The I-Don't-Know-If-I-Am-Talking-To-The-Right-Person Call

This one is similar to the detective call. We use this script in conjunction with good mailing lists. However, the best lists in the world often deliver our brochure to people who either do not handle the decision or people who are no longer employed at the company. This script will even update your mailing list if you want to do that as well.

"Hi, this is Mike Craig with Danielle Kennedy Productions and I am a little confused and not sure whether I am speaking to the right person or not."

He sounds a little breathless and stupid, which usually elicits this response:

"I don't know if you are either, but try me."

"Well, I represent a lecturer and author named Danielle Kennedy. Are you involved in booking speakers for programs that your company or association puts together for their sales people (or members)?"

If that organization has no use at all for your service, then there is no point in continuing the conversation any longer than it takes to politely end it. If we are using a good mailing list, quite a few of these conversations will lead to future business. Then decide what to do. You can:

1. Send them a brochure or more information including a press kit.

2. Set up an appointment.

3. Send them a quotation or fee schedule.

4. Design an outline of a customized program for their company.

5. Put a card about them in your tickler file to call at a specific time.

6. Contact someone else in the organization for an appointment. If you get a positive response, send a thank you note.
"I didn't know who I was talking to when I first called you, but you sure turned out to be very kind and helpful."

This also covers you when the person directs the call to someone else. Perhaps she tipped you off like this:

"Talk to Kate O'Brien. She hires all the speakers. Let me warn you that she hates dealing with most motivational people like yourself. But I know for a fact she has heard of Danielle Kennedy and it is time for her to put together next year's sales rally. Call back at her extension in 10 minutes. I will mention I was talking to you and suggested you speak to her directly."

The Follow-Up Phone Call

This call is made within 5 days after the prospect receives the information you sent.

"Hi Mr. Chester. This is Fearless Flyer with Detachable Wings, Inc. I talked to you last week. I mailed you some information about our new models. Did you have a chance to review the brochure?"

Do not send out direct mail pieces or huge bulk mailings unless you intend to incorporate some type of follow-up system by telephone. Read "The Great American Telephone Blitz" at the end of this chapter.

The I've-Got-A-Problem-Call

I began warm calling my past satisfied customers years ago using this dialogue. It was strictly the selling instinct doing its job. I was sitting at my desk talking to myself: "You know I have a real problem here. I need to enlist the help of my supporters." With that, I started leafing through my card file and identified my happiest customers. I wrote the date in red ink next to their name and called them.

Each quarter or half-year period after that I would check the red date on the file cards and remember it was time to tell them my problem again. A few always came through for me.

"Hi, Mitch. This is Danielle Kennedy. Boy, have I got a problem."

"What's up, kiddo?"

"Well, you have given me a lot of business in the past and so I am assuming that is a sign that you have been satisfied with our business relationship. Therefore, I want to take advantage of the good standing I have with you and enlist your help. I need to contact some hot prospects who might be interested in my service. Do you know of anyone who may have that kind of potential or even be remotely interested?"

It never hurts to ask—especially those people that you have served well.

The Shot In The Dark Script

This dialogue can be tested on both the cold and warm call. With the warm call (such as the past client), a referral may be the result of this off-the-wall conversation.

The stranger you call off a target list or your specific territory may respond, too. The tone here is very "phone home." Before you try it, imagine you are calling on your next door neighbor. You just discovered you need an egg to make the pancakes. Or perhaps you are in the garage looking for a drill to finish a repair job, and you remember your son borrowed it and he's 20 miles away.

"Hi Bud. (or Mr. Stranger) I am Mary Magic with Flying Carpets Unlimited. This is strictly a shot in the dark, but I am always hunting for new prospects to spread good rumors to about the wonderful product or service I represent. Do you have any names to pass on so I can get to work?"

I got a big sale from this call once. I was driving down the street one Saturday afternoon in my territory and something told me to pull off the road, go to a pay phone and call this certain customer of mine. As soon as I finished the "Shot In The Dark" dialogue, my man said to me, "I can't believe you are calling us today, Kennedy."

I asked him why and he told me that he and his wife had just mentioned they were going to give me a call because they wanted me to come over and do a presentation for some friends who were staying with them from the East Coast.

We all have an inner trainer or coach dropping little hints into our head. Many times when I do not follow my inner selling sense, I find out that the person I was considering calling just went out and did business with someone else. If I had followed my instincts, the business could have been mine.

The Jump-Up Call

While phone prospecting, be prepared to drop everything at a minute's notice to react if the caller sounds ready for an appointment. Here's how I once handled a phone lead that was ready for action.

I was talking on the telephone to the chairman of the board of a major national consulting firm. I heard he had just finished my book and was passing it around to his staff. I called to voice my appreciation.

Our conversation was filled with good feelings. I doubt I would have said what I did if I had sensed a lack of admiration on his part. We were just about to end the conversation when he said:

"Perhaps we can get together sometime. I would love to give you a tour of our new corporate offices, which I understand are very close to your home."

I jumped on the offer. "How about this afternoon? I can change my schedule, if you can fit me in."

The man was amazed. He was caught a bit off guard, but responded enthusiastically with, "Sure. What time? Say three or four this afternoon?"

I took it from there. Because I jumped at the chance to meet the main man, I landed a major national account.

The What-Do-You-Think-Call

Years ago, when the mayor of New York City ran up and down the streets asking the people, "How am I doing?" he gained much attention. There is something courageous about this question that people on the receiving end cannot resist. It has the "C'mon, I can take it" sound. "You can tell me the truth about how you feel about this product and we will do everything in our power to improve what we offer you."

Here is how to use this script over the phone.

"Hi, Mrs. Mitchell. This is Krystal Klear with Window Washers Anonymous. What do you think?"

Pause for a few seconds. (You have to be in a slightly silly mood when you do this script.)

She replies with: "What are you talking about?"

You respond: "What do you think of our reputation as a company in the community? Have you noticed our newspaper ads? Do any of your neighbors use my service?"

The responses range from outstanding to obnoxious. In all cases, I have discovered that most people appreciate the opportunity to be heard. No one seems to care about people's personal opinions anymore. The real message behind this question is: We care enough to ask you how we are doing and how we can improve.

I assigned this phone script to my sales students at the Kennedy Clinic For Real Estate Professionals last summer. They were instructed to go home and cold call "For Sale By Owner" ads in the papers until they connected with at least one person who would respond to the following dialogue.

"Hi, I am Laura Lister, a real estate professional, but I am not calling to solicit a listing. For the past two days I have been attending an educational conference here in the area and one of my homework assignments is to call people who are trying to market their own home and ask them: 'What do you think?' So, what do you think?"

One man said: "What do I think about what?"

My salesperson replied with: "What do you think about the real estate industry in general? Do you have a poor opinion about the service we offer?"

One student reported the following conversation to my class the next morning:

"The man I called explained to me all the reasons he did not like or want to do business with realtors. This is my first month in selling and I have always feared the telephone. I hate it when people get mad. This has been a great approach script for me because I didn't have to ask the man to buy anything and I really got an idea of why he dislikes salespeople.

"By the end of our talk, he invited me to come see his home and was asking me a million questions. His final comment was 'Your approach is refreshing.'"

Here's another way to use this script. Suppose you sell cellular car phones. First, get your hands on an up-to-date list of a target audience who have the need for a car phone. It would include salespeople from certain industries such as insurance, travel agencies, and advertising.

"Hi, I am Frank Carphoney with Over The Off Ramp Cellular Phones. What do you think of our product?"

"Never heard of it."

"What do you think of car phones in general?"

"I heard they are expensive, but convenient."

"This is exactly why I need to make calls like this, sir. False rumors spread about valuable products, and people such as yourself who may have a need for the convenience of a car phone, never get a chance to learn how really affordable it can be to own one."

Remember, you are asking for trouble with this script if you do not know what you are talking about. If you are on top of your service, callers admire your courage. I have made a lot of money from this script.

A word of caution: End the conversation gracefully when it starts going nowhere fast. Ask yourself: "Is this conversation going to make me any money?"

The Be-On-The-Lookout Call

This is a networking call. It works well with people who seem to know everybody and exactly what's happening at all times. There are some people I know that are fountains of information. The best way to describe this group is to call them "the informers." They are very generous, so please return the generosity whenever possible. Whenever I need to get the word out, I know it is time to call the informers.

"Hi, George. This is Danielle Kennedy. You seem to have a handle on the latest trends in speaking and what the hot topics are. I have a new marketing program for the health industry that is very exciting. Be on the lookout for people or any information leading to people who may need my services. As a matter of fact, if you have time, I would love to take you to lunch or buy you a cup of coffee and fill you in."

Sometimes, one call like this can put you in front of a decision maker or direct you to one.

Have-You-Heard-The-Latest Script

This updates your clients on your product line. You must take the position that if you don't keep them informed, they will think that you are falling down on your service.

"Hi, Mary. This is Faye at Danielle Kennedy Productions. Have you heard the latest about the new addition to Danielle's video library?"

"I thought I had all of her tapes."

"All, but her newest one. It's called 'Leading the Double Life Between Family and Career.' She gives working parents specific ways to eliminate unnecessary guilt, better ways to delegate, and positive communication skills to use with one's children. Her whole family is interviewed on the program.

We've been getting rave reviews from those who invest in it. I know you will want this in your library. If you buy it today, you can save 30% off the retail price of $125. Shall I charge it to your corporate account or do you want more information?"

You can use the "Have-You-Heard-The-Latest" script for telemarketing all of your products. Make a twelve-month calendar and offer special savings every 30 days on one of several products. This works very effectively at my company.

We choose to run specials on products that would benefit salespeople at certain times of the year. My time planner is offered at a savings near Christmas. They make wonderful presents and during that time of the year people are shopping for planners. My business development video and audio tapes are offered at a special price in January, when salespeople are working on getting back their focus after the holiday season.

The I-Can-Protect-Your-Money Affluent Call

Remember Dorothy and her friends in the movie, *The Wizard of Oz?* Think back to how desperately they wanted to see the all-powerful Oz in person. He would solve all their problems. But they were shaking in their boots thinking about the confrontation. Once they met him, they discovered he was just as nervous as they were.

I try to remember that story when I call on the men and women in the "ivory towers" across America. They are people just like you and me. The biggest challenge we have when prospecting the affluent is getting in touch with them directly. They have a strong protection team around them and they do not work the same hours as the average person on the street.

However, the self-made millionaires and billionaires of our time admire hard work, salesmanship, and courage. Once you get their ear, I find them the best prospects of all.

Among the affluent are business owners, high producing commissioned salespeople, employees at both large companies and growing smaller businesses who receive yearly bonus compensation, entrepreneurs, and artists.

Many salespeople do not think they have a chance to connect with these prospects. The trick is to study and understand their lifestyles. Because they typically work very hard and in spurts, if you contact them by phone, do so at their office before 8:00 A.M. They are often the first in the office and the last to leave at night.

Before you make the call, you need to know as much about their situation as possible. If you have a mentor or some common ground, it helps. The primary purpose of your call is to get an appointment. There is no substitute for face-to-face contact.

The affluent call requires that you take a great deal of time to research needs and develop an understanding of desires and risk-taking propensities of your prospect.

You must be sensitive to timing with your wealthy prospect. One single period during the entire year may be the only time to strike with your call or offer. This period of sensitivity may only last for two or three weeks. You may find yourself calling 30 affluent people, but only one is interested in your offer. Take the time in your phone dialogue with these people to ask when a better time would be to call them back and reopen the conversation.

"Hi. I am Morticia Martin with Dead-Beat Estate Planning. How fortunate to catch you, but I know how busy you are so I will make this brief. Often, people in your position are helping everyone else protect their investments but don't have the time to concentrate on their own.

"The Retirement Plan Charitable Remainder Unitrust is the latest and best solution to protecting your income. When compared to a qualified retirement plan, the benefits far outweigh anything else out there. But, I need to sit down with you for 30 minutes and explain. I could speed the process up by sending you my prospectus before we meet. What do you think?"

The affluent move and act fast once they decide to buy. One of my "naturals" in the car industry helped a well-off executive get exactly what she wanted recently because he moved swiftly at the right time.

He told me: "A woman called me one morning and she was in a big hurry. She asked about the Classic 1967 Mercedes convertible that she saw in our showroom window.

"I told her the owner's son collects cars and then sells them. Initially, he hadn't intended to sell this one because it was hard to come by, but at the last minute he changed his mind. My prospect told me she was leasing a Mercedes and the lease was up this month. She had to make a decision about whether to buy that one or get another car. She had been looking for this rare model for a long time and was surprised when she drove by and saw it in our window.

"She needed the information sent to her accountant immediately. She was going out of town on a business trip in three days and wanted to make the decision by then.

"I got her into the showroom within an hour; introduced her to the owner of the car (car collectors are very picky about who buys their gems); hand-carried the car papers and work sheet to her accountant; and delivered the car to her door three days later—two hours before her flight out of town."

When a busy executive wants action, the Natural is ready to go for the natural high!

The Information Call

This call is excellent for both large department stores and exclusive neighborhood boutiques. The call can be made to both the regular client and the prospect who has filled out a card for your mailing list.

"Hi, Marian. This is Ruth from Radical Rags. Our fall collection of suits is in and I thought you might want to know about it. The selections are stunning, so please don't miss the chance to take a peek. Our hours are——.

"I am in every day except Thursday, so please try to come in any day but that one. I always enjoy giving you special attention."

Send an announcement or a follow-up "Thanks-for-talking-to-me" note.

So far, all of these prospecting calls have one goal in mind—to discover a need and get an appointment. If a salesperson has a third party endorsement, his chances of getting that appointment are almost assured if he follows my mentor calling program.

The Mentor Call That Counts

After I became fairly successful in selling, satisfied customers began calling me with referrals. I learned that just taking the person's name and number and trying to work the lead on my own was not productive without enlisting the assistance of my mentor.

One day I got a mentor call from a customer of mine.

He said: "Danny, Dr. Smith is going to call you with a lead. I told him how great you are."

I was shocked. "Are you sure it's Dr. Smith?" I asked. "He normally works with Paula Peterson, a competitor of mine."

My friend told me: "He hasn't worked with her for several months. When he first gave her leads, she was very grateful, but now that she has become successful, her follow-up is poor and she doesn't seem to be appreciative of the business. She also gave him the third degree every time he dropped a lead on her lap. If the prospect wasn't ready to buy that day, she didn't want to bother with them."

After hearing that, I realized that mentors can be touchy—and rightly so. First of all, they do not have to take the time to call you at all. They do this out of the generosity of their hearts. There are many salespeople out there who would love to get their business. Once they choose you, show appreciation no matter what happens.

Then I thought about how important it is to reassure that mentor that we will not let him or her down once we make the contact. It's very embarrassing for a mentor to get a bad report about his recommendation. The following script covers all the bases:

"Thanks so much for calling me. There are so many people in the insurance business these days, you could have called any number of them. I will make sure you won't be sorry you contacted me.

"I have a double responsibility now. I have to do a good job not only for the lead's sake, but for your sake because your name and reputation are on the line.

"But I'm curious. How did you hear about me? (If they have called you with leads before say: What have you liked about doing business with me in the past that has motivated you to call me again? I'd like to know what I am doing right.)"

They might say: "We heard you are more interested in serving the customer than anything else."

Or if they know you well:

"Remember when you sold us our policy? We must have talked to a million agents and we kept coming back to you. You were so patient and knowledgeable. You answered every objection very logically, too."

Then I would go on: "Do me a favor. In the next two hours, can you call Mr. or Ms. Lead and tell them what you just told me? Spread a good rumor for me. They will feel so much more comfortable with my call when I touch base with them."

I always get a positive response: "No problem, Danny."

"Thank you. I will call them by 3:00. Does that give you enough time to make your call first?"

Then they call the lead. I call that prospect shortly after they do and say:

"Hi, Mr. Lead. I am Danielle Kennedy, the representative from Detachable Wings that Mr. Mentor told you about. Keep in mind I have a double responsibility to both you and Mr. Mentor now. If I don't take good care of you, I will never hear the end of it."

This makes the prospect feel very safe. Before a customer tells a salesperson the truth about his needs, it is important to be seen in that customer's eyes as someone he can trust. The mentor helps build the foundation for you.

The Testimonial Letter Call

I use testimonial conversations and testimonial letters to build a 100% referral business in every new career I develop. Here is how to overcome false modesty and collect more testimonial letters than you have room to file.

A customer compliments me: "Danielle, you did a great job. The service was perfect and your communication with us meant so much."

DK: "Mr. Customer, I have an URGENT request. Can you put that compliment down in writing in the next 24 hours? Perhaps you could dictate a letter to your secretary and I could work with her on picking it up by tomorrow after 5:00."

Customer: "Okay. But what is your hurry?"

DK: "Well, I go out on job interviews every time I have an appointment with a prospect. All salespeople really hire and fire themselves based on their attitude, knowledge, and ability to promote. No one would think of going on a job interview without a reference letter. Your testimonial will be my reference letter. I like to ask when my clients' enthusiasm is high—strike while the iron is hot, you might say."

I always get a "No problem" response.

The-Do-You-Love-Me-Call

Whenever you are having one of those down days with cold calling, you can pick up your mood fast by calling a satisfied client to find out how they're doing, and get a free "feel good" for your ego.

"Hi Julie, this is Denise Delirious. Am I still your favorite Rubber Room salesperson?"

"Hey, Delirious you devil. What's happening, girl? Are you still setting the world on fire? Seems like we heard you just won some big sales award."

"Well, I could use a little encouragement today. I have been calling people searching for leads and nobody will talk to me. Are you still happy with your Rubber Room (car, house, computer, carpeting)?"

"Absolutely."

"Can you think of anyone who might be getting ready to buy?"

"Now, let me think . . ."

The next thing you know, I am in much better spirits because I just hung up with a hot tip from an old buddy.

The Deadline Call

One of my students who sells life insurance told me my deadline script had really increased her income. I suggested that one of the first questions she should ask her prospects over the phone is their birthday. Then I told her to organize her customer/prospect files by date so she is reminded to call on her prospects two weeks before their next birthday. Why? So she can say:

"Ms. Jones, I understand that Pete will be forty years old in two weeks. At that time the rates will go up. But, if we put this policy through right now, it will take the rate for age 39, and save you quite a bit of money. We need to get the application in right away to get it approved before Pete's next birthday."

This script works because it puts enough time pressure on people to break through their inertia. You are also doing your customer a favor. Do you realize the number of people who depend on honest salespeople and other service representatives to keep their lives squared away?

The Limited-Supply Call

"Limited edition. The mold will be destroyed after only 23 copies are cast."

"Only five more building lots in this prestigious location."

"The only one of its kind in existence."

All of us have seen advertising like this. The customer who is ready to buy now wants the product. If it looks like the supply may be running out it makes people nervous. I respond to this myself. As long as this is not used to take advantage of the customer or as a ploy, I think you owe it to the customer to let him know that this could be his last chance for such a great opportunity.

"We are getting a limited number of Land Cruisers in during the next two weeks. I can't keep these cars in my lot they move so fast. I know you showed interest. If you are sincere about purchasing one, come in Wednesday around 2 o'clock in the afternoon."

Telemarketing tickets to seminars requires many deadline scripts to get the people to attend. I tell my sales staff that they have to imagine how angry the person they are calling is going to be when one of his associates comes back from my sales retreat bragging about how much he learned. If my telemarketer is not fired up, he or she is not going to fire up the caller.

"This event is almost sold out. You must reserve your seat. Believe me, someday you will thank me for getting you to this valuable educational experience."

The Early-Bird-Special Call

If you are selling a travel package, a ticket to a convention, seminar, or a retail item try this phone script either before or after you do a mailing.

"We have a marvelous offer for all the senior citizens who live in Happy Heights. We are booking a two-week cruise to the Greek Islands for June of next year. If you sign up for this trip before March 31, you will save $575—the price goes up to $14,000 a couple, and $7,000 for singles after that date."

If you are selling high ticket items, there could be a substantial savings involved when someone takes advantage of the early bird special. Do not assume this approach only appeals to the more conservative or moderate of income. The affluent are conservative about spending money. They are also looking for savings.

Telemarketing for Appointments

There are two types of telemarketing calls: the kind you make when you want to sell the product on the spot, or the kind you make to get an appointment with the customer.

This script will work for the public relations person who is going after a business account, or the pure telemarketing specialist who never makes in-person calls, but whose sole purpose is to book appointments for other members of the sales staff.

"Hi, I'm Mary Wright and I represent Danielle Kennedy—considered by many to be the Mother of Sales Development. Are you familiar with her teachings or work?"

"Yes, I have read her book."

"Wonderful. Let me ask you, how many salespeople do you have on your staff at Paper Planes Unlimited?"

"Ten."

"Would you be interested in learning more about how your ten salespeople can make more sales and experience fewer sales slumps with the personal coaching of Ms. Kennedy?"

"Perhaps."

"Danielle is coming to St. Paul on January 28th. One of the members of her sales team will be in your area in the next ten days and would like to stop by and give you and the staff a short presentation on how to get involved in this great event. There is no obligation and the presentation will be very informative whether you decide to go see Danielle or not. Can we pick a time and date right now?"

"How about after our sales meeting on the first Monday of this month?"

The Wait-Until-You-See Call

I learned this dandy from my eight kids—the naturals of all time.

"Mother, come here. Wait until you see this."

The next thing you know, I am standing next to an 11 × 14 ski poster of some handsome dude coming down the slopes at Snowbird, Utah.

"Picture this, Mombo. It's almost Christmas. You are not stuck in the malls running around at the last minute like a madwoman. Instead, you are sitting on the floor next to a sky-high, wood-burning fireplace up in a mountain cabin. The snowflakes gently fall in front of your window, while the fire crackles and the aroma of turkey cooking in the oven pleases you. Your children have left you alone in peace, while they merrily ski down the powdered slopes.

"If you sell about six houses between now and November 1st, we can all live like that over the holidays."

The "Wait-Until-You-See Script" gets the prospect speculating with his imagination. I started using their "Wait Until You See" script on the telephones like crazy. Let's say I was keeping an eye open for a certain type of home for one of my prospects. Perhaps, the client insisted on a home with a pool, a view, and plenty of privacy.

"Harold, put Mary on the other phone," I would say.

"I'm here, Danielle. What's going on?" asks Mary.

"I found something perfect. Wait until you see this little spot of heaven about two blocks up from the beach. It sits on the hill at the end of a cul-de-sac. You have complete privacy because the home is surrounded by tall green pine trees and there isn't one single neighbor within eyeshot. You can skip-and-go-naked and no one will know the difference. Oh, and the pool . . . wait until you see that. It's a free form with the most beautiful Mexican tile finish I have ever seen."

Pretty soon he can't stand the suspense and interrupts my dialogue to say:

"I can't wait. Can I make an appointment to see you right now?" Those nasty kids of mine have taught me some powerful stuff.

THE GREAT AMERICAN THREE-METHOD TELEPHONE BLITZ

Now that you have the scripts to get you on the telephone, the next step is selecting the best tracking method to organize your prospect calls and maintain a rapid follow-up system. There are three common methods of telephone prospecting:

1. Mail—Phone
2. Phone—Mail—Phone *or*
   Phone—Fax—Phone
3. Phone only

The most effective of the three types is the phone—mail—phone method. Study all three types and choose your plan.

1. *Mail—Phone Campaign.* The salesperson procures a targeted list of prospective names, addresses, and telephone numbers.
   Step One: Mail a brochure, flyer, or teaser piece of advertising to each listed name.
   Step Two: Make a follow-up phone call within five days of the date you estimate that they will receive your mail. The dialogue goes like this:
   "Hi, this is Kelly Craig with DRK Productions. Did you receive my brochure regarding the Kennedy Clinic for Sales Professionals?"
   Disadvantage: They never received your piece because either the wrong person intercepted the information, they never opened the envelope and it's still sitting in the individual's in-basket, or the material was thrown away.
   The Mail—Phone campaign usually turns out to be a Phone—Mail—Phone campaign and the dialogue ends up like this:
   "Did you receive my brochure about the upcoming Kennedy Clinic for Sales Professionals?"
   "Never saw it."
   "Have you ever heard of Danielle Kennedy?"
   "I'm not sure."
   "She's the Mother of Sales Development across America today. You'll kick yourself later knowing she was in your area and you didn't take the opportunity to send your sales force to hear her. Sales managers are reporting sizeable increases in productivity after

their salespeople return from her programs. How many salespeople work for you?"

"Twenty."

"I'd like to send you a detailed brochure about this educational opportunity—with no obligation, of course. You owe it to your staff to review the material. How can I be sure it *gets in your hands* this time?"

"Send it to the attention of . . . "

2. *The Phone—Mail—Phone campaign.* You still work the list, but use the "I don't-know-if-I-am-talking-to-the-right-person" script. This puts you in touch with the appropriate contact before you mail anything.

If you already know who that person is, try this dialogue:

"Hi, John. I'm Dixie Robb with The Danielle Kennedy Education Systems. Have you ever heard of Danielle Kennedy?"

"No." Then continue with the previous dialogue.

Follow up within five days from the date they received the piece, using my "What do you think?" dialogue.

Decide whether you should send any information, and if you do, who should receive it.

Advantage: Pre-screening the prospect gives you an idea if the interest is there. With this method, you avoid wasting money on blind mailings.

Phone—Fax—Phone. This is the same as Phone—Mail—Phone, except you ask them their fax number and send out the information by fax. The reaction time is faster and more effective.

3. *Phone only Campaign.* Take a crisscross directory or targeted list and start calling at random. This works if you are known in a certain territory. Make this type of call at an appropriate time when you are not catching people in the middle of meetings, meals, or bad moods.

There has to be at least one dialogue in this chapter you feel comfortable transplanting into your quiver immediately. Remember, these scripts work for any product or service. Just customize and enter them into your personal journals. Like anything else, they will not do you much good if you only write them down or just self-talk them. Go ahead and grab that phone NOW.

Once you connect with some hot phone prospects, it is time to hit the streets and go face-to-face with your adoring future customers. Watch how we two-step into their life in the next chapter.

4 Natural Networking: How to Create Enormous Profit When You Own the Marketplace

"Eighty percent of success is showing up."

WOODY ALLEN

You will never live the good selling life and breathe the pure air of prosperity unless you commit yourself to face-to-face customer prospecting. Some salespeople refuse to knock, walk, and talk, claiming that such "shmoozing" is beneath them.

"It's already been overdone."

"It doesn't work for my product."

It isn't worth doing."

The bottom line is that any salesperson who refuses to get out and meet the people is either afraid or ashamed. If you are ashamed and you feel bad and embarrassed about working your territory, I cannot help you with that problem. You are either trying to sell something you do not ardently believe in, or selling, as a vocation, is not your style.

If fear is stopping your progress, I can help you. Nobody was more frightened than I was when I asked my first sales manager how to get some customers and she told me to go hit the streets and start door-knocking. I was six months pregnant and there were very few women in the selling field and I didn't know of one other pregnant door-knocker.

Since I had no choice, I forced myself out in the marketplace like a baby struggling to walk or talk—I picked myself up after the fall, and pounded the streets again. Once I got the hang of mingling with the masses, I felt at home networking anywhere, any time, or any place.

Many Naturals have overcome personal fears and mastered the art of confrontation. My friend Tom Hopkins is one of the great sales trainers of our time. He has achieved such tremendous success in his career by honing his selling skills so naturally that he could stop working tomorrow

61

and live very well off for the rest of his life. He doesn't stop, though, because he so loves the field of sales and helping others achieve success in sales. His career hasn't always been so rosy, though. He began his door-knocking at age 18 when he was so broke he could not afford to buy a suit. That did not stop him. He decided to wear his band uniform. He learned how to work the territory effortlessly. Recently I watched Tom take a total stranger through the process of prospecting, presenting, and closing within two hours. By the way, this was on his day off right before he started a round of golf.

My husband and I had a golf date scheduled with Tom and his wife Debbie. Several months earlier his intuition was beginning to guide him in the area of skillful bartering.

"This golf game won't cost you a penny," he announced.

I thanked him for offering to pay our way but he corrected me: "I'm not paying anybody's way. I am going to trade my training materials with the golf pro for greens fees."

My husband and I looked at his wife and rolled our eyes. We thought maybe he had been on the road too long. I also wondered how he was going to embarrass us in the pro shop.

Debbie explained that Tom was dead serious about bartering. Since he had become a golf fanatic, he had noticed how the sales staff at golf shops never attempted to sell him their merchandise. This complacency bothered him, and he was convinced they needed his sales training.

She told us that Tom started asking around at different courses and everyone admitted they were very naive about sales. He was told that if someone comes in and wants something, the staff accepts the money and hands over the merchandise. They did not realize that with a little help, the golf shop could make a profit.

The first thing Tom did was call the golf course about one hour before our tee-off time. He asked the switchboard operator for the name of the golf director and the time he was expected to arrive. She told him he was there and she would connect him.

Tom said: "Hi, Jack. My name is Tom Hopkins and I want to stop by with a free gift for you this morning before I tee off at your course around 10:30. I golf all over the world and have presented this gift to many pros like yourself. They all love it. Can I drop it off at about 10:15?"

He agreed to see Tom.

I believe in natural selling, but I thought Hopkins had gone over the edge this time. In the car, on the way over to the course, he explained to us how well this plan was working out for all the people involved.

"I get to play golf and pro shops finally start making some profits."

By the time we got to the golf course I just wanted to go in and pay for my golf game and pray that Hopkins would not embarrass us. He marched up to the pro and said:

"Hi, Jack, I am Tom Hopkins who called about 30 minutes ago. I have a gift for you. Can I take it into your office?"

Inside of a big box was his complete sales training library on 12 audio tapes, including workbooks. This program was based on his best-selling book *How To Master The Art of Selling*. The program retailed for the same price as the cost of green fees for all four of us.

I eavesdropped outside of the pro's office to find out the greens fee verdict. I can honestly say it was one of the most natural sales presentations I have ever listened to in my life. Here is what I overheard.

"Jack, I am Tom Hopkins and I am in the teaching profession just like you. I don't give golf lessons—I give selling lessons. I travel all over the world and play a lot of golf in between my speaking engagements.

"Because my whole life is about selling, I always watch to see how people sell to others. This is instinctive to me just like observing a golfer's style is instinctive to you.

"I must admit that I have never been to a pro shop where the staff is interested in selling their products to the public. Do you have any idea how much this company could increase its profits if some sales efforts were made in your pro shop?"

Jack agreed and mentioned that the owners were always complaining that the pro shop never made much money, especially since discount golf stores opened.

Tom said: "I want to make you a proposition. It costs $395 to send a salesperson to my boot camp in Arizona for three days and that does not include airfare, hotel, and food. Those salespeople who attend turn company profits around once they have graduated from my program."

Tom then put his beautifully-packaged materials on the desk and said: "This is the complete curriculum that I cover and it sells for $299. It is yours free.

"All that I ask is for an invitation to play a free round of golf for myself, my wife, and my friends today. Does that seem like a fair exchange to you?"

Jack replied enthusiastically. "Absolutely. As a matter of fact my brother-in-law sells insurance and he has your book on his bedroom shelf. He won't believe I met you."

At this point these two buddies walked out of Jack's office talking drives, putts, and scores. For the rest of the day, Hopkins kept repeating the same question to me over and over:

"How many hours of opportunity to SELL exist in a given day, Kennedy?"

"Twenty-four, teacher—24 beautiful hours."

THE QUICK "ANYBODY-I-KNOW" NETWORK

It does not matter what you sell, networking starts with a list and the best resource for names on that list is you. I can still remember the cards in my green cardboard box filed from A to Z. I just started filling out cards with names of people that I could recall all the way back to grade school.

If funds are a problem, use a shoe box with 4 × 6 index cards. If you are established, input the names in a data base on the computer. Start by copying current addresses off of your Christmas card list and whatever address books you have.

Expand your list by including your current client list. Also include the local hairdresser, barber, dentist, doctor, service station owner, your children's teachers, coaches, the pastor and staff at your place of worship, and anyone you know. Try to add three names to your list each day.

Networking starts in your own backyard. Whenever I took my children to the pediatrician, I made a prospecting call too. The first time I approached the doctor, he made the mistake of asking: "How's life treating you, Mom?"

I replied: "Pretty darn good since I started selling houses all over town to beat the band."

Doctors are real estate addicts. "No kidding. You know Vera and I want to move into something a little bit bigger if we can afford it. Maybe you can help us."

Without missing a beat I asked: "What day are you off?"

"Wednesday and Thursday afternoons."

"Why don't we go exploring Wednesday afternoon?"

"Let me talk to my wife. Can you call me here later today, say about 4:30?"

I moved the good doctor and his two partners in and out of houses for 10 years. All I had to do was ask once. I would have brought the topic up whenever I had to in order to remind him to spread a few good rumors about me, but he always initiated the conversation:

"Still selling like a madwoman, Danny?" he said.

"You betcha, Doc. It may be time for you to think about another investment. What do you think?"

or sometimes I said:

"Do you have any new patients who may need my services?"

As my doctor's practice grew, so did mine. However, my children got a little tired of my fanatic behavior regarding their health. Especially the day I insisted taking one of them to the doctor to have a mosquito bite examined!

Networking is a simple two-step process:

1. Take people out of the dark and tell them what you sell.

2. If it feels right, ask them for an appointment.

This advice applies to anyone. Whether you sell insurance or fine art, you can spread the word. At first it takes courage, but begin to spot and take your best chances anytime the opportunity presents itself.

I learned this Anybody-I-Know-Lesson the hard way. Shortly after I began selling homes, someone in my parish moved and used the services of a competitor. I did not know about it until I ran into these people a year later at the mall. While we were engaged in casual conversation, they mentioned that they had moved into a new home.

When I told them I was selling real estate they actually hit the roof.

"If only we had known. We didn't know one person to call so we blindly picked up a newspaper and called the first company we saw advertised. It was a terrible experience. Before we made the call we kept racking our brains trying to think of someone in the parish we could call."

A word of caution here: It is important to get the word out by foot, phone, and postal service to everyone you know or remotely know, but keep in mind, your best friends may not come through for you. They might not trust your new vocation and question your survival. If you are a former teacher or engineer they cannot picture you making a go at this new life of selling. This reaction also applies if you are in the middle of starting up a new business and trying to get a customer base going. The last people to come through are often those closest to you. But do not let that stop you from asking for their business. Sometimes those we know the best want us to prove our worth before they give us a chance. Try not to take it personally because it is a very common occurrence. If you are good, sooner or later they will come around.

MAKING CONNECTIONS IN YOUR TERRITORIAL NETWORK

The Anybody-I-Know-Network is a large group of people scattered all over your life as far back as you can remember. The Territorial Network is a defined, targeted audience that consists of strangers in its early stages of development. Examples include: the pharmaceutical salesperson's list of doctors' offices; the Avon lady's 300 homes in a targeted neighborhood; the computer salesperson's list of corporations and various size businesses; the real estate office that the title representative visits; and the community that the owners of hair salons or print shops serve.

You have to build a territory from scratch. You cannot rely solely on old friends or the Anybody-I-Know-Network. I can show you how to gain a big share of the market if you discipline yourself and follow my proven marketing theories.

FOOLPROOF WAYS OF DEFINING YOUR MARKET

Where do you want to go to get business? If you are assigned a territory, many of the marketing methods in this chapter will assist you. However, if you are in direct sales such as the Discovery Toys educational consultants or the A. L. Williams insurance representatives, you must choose the best spot on the lake before you drop in your line and start fishing.

I started with 300 homes that consisted of educated baby boomers who were on their way up the corporate ladder and right in the middle of producing families. I understood these people because we were nearly the same age with the same ambitions. I would have looked very stupid prospecting door-to-door in a singles condominium area when I was six months pregnant.

Be sure you have at least a degree of *kinship* for the people and the places you are going to prospect. Why would a salesperson interrupt a young mother and try to sell her a vacuum cleaner that she cannot afford? Know your audience before attempting to sell.

The following true story proves my point. I will never forget the afternoon a vacuum cleaner salesman woke me up from a nap two days after I got out of the hospital with my newborn son Joe. I was irritated all the way to the door because he kept pressing my bell like it was a fire alarm. When I opened the door, he scared me to death:

"Well, hello there, little lady. I'm Hideous Harry. Do you have any idea how many times each day across this fair land women who think they are sucking up dirt off their carpet are merely kidding themselves?"

I was stunned, and because I couldn't open my mouth he figured it was okay to move right in and take control:

"Step aside, my dear," he arrogantly said as he began studying my carpeting while heading to the living room.

Like an idiot I followed this pitch-man and watched him drag out his paraphernalia.

"Now I don't know what kind of vacuum you use, I can just tell it isn't doing the job."

I didn't want him to know that I had not vacuumed since Christmas, so I just kept quiet.

He then dropped half a bag of dirt on my already filthy carpet. Then the baby started crying in the background. I told him I had to tend to my child but he acted like he did not hear me and started dragging out some equipment. It looked like he was going to assemble a car and drive it across my living room rug.

I ran into the bedroom to get the baby.

When I came back he plugged in his system. It was so powerful I thought I would be sucked up and squeezed into the bag.

"Have you ever seen anything like this machinery, sweetie?"

"How much is it?" I replied.

"Normally $1095. If you buy it today, the price is $875 cash."

I was right. It was a car.

I told him I was sorry but I could not afford an expensive vacuum cleaner. I asked him to leave because I had to feed my baby.

Finally after he tried 30 different attempts to get my nonexistent money, he began to mumble to himself and head for the door. His parting words were: "I'll come back Saturday when the man of the house is home."

This salesman felt no kinship for any prospect. He worked his territory like an animal looking for prey.

Once you find a territory that you have a natural attraction for, do some research on the future promise it holds for you.

Are the market conditions stable in the area? If you are working direct sales, it is important to know the income level of the homeowners and their level of discretionary income. You can find out this information in a number of ways. If you are friendly with a local realtor, she can tell you the price ranges of homes in that area and approximately what the average income is of people moving in and out. She can do this without giving away confidential information. Sometimes the Chamber of Commerce has statistical information about community members.

If you call on companies, use budget reports or company history and profile information to assist you in making a good networking decision. The more pre-qualifying you can do in your territory, the easier it will be to get your toe in the door.

As you attempt to select your territory, do not overlook the *competition and their present market share of business.* Do not let false rumors scare you away from pursuing a network that you know would be right for you.

I had my eye on a territory that was supposedly being conquered by a competitor of mine. Once I began investigating the actual amount of business that this salesperson was taking out of the area, I realized he had not begun to make a dent in that market. Never believe rumors, and always study the facts and statistics.

If someone really is doing the job in the territory, decide if you want to compete or go find a virgin spot that would not be as difficult to dominate. This decision depends on how badly you want the location and how willing you are to overcome the objections you will receive from the competition.

THE WORLD'S BEST METHOD OF ORGANIZATION

The best way to get organized is your way. Do not copy someone else's system unless the two of you have a similar style of doing things. Sometimes people think I am very unorganized because I have little pieces of scratch paper and sticky notes all over my desk, in the bottom of my purse, or in the car with prospective leads written on them. But I know where every little piece of paper is and if anyone touches my notes, it breaks my train of thought.

I am going to pass on what I know about organizing a territory and then the rest is up to you.

I have used three different methods of keeping track of prospects:

1. The card file (3 × 5) (which is also on the computer)
2. The address book
3. The communication register and the three-ring notebook binder.

The card file can stay on your desk. Past clients' names are placed in that file. All prospects who turn into legitimate customers get transferred to that file. When time permits the names are also input into the computer. Always keep a hard copy of your computer file.

The address book contains current hot, warm, and cool leads, which I can take anywhere. When I get the urge to do some foot or phone work, all the information I need is at my fingertips.

The communications register (see Figure 4-1 page 69) is a form kept in a three-ring notebook binder. When you are out in the territory, you can log in conversations, updates, and changes that occur between you and the prospect. This notebook becomes your other self. When you are working on getting a customer's business and the relationship is taking a long time to develop, you will be happy that you kept notes along the way to remind you of certain conversations.

A glance at your notations, including the last time you called on the prospect, enables you to begin each new call right where you left off. You will find that people pay friendly attention to you because you are paying close attention to details.

THE SOW-AND-REAP NETWORKING METHOD BY FOOT

There are three common methods of networking. They are

1. "I'll do it but I am not happy about it." This is the easy way out. The salesperson rarely visits the territory but guards it with deep suspicion. If anyone else in the sales organization gets a bona fide lead in

CLIENT/SUBJECT				TRANSACTION TO	

COMMUNICATIONS REGISTER

START TIME	DATE	STOP TIME	CODE: ODE	OC/outgoing phone call V/visit L/letter IC/incoming phone call	
				GIST OF EACH COMMUNICATION AND NAME OF PERSON CALLED	

Figure 4-1

his territory, he becomes infuriated. He does not want to work it, but nobody else better go near it either.

2. "I really tried it—once." Nothing happened, so they figure it is useless to continue. They door-knock when there is nothing better to do, or send some delivery boy to pass out a few newsletters or flyers at local businesses or to residents. For them, pounding the pavement is a waste of time.

3. The sow-and-reap method. The goal is complete control of the territory. Salespeople who use this method are convinced that they are the best person to do business with and they have a responsibility to get that word out in their territory. They see the big picture and the huge profit-making potential. Their communication is steady, consistent, and methodical. Every day they follow the "Just do it" law of discipline.

BE LIGHT AND BREEZY, NOT HEAVY AND HARD

Approach each prospect in the field with a sense of humor and a very light conversational approach—not overly friendly, but just matter-of-fact and happy-go-lucky.

Recently some kids came to my door selling magazine subscriptions and CDs out of a catalog to raise money for their building fund. They were a brother and sister and it was fun to talk to them.

"How's it going?" I asked.

"This is so easy to do," the brother commented, "I've already sold to nine people today. I just casually ask people if they want to help us out. They always come back with a 'why not and how much?' response."

Then his sister piped in: "Yeah, no big deal if they don't feel like buying but most of them want to buy at least one CD. What we can't figure out is why we haven't run into more kids from our school trying to do the same thing."

I wondered the same thing when I started working my territory. Once I practiced "sowing and reaping," I found out how little competition I had and how easy it was to go beyond the ordinary expectations that people set out for themselves.

WALK IN LIKE YOU OWN THE PLACE

My father gave me great advice about 30 years ago: "Don't ever think you are better than anyone else, just a lot like them. When you think like that, then it is easy for you to walk into any strange neighborhood or city and feel like you belong there. Just walk in like you own the place, and more times than not, people will assume that you do."

Today I travel all over the world and feel that way. The kids at my door had that same attitude when they were selling their magazines. They just *assumed* somebody might want to help them out. When you come across that way in your territory, you turn strangers into helpers.

If your sales manager or another colleague is a natural, beg him or her to take you out on a couple of routine calls. The best education in the world is passed on through role modeling. When I had the opportunity to go in the field with one of the legends of my industry, I learned more on one call with him than I could have studying theory for a year in the classroom.

MAKE A STANDING DATE TO NETWORK

Make an appointment with yourself to door-knock just as you would any other important commitment. Once a year sit down at the calendar and mark the time, dates, and area you intend to network during the following 12 months. At the beginning of each month, check your networking dates for the next 30 days to make sure that you can keep those appointments. You may have to do that check-up once a week as well. If appointments and important clients come on the scene, do not pass on networking in your territory for that week or month, just reschedule the dates.

FAST, FASTER, FASTEST

Speed counts when you are working the territory. Do not socialize with your prospects at their places of business or in their homes. Always be in a hurry to move on to the next commitment. If you do not have a good reason to get in and out of there fast, they will wonder about you. "When does she sell anything? All Danielle does is visit and chat."

The other reason you move fast is because you have many people to see, and networking is first and foremost a numbers game. That means you have to find a few "no thank you's" before you discover a "yes" or a "maybe."

THE PRIMITIVE POWER OF FAILING FORWARD

Babe Ruth struck out 1,306 times in spite of his 714 home run record. The writer of the television series *M*A*S*H* received 67 rejections before he made the deal. Right before he submitted his script for the 68th time, he decided that he would only try one more time. The rest is television history.

It is critical when you are networking that you do not take the prospect's rejection personally. You cannot dwell in the past. Just tell yourself, I am one call closer to a legitimate prospect."

TIMING AND PERSISTENCE IS EVERYTHING

When is the best time of the day, week, or month for you to visit your territory? In the beginning, just go out and see for yourself. When I first started door-knocking, I took the "survey approach" and began to study the habits of my prospects. I discovered that Friday and Saturday afternoons were the best times to sell.

The best time to sell depends on what you sell and your audience. If you are networking businesses, it is better to stop in when their customer traffic is down. If you call on doctors and interface with the nurses and receptionists, schedule times when the waiting room is not jammed or the doctor is in surgery.

If you are in the title or advertising business, the challenge is to visit other offices when the salespeople are there. They are in the field most of the time except on the day they come in to the office for a sales meeting. Find out what day that is, and time your visit directly after the meeting adjourns.

If you call on homeowners you may face the same problem as the title representatives or advertising people. Today 80% of homes have two wage earners. If both people work and the children are all in school, you must limit your visits to weekends or evenings.

The only way you can find out people's schedules is to go out into the territory and ask questions. My Progressive Networking System will give you a profitable working plan.

THE PROGRESSIVE NETWORK: A SIMPLE THREE STEP-UP PROGRAM

Working a territory consistently and correctly is rare in the selling business. People doubt the effectiveness of this practice. Yet, if you gain complete market penetration with a targeted audience of prospects, you will get rich. Even the entertainment industry's biggest stars use target marketing. Two names you may recognize are Madonna and Oprah Winfrey.

It takes time and a great deal of patience to network effectively.

Everything in life is about process—the natural process of letting time pass and allowing change to take place. I call it "going the distance" and "having staying power." I am glad I started to run over 10 years ago. Today my resting heart rate is forty-two beats per minute. Sticking to process works. It develops my willpower, too. I have noticed that the first two miles are always tough.

As I run, my self-talk is negative. "I don't have to run today. I'll skip this until tomorrow. My body is fighting me. I can feel it, so why push it?"

I just let myself rattle on and I keep running. My system is warming up and pretty soon I do not notice the discomfort. By the time I have run about two miles, I am feeling better. My imagination starts to take over and I forget about running. I look around and enjoy the scenery, let my mind daydream, and usually accomplish some creative problem solving.

The Progressive Network Plan may be very unpleasant work for you during the first several months. That is why so many salespeople begin, but never stick with, this important sales habit. Like running, it takes a while to get going but the rewards are well-worth the early displeasure. Use the following guidelines to motivate you to continue networking despite setbacks.

Level One: Recognition

After my manager instructed me to generate business on my own, I selected a 300 house territory and wasted no time getting to know the people in my area. From the beginning, my attitude and approach was one of appreciation. Acting appreciative is different than acting beholden to someone. I was not looking for a hand-out because I knew I would earn their respect—I was prepared to pay the price. My upbeat attitude is quickly noticed by the customer.

I like to give things away when I sell. This approach sets the mood for the relationship with my client. I bought 1,000 imprinted scratch pads with my picture, name, address, and phone number for $200. Homeowners used them for grocery lists and notes to their children. My face was all over the neighborhood in a variety of places in each home.

One of my customers called me one day and said "I have been staring at your face every morning for the last 10 years. My wife leaves for work before I do and she always leaves a note for me on the bathroom mirror, written on one of your scratch pads. I feel like I know you, so come on over, and sell my house."

Wrigley Chewing Gum began as a giveaway when the customer bought a bar of Wrigley soap. Mr. Wrigley could not sell his soap until he got the brainstorm to include a free piece of chewing gum with each bar of soap. When the gum became more popular than the soap, he started selling chewing gum.

Other businesses also use the giveaway approach. The Fuller Brush man always carried free samples. Department stores give away sprays of perfume, grocery stores give away coupons, magazines and newspapers give away pages of advertising, and airlines give away first class upgrade certificates.

Use this dialogue at the Recognition Level when you call on your prospects bearing gifts:

"I want to introduce myself. My name is Pete Best, with Harmon Homes Magazine. Please accept my free gift to you—*The Harmon Guide on Writing Creative Ads.* We are offering this with no obligation, in the hopes that you will get to know us better. Thanks for listening to me."

Or:

"Hi, Mr. Meeting Planner. I'm Ruth King, director of sales at the Holiday Inn down the street. On behalf of the Holiday Inn and myself, we welcome you to the city of St. Joe. Please accept this invitation to stop by our cocktail lounge any weekday this month between 4 and 6 P.M. for free hors d'oeuvres. This invitation admits you and a guest.

"I would be glad to give you a quick tour of our first-class meeting rooms. We hope if you ever need our services, you will remember the Holiday Inn."

The "Survey Dialogue" is also helpful at level one.

"Hi, I'm Laura Gilbert with Homes Magazine. I am surveying local businesses to see where they put their advertising dollars. Are you presently advertising in any publications? Are you satisfied with their rates? Service? Response?

"Thank you for your cooperation. Here is a gift to show my appreciation. If you ever decide to use additional magazine advertising, I hope you will remember us."

During this level of networking, be on the lookout for mentors. Easy-to-approach prospects in your territory are great sources of information and future mentors. The "Mentor Dialogue" in Chapter 3 is easily converted to a face-to-face script when the occasion arises in your territory.

Be patient during this stage of development. Many salespeople stop networking because they are not getting quick results. I have watched title representatives call on real estate offices for over a year without receiving one order. Every week they would call on their prospects, hand them a schedule of their rates, a note pad, and a business card and ask to be remembered. But one week during a regular visit, an agent trying to close a transaction runs into an emergency and needs someone to drive loan documents to a bank before 5:00 P.M. The friendly title representative jumps in and saves the day. That is the beginning of his penetration into a very tough market. He's on his way now to level two.

Level Two: Credibility

"Staying power" brings you to level two. Many salespeople do not get this far because they start whining and complaining like a spoiled child who wants his way. One method that kept me alive until I reached the credibility level was the "Miss America Drive." On Saturdays I would drive through my territory and wave to homeowners out in their yards. They recognized my car and eventually when people saw me driving around they assumed somebody must be getting ready to sell.

One particular Saturday I was driving and a woman recognized me, waved me down, and asked for a favor. Her husband was in the kitchen filling out a loan application for a backyard pool and they needed to include a report from a local realtor of recently sold properties and sales prices. I delivered a completed report to her within one hour. She thanked me and I never gave it another thought until she called me again a year later.

"Danny, do you remember that day last year I stopped you when you were driving by our house and I asked you to prepare a property report for us?"

"Vaguely."

"My husband and I were so impressed with your quick reaction to our request. We got our loan and we enjoy our pool tremendously. My brother-in-law is here from Alabama and he and his family want to buy a home this weekend in my neighborhood. Do you have time to sell him one?"

I could not believe my ears. The "Miss America Drive" led me down the boulevard of dollars and sense.

Spot check your mentors at this level. Use the same scripts in person that I recommend in Chapter 3 for the telephone (e.g., the "I've Got A Problem" and the "What Do You Think?" dialogues).

Be patient. After twelve months of strong networking many salespeople drop their territory and seek greener pastures. This impatience is a mistake because the territory may be about to open up for you.

I did volunteer work when I was at my "credibility level." Become involved with the same philanthropic efforts as your customers. Organize the 10K runs for Easter Seals or lead the "Dance-For-Heart" crusade against heart disease. Create opportunities to increase your credibility and compassion. When you love your customers, you know how to give until it hurts.

Level Three: Authority

You rule the roost now. Everywhere you go your customers greet you with open arms. Business is booming, but remember to keep your servicing circle pumped. Follow-up is the key at this stage. One bad rumor can ruin your career.

I saw this kind of destruction occur in real estate. A salesperson had complete control of 200 homes in an affluent area. Her follow-up weakened because she refused to hire a personal secretary to help her with the overload. She neglected returning calls and paper was stacked up for weeks. One day she found out she missed a big sale because the prospect who was considering doing business with her called one of the homeowners in her territory.

"My homeowner gave me a bad report. She told the prospective client that I was very good before I got too big for my britches. She suggested the woman do business with someone who would return her calls and give her more personalized attention."

Success should breed success and it will if you build the support system to help you with the extra business. When I reached the Authority Level, I began to win awards and my picture appeared in the local newspapers. I enclosed the clipping with a note to the mentors in my territory.

"If it wasn't for your recommendations, where would I be today? Thanks for keeping me in the public eye."

It is time to open a special bank account for yearly "thank you" promotions in your territory. When I was a business owner, we brought Santa Claus to our office on the first weekend of December. The salespeople would deliver invitations to their territories the last two weeks of November stating that free photos would be taken of their children with Santa Claus and that refreshments would be served. The invitation stated the date, time, and place and explained, "This is our way of saying thank you for being such a great customer." The response was overwhelming each year.

My Networker's Almanac, described below, is recommended once you have built a solid client base. It is designed to be a consistent plan of appreciation to use with satisfied customers. Entrepreneurs, business owners, commissioned or salary-plus-bonus individuals, direct-sales people, free-lance artists, and independent contractors are candidates for the almanac. Pick and choose one or more of the giveaways, dialogues, complete monthly concept, or whatever method works for you and start spreading some good rumors about yourself.

THE DANIELLE KENNEDY TWELVE-MONTH NETWORKER'S ALMANAC

I wrote my first almanac after making a great deal of money in my territory for a solid year. Build a reputation based on quality service, not giveaways. These gift ideas and the networking almanac are meant to stimulate your creative gift giving nature as a way to say "Thank You" to those who have put faith in you and made your income possible. Please check with your industry and make sure none of these ideas would be considered illegal or a form of payola.

Remember, the more your income grows, the more you should concentrate on ways of re-investing the money in your business. Do not become attached to the material benefits of success. Enjoy the perks that success brings, but continue to focus on the customer and maintaining quality service. Such is the true meaning of success and financial security. Consider this almanac as a method of repayment to the people who make your livelihood possible.

Use my twelve-month almanac or make up your own. Maybe you will create a combination plan including some of my ideas and your own. Follow a plan and lay it out a year in advance. The first one you do can be very simple. Take a sheet of paper and list the twelve months of the year on one side of the paper. Next to each month include a dialogue, giveaway, and an optional promotion. In the middle of each month review the next month's activities.

Make sure the networking activity makes business sense. What good is sponsoring a big breakfast for the local chamber of commerce if it has been happily doing business with your competitors for years? The result may be a conversation like this:

"That was a lovely breakfast. I think Quick Press picked up the tab for the whole shooting match. I am so glad we give them all our printing business."

You own Mr. Quick Printing and after hearing that comment you are ready to change the company name to "Mr. Slow and Stupid Printing." The moral: first determine that you've targeted your prospects wisely and then make sure you're clearly identified with the event. Otherwise, you will have wasted your time and money.

JANUARY

Promotional Options:
Deluxe budget: Sponsor the kick-off-the-year sales meeting breakfast at the local hotel/restaurant for your best client in the territory. (Prices vary but estimate $10.00 a plate. If they have 30 people on their staff, the cost could run about $300.00.) If you are getting their business exclusively, disregard the cost.

Medium-size budget: Buy tickets to sports events, concerts, ice shows, and the circus for the top 10 customers in your territory. Be familiar with their favorite teams, entertainers or interests and surprise them with plenty of advance notice.

Start-up budget: Make a surprise popcorn or pizza delivery to the offices you call on. Right after the holidays, the staff will enjoy a pick-me-up.

Giveaway Ideas: Imprinted scratch pads. A calendar of upcoming sports and cultural events. Miniature sewing kit.

Prepared Dialogue: "Happy New Year from ABC Manufacturing Company and little old me. Thanks for all the past year's business but it's a new year and we will serve you better than ever before."

FEBRUARY

Promotional Options: Deluxe budget: An evening at the theater. Rent a bus and take your best customers to the most exciting play in town.

Medium-size budget: Plan a bowling party. Pay for three games and three drinks. Arrange team challenges.

Start-up budget: Throw a Valentine's Day party. Provide red punch, heart cookies. Have a "secret pal" drawing a week before the party, so everyone can pick the name of a person for whom she can buy a Valentine (under $10.00).

Giveaway Ideas: A heart-shaped perfumed sachet. A single audio-cassette, e.g., "Serenity" by Leigh Taylor Young, "Seeds of Greatness" by Denis Waitley, or Earl Nightingale's "The Strangest Secret." Old-fashion candy apples with nuts. Marshall Field's Chocolate Frango Mints.

Prepared Dialogue: "Hi everybody. I'm here to sweeten you up for the month of February with candy apples and tangerines. We have a special valentine advertising rate exclusively for our customers because you are all such sweethearts."

MARCH

Promotional Options: Deluxe budget: Organize an annual St. Patrick's Day Golf Tournament. Customers decorate their golf carts and themselves in green. Serve a corned beef and cabbage dinner after the game and pass out awards for best games.

Medium-size budget:	Have a Spring Fashion show and luncheon. Enlist other sponsors to reduce expenses.
Start-up budget:	Mass deliver green carnations on St. Pat's Day.
Giveaway Ideas:	Kites for the kids. Fuzzy green shamrock for the lapel. A green bucket of Golf Tee Trivia. (American Traveler Magazine 3825 West Green Tree Rd. P.O. Box 17001 Milwaukee, WI 53217)
Prepared Dialogue:	"This is Joe from Mr. Quick Printing. I just want to remind you that we always consider it a *privilege* to do business with you. Hope the kids enjoy these kites, compliments of me and Mr. Quick."

APRIL

Promotional Options: Deluxe budget:	A classic car weekend. Give your best customers the opportunity to drive a classic car around town for the weekend. Ferraris, Lamborghinis, Rolls Royce, Mercedes, Corvettes. They'll get a kick out of taking their spouse to an exclusive restaurant or play on a warm spring evening in a classic.
Medium-size budget:	Send the Easter Bunny around or bring him to your store. Samples of lotion, perfumes, chocolate eggs. Be creative and make up inexpensive but colorful gifts.
Start-up budget:	Stage an Easter Egg Hunt at a local park or recreational facility. Customers bring the kids.
Giveaway Ideas:	Rain hats. Flower seeds. Spring Fling Litter Bags, with your name and logo.
Prepared Dialogue:	"You and the family are invited to stop in the store all weekend. The Easter Bunny will be there giving free prizes away."

MAY

Promotional Options: Deluxe budget:	Organize a charter boat and take your customers on a four hour fishing trip. Supply the food and drink. Have a fishing tournament and give a prize to the person landing the biggest fish.

Medium-size budget:	A picnic in the park. Everyone brings a dish but you provide the main barbecue ingredients. Organize games like: egg toss, grape toss, volleyball, relay races.
Start-up budget:	Organize a 10K run around the lake, park, or harbor for a local charity or hospital building fund. Get all your customers to donate everything from tee shirts to refreshments.
Giveaway Ideas:	Mother's Day Plants. Pens with your name and company imprinted on them.
Prepared Dialogue:	"Hi, Marv. I've got a problem. My new spring line just came in and I can't tell enough people fast enough. Please stop by and bring a few friends. You won't be sorry you did because the prices on some of the serigraphs are absolute steals."

JUNE

Promotional Options: **Deluxe budget:**	Sponsor a Sailing Regatta. Provide skippers if some of your customers do not sail. Have teams and award prizes for the winners. Provide refreshments and enjoy a fun afternoon on the sea or lake.
Medium-size budget:	Publicize a free drawing. Winner gets a free weekend for two (food and two nights lodging) at the closest local resort. (Include reliable babysitters. Great promotions for first-year parents.)
Start-up budget:	Free maid service for two months for your' best customer.
Giveaway Ideas:	Father's Day plastic drink holders. Barbecue apron for dad. Imprinted scratch pads.
Prepared Dialogue:	"East Marine and I really appreciate your past patronage. Here's a special Father's Day gift. We hope you will think of us when you are in the market for a new boat."

JULY

Promotional Options: **Deluxe budget:**	An evening at the ballpark. Rent a bus and take everybody out to the ballgame.
Medium-size budget:	Call on customers with a cooler full of treats—ice fruit bars, cold root beer, and fat-free ice-cream. Serve floats in the middle of a hot day. Surprise people and treat them with kindness.
Start-up budget:	Blitz your territory with a newly-released paperback novel that they will not be able to put down.
Giveaway Ideas:	Safety tip booklets. Mini First Aid Kits. Small hand-made fans.
Prepared Dialogue:	"Hope you are staying cool and enjoying the summer. We have a special sale on educational games in our catalogue. Since it's mid-summer, the kids need something new to keep their attention for long car rides. I brought the Toy Catalogue with me if you care to take a peek."

AUGUST

Promotional Options: **Deluxe budget:**	Rent out the local cinema for a free morning at the movies for kids. Make sure they put your name up on the marquee. Plan this six months in advance.
Medium-size budget:	Stage a romantic evening hayride for customers and their spouses. Arrange with local stable. Find a guitarist you can all sing-a-long with.
Start-up budget:	Compile a babysitting network resource guide. All the excellent licensed day care centers as well as private offerings with good reputations and references.
Giveaway Ideas:	Cookbooks. A book list that includes both fiction and nonfiction best selections. A list of inspirational audio tapes organized by topic.
Prepared Dialogue:	"We value your business and because we do, we want to earn more opportunities to prove that we know what we are doing. There is an excellent strategic income plan brochure I brought by for

you to peruse. I always watch out for you, so trust me, and take five minutes to look at this."

SEPTEMBER

Promotional Options:
Deluxe budget: Hire an expert or form a panel of experts and organize a free seminar on a hot topic pertinent to your customers.

Medium-size budget: Volunteer to give a free seminar to your customers and their employees. If you sold them computers, either you or the service representative from your company could make a visit to brief new employees on the programs. Include refreshments.

Start-up budget: Monday Night Football Party. Provide chili, popcorn, and refreshments.

Giveaway Ideas: Football schedules. A subscription to "Insight" (A monthly audio magazine from Nightingale-Conant).

Prepared Dialogue: "Don't miss our Monday Night Football Party. Let me warn you, we have just received some new samples and I will want you to take a peek while we watch the game."

OCTOBER

Promotional Options:
Deluxe budget: A trip to a comedy club with customers. Rent a bus or organize a caravan of cars.

Medium-size budget: A day of beauty. Send a favorite customer for a facial, massage, and hair style. Great for new moms who are also your customers.

Start-up budget: An exclusive lunch or dinner for two. Send your favorite couple out on the town.

Giveaway Ideas: Food coupons of all types, including fast food. A video tape classic such as *Peter Pan.*

Prepared Dialogue: "Next time you make a hair appointment with us, take advantage of the free manicure we are offering to special customers this month."

NOVEMBER

Promotional Options:
Deluxe budget: Give away free turkeys to 25 of your best customers. Or hold a drawing and give away 25 turkeys from the names selected.

Start-up budget: Organize a trip to a poor section of town or just give a food package to an anonymous family for the holidays. Get your customers involved.

Giveaway Ideas: Pies, cakes, cookies for holidays.

Prepared Dialogue: "This is the time to say thank you. Here is a small remembrance for all your support throughout the year."

DECEMBER

Promotional Options: Ice skating Party, Christmas Party, and grab bag. Toys for Tots Program. Visit hospitals or the homeless with your customers.

Giveaway Ideas: Holly trees. Personalized Christmas ornaments. Set of Christmas cookie cutters. Spirits and other refreshments.

Prepared Dialogue: "Thank you for letting us serve you all this year. During this holiday season, we wish you the happiest of times. Here's a small sign of our appreciation for your business."

Don't let this almanac scare you. It is just meant to guide your right brain in the creative department. Gift-giving can sometimes be time-consuming, especially if you can't think of something exciting. There are thousands of companies and catalogues that will help you come up with ideas just right for your customers. They will do anything from delivering breakfast in bed to sending a movie star look-alike to a secretary's office birthday party. The time to get involved in gift-giving is after you have earned your customers' good will and a decent income.

There is no substitute for consistently contacting prospects face-to-face. But we need the telephones and the mail to keep the interest and the excitement mounting. Find out how powerful the pen can be in creating a personal promotion package of significant value in Chapter 5.

5 How to Mastermind and Market Your Natural Style With the Persuasive Power, of the Pen

"My tongue is the pen of a ready writer."

THE HOLY BIBLE: Psalms, 45:1

What do bestselling authors Stephen King, Tom Clancy, Danielle Steele, and Jean Auel have in common? Natural selling. We know that natural selling is a state-of-the-art form of persuasive communication. The bestsellers use the written word so powerfully that the public accepts their work with no questions. Carol Schneider, vice president for publicity at Random House, claims fans of James Michener and Robert Ludlum make phone calls to her office and say: "My father's in the hospital dying. Couldn't you just get it to me ahead of time so he can read it before he goes?"

Some writers like Steele, Clancy, and King remain silent to the public and do not hit the interview trail or do book signings. They have created an intense and loyal following of fans strictly by using their pen, assuring the publisher that they are bankable.

These persuaders cause the word to jump off the page, grab you by the collar, keep you up all night, and refuse to let you go until the story is over. Many a sleepless night I have fallen victim, escaping into the enchanting worlds of complex characters and plots. What can these masters of natural selling teach us about the writing craft?

BECOME A WORD CONNOISSEUR

A word culturist cultivates a knowledge of the language, and develops an intimate sense of the meaning of words that enables him or her to choose the word that best fits the sentence. This selection can determine how persuasive your writing is and how much force and impact it will have on the customer.

Naturals cultivate extensive vocabularies for their presentations. You must always look for the best word for the occasion or the merchandise you are describing. This is not an easy task because words have many meanings. For example, the word *colony* can refer to a pioneer community or swarms of buzzing bees.

My writing education will be continuous. The more precise my writing becomes, the clearer my verbal communication and sales skills become. Writing forces me to live in the present moment.

Start improving your vocabulary by following these guidelines:

1. Carry a pocket dictionary in your purse or briefcase.

2. When you do not know the meaning of a word you hear or read, stop and look up the definition.

3. Read the editorial section of the daily newspaper. Look up all the words you do not understand.

4. Build a reference library of dictionaries, thesauruses, and books about word power and words that sell.

5. Pretend you must take the Scholastic Aptitude Test (SAT) or Graduate Record Exam (GRE). Go to a college or local bookstore and buy test preparation books. Study the vocabulary section. Use 3″ × 5″ cards and write one word on each index card, turn the card over, and write the definition. Then start memorizing your new vocabulary. Take the cards with you and study them whenever you have time.

6. Enroll in a basic English or creative writing course at a community college.

7. Read at least one new book a month. Choose a variety of books, such as fiction, non-fiction, self-help, reference materials, poetry, and short stories. There are marvelous ideas and words in many genres that will trigger your imagination.

8. Use your journal to record ideas that sell. Don't miss the opportunity to write down any brilliant flash you may have.

9. Start an advertising scrapbook. Collect zinger ads from magazines, newspapers, and individual brochures and mail-outs. Don't discriminate—just take ideas from everywhere.

10. Simple words and sentences create the best sales effect. An overdressed thought can be as distracting as an overdressed person. If, when you called on a customer, you wore a tailored suit with a chartreuse necktie and lots of jewelry, your accessories might be so distracting to the customer during your interview and presentation

that they would detract from the message you were trying to deliver. The same rules apply to using words.

11. Learn rules and definitions. Invest in a handbook that explains the use of language. Check with a local college bookstore and ask for a writer's guidelines.

12. The best rule of composition is to write about a subject that you know. If this element is missing, all of the reference materials and impressive words will not make your composition interesting.

13. Write a passionate letter to your lover. Some of my best writing is found in personal love letters. Because the feelings run deep, my "voice" comes through on paper. I never hold back what I want to say. Try it. Read it out loud to yourself. Then write a passionate letter to a customer describing your service or product with the same intensity.

NATURALS HAVE WRITING STYLE

Written style is the particular manner in which you combine words, phrases, and clauses into sentences. Natural salespeople have their own characteristic tone in what they say and how they say it. This manner is present in both their written and verbal communication and I believe the uniqueness comes from trusting intuition and then developing it through the educational process. Part of creating your own style comes from your ability to think clearly and then express yourself in convincing language. Organize your ideas, put your own enthusiasm and personality into your writing, and become an avid observer of everyday circumstances.

The purpose of language is to communicate your ideas to others or to persuade them. When you communicate a message authentically, it means your individual style reached the listener because you used your own, not somebody else's words. Your message can often create the strongest impact if you keep the language very simple. Slick ad writers sometimes forget that elegant techniques often get in the way of a "selling message."

Through the years, I have created all the advertising and marketing promotions at each company that I have owned. I entered my work in statewide contests and won awards or received honorable mention. I allowed my inner coach to guide me by writing down my own words to persuade others. When I opened my first company, I wanted a logo that communicated the importance of repeat business and quality service. One of the messages I found myself repeating to the customer was "remember me." So I decided to use that theme in all the printed matter the company sent out.

I had a graphic artist design a simple forget-me-not flower that was placed under an oval picture of each salesperson on our staff. The words "forget-me-not" were written next to the flower. This message appeared on all advertising and stationery. Muted blue and gray colors were used to soft sell our approach.

The original ads announcing our opening ran in the local newspaper and showed all five owners' profiles sketched in charcoal gray pencil with the forget-me-not flower and words appearing under the photo. We kept to that theme by passing out forget-me-not flower seeds in our territories and always reminding potential customers that if they gave us a chance, we would deliver "forget-me-not" service.

At that time sales companies used photos of their top producers all over the page, stating how many millions each salesperson had produced in a given month. I wanted to play up the customer and our role in providing them with quality service, not sales figures.

Our first 18 months in the business, we became one of the top three sales companies in market share in our town. Throughout the community, everyone said: "They are different. They really care." Originally many of our critics told us the message was too weak and not impressive enough, but our customers disagreed with them.

WRITE TO BE UNDERSTOOD

All of us want our advertising messages to be understood. I collect great ads because it sparks my own personal idea machine. Ford Motor Company recently did a full-page double-truck ad in a national newspaper. It was a wide black and white photo of an empty, open road lined with pine trees. The bold, black copy read: "You're Looking At All The Trucks That Outsell Ford." The ad talked about why no one else was even in the picture, the "Ford-Tough" credibility, and the loyalty of the Ford customers over the last several decades.

The best advertisers write so that no reader is conscious of any style. The reader catches what the writer is trying to say without thinking about how it is being said. Whether you are writing copy for an ad, brochure, letter, catalogue or resume, remember your motive is to sell the customer. Choose your words with thought and care and always consider what the customer wants.

USE THE LANGUAGE OF THE PEOPLE

Another way of adopting the language of the people is to express your words from their point of view. Ask yourself questions like:

Why would I buy this product?
How long will this product last?

What will I use it for?

Then select a combination of long and short sentences and write your proposition. Have resource books like the dictionary or a thesaurus handy so you can build your sentences swiftly and accurately.

Don't beat around the bush—just get right to the point of your appeal. Nike's "Just Do It." advertising campaign motivated thousands of runners to get off the couch and do a few laps.

SPEED WRITING 101: A THREE-WEEK ADVENTURE IN BUSINESS WRITING

I am a lifelong student of writing and, once again, the good nuns must be given credit for my early introduction into the world of words. As far as they were concerned, if their students didn't have a good grasp of the English language, have a desire to read books as much as they desired food, and couldn't compose something of importance by the time they graduated, the nuns considered themselves failures as teachers.

The process of becoming a good speaker has been an easier one than becoming a more skillful writer. When I talk, I have my facial expressions, body, voice inflection, and dramatic pauses to lean on to get my point across. When I write, I just have a blank page and an unused batch of words to play around with.

All through college I kept taking writing classes. Recently I worked on my Masters in Professional Writing at the University of Southern California. If you do not have the time or money right now to pursue more formal education in writing, use my SPEED WRITING 101 class to get you pointed in the right direction. The following class is a quick overview of all the tips I have picked up from teachers, experience, self-correction, and other writers.

You can do your homework on a word processor if you have one. You will need plenty of legal-size pads, a journal, a typewriter, (if you don't use a computer) and a three-ring binder for notes.

Class Schedule

Week One: Conceiving the idea. How to brainstorm on paper. Various methods of conceptualizing are introduced to enable you to take one idea and turn it into a product, ad campaign, personal promotion, newsletter, or the development of new sales dialogue.

Week Two: Outlining, sketching, and preliminary writing. How to draft an introduction, body, and conclusion. Paragraph unity, length, development, and organization are discussed.

Week Three: Tweaking and toning. How to rewrite and refine your first draft. Methods of chunking and linking are presented to assist you in presenting clear messages to your readers.

Week One

Welcome to Speed Writing 101. We will use a legitimate company as our model to assist us in conceptualizing, outlining, and tweaking our sales writing assignment over the next three weeks. I have chosen NoJo, Inc.®, located in Irvine, California.

In the early 1970s NoJo, Inc.® was founded by two women. Their business started at the same location as mine—the kitchen table. One hot summer morning, these two women were drinking coffee, feeding their babies, and visiting with each other when they got an idea. It was sparked because they noticed their babies, both sitting in infant seats, were acting fussy and perspiring. The backs of their infant seats were lined in plastic padding, which was extremely uncomfortable.

"Let's sew some infant seat covers," they said.

After they made some for their own babies, each of their expectant friends wanted one. They were made of terry cloth and other soft fabrics in many colors. They gave them away at baby showers and everyone who saw how pretty and practical they were offered to pay for them.

Finally, these women decided to take a few handmade infant seat covers to the local mall and visit the saleswoman in the infant department. She put the seat covers on display and within 24 hours they were sold. The buyer at this major department store called and wanted to order 100 coverlets and needed a flyer or brochure to display in the store.

Imagine that we find ourselves in the same position these two women were in at that time: unskilled in sales and marketing, but forced to write an attention-getting brochure. Let's analyze the best way to handle this task and then you can apply these principles when you find yourself in the same situation.

1. Ask yourself if your idea fills a need or a gap in the market place. Visit dozens of baby shops and department stores to see if there is anything close to this designer infant seat cover available.

   Listen to other mothers and ask for feedback. Some of this feedback can be included in the brochure. All good sales copy shows the value of the merchandise or service from the customer's viewpoint. It is impossible to communicate that viewpoint on paper unless you listen to what the customers are saying.

2. Break down your writing problem into five parts: (I got this idea in a book entitled *A Writer's Reference* by Diana Hacker.)

   Subject: How much information is needed in the brochure

about the infant seat cover? Where will you gather information? Personal experience? Other mothers? Direct observation? Surveys mailed to a select group of parents?

Remember the NoJo® women based most of their writing about the subject on personal experience, observation, and comments from other mothers, as well as some research and development into the stores. If they had just written from personal experience, the words might have been less powerful.

Purpose: The purpose of the writing should answer the question "Why?" Are you trying to inform, persuade, or entertain? Motivate the customer to buy your product right now. The NoJo® women wanted to inform, persuade, and call to action to a need for infant seat covers.

Audience: Who will be reading your brochure? How informed are they and will they resist the strong message you wish to convey? Use a direct appeal written in an intimate mother-to-mother style.

Length and format: How much copy is necessary? It is important to include enough information about the practicality of the covers and a photo of the product. Would a closeup photo of a fluffy, soft, pastel-colored infant seat cover make a parent's mouth water? A picture can be better than a thousand words.

3. Brainstorm with a pen and paper. There are all kinds of ways to do this. Write down the first thing that comes to your mind. Let's try it:
   Infant seat covers—a marketable product?

— Baby will love the softness of flannel, terry cloth, or light-weight cotton.

— Baby will love the colorful patterns. Use nursery rhyme sketches, animals, children, bright rainbow patterns, or pastels.

— Mothers will love the wash and wear quality of the cover.

— Mothers hate those hot plastic pads that stick to the baby's back if the baby isn't wearing an undershirt.

— The baby can relax in just a diaper and bib and enjoy the comfort of a soft material padding against his or her body instead of a hot plastic pad.

— The plastic pads are unsanitary after some use.

— Baby stores, baby departments, gift shops in hospitals, small gift boutiques, mail order, word-of-mouth.

Brainstorming is not a formal outline. Later you can go back and organize and rearrange any of the items you listed. Every salesperson or business owner must envision himself or herself as an entrepreneur and spend at least once a month in a brainstorming session, either alone or with a management team. I brainstorm constantly, either in my journal or on a legal pad. I have a certain place in my file cabinet that has nothing but legal pads filled with ideas. I may not come back to the ideas for several months, but when it's time to start the project I am ahead of the game.

We are working on the baby covers brochure in class, but your assignment for this course is to take your idea for a brochure or direct mail piece and follow the same methods introduced to you in this course.

4. Calm the brainstorms. Organize the items into sections. For instance, all the benefits of the coverlet for the baby would be listed in one column; all the benefits for the mother in a column; and all the locations the item can be sold in another. I like to categorize each column by giving it a name. The baby column can be called "Why babies love NoJo®," Then the mother's column "Why mothers love NoJo®," and finally, "Where you can find NoJo®." By the way, the name NoJo came out of a brainstorming session too. The company was named after the two founders' babies who used the first coverlets. One baby was named Noel and the other baby was Joanna.

5. Interview yourself and write down your findings. Ask yourself typical questions such as: How will I describe these covers in my brochure? Who am I trying to persuade? Just mothers or both parents? Why should a prospective buyer read my brochure? What will I write about the product? The price? Special offers? Where can they get the covers?

I am always amazed when I pick up brochures that are missing phone numbers, addresses, or prices. This type of information is critical to the return response of the piece. The best way to avoid this oversight is to use Who? What? Where? and Why? questions before composing your flyer.

6. Write a thesis sentence to describe the main point of your brochure. A NoJo's thesis statement: An infant seat cover made out of soft fabrics, instead of plastic padding, is well worth the additional expense because of its practicality, comfort, and beauty.

Formulate your thesis early in your writing but don't be afraid to change it as the piece evolves. This statement will keep you focused during the writing. Sometimes people forget that sales literature is meant to sell the product and not just describe it.

7. Now you are ready to do a rough outline of the brochure. Use the suggested steps to assist you with this first draft blueprint of your piece. The NoJo® brochure outline looks like this:

Thesis: A NoJo® infant seat cover made out of soft fabrics, instead of plastic padding, is well worth the price because of its practicality, comfort, and beauty.

Now I use the standard outline numbers and letters to focus my piece:

I. The NoJo® mothers' story
   A. The birth of two babies and one idea
   B. The first infant seat covers
   C. Testing the marketplace
II. Creating a quality product
   A. Expensive and durable fabrics
   B. Colorful designs for the nursery
   C. Money-back guarantee offers
III. Call for action
   A. Cost versus value
      1. Baby comfort
         a. Body stays cool and comfortable
         b. Germ-free and safe
      2. Less worry and bother for mother
         a. Washable
         b. Attractive designs
   B. How to order yours today
      1. Check or credit card
      2. Fill out return postage-paid form
      3. Price plus shipping and handling

All the steps to conceptualize our idea can be followed when writing other pieces such as dialogues, newsletters, and various types of advertising campaigns.

Week Two

You will need all the materials and information that you accumulated while brainstorming last week. While you prepare the NoJo® brochure, keep in mind that once you start writing, keep going. You can always go back and clean up the copy next week.

Introduction: First draft the introduction, which states the main point of your sales piece. You continue to develop that theme or thesis throughout the entire brochure, but you must catch your reader's attention early. I like to leave the strongest points until late in the body or in the conclusion in order to motivate the prospective customers to take action immediately after they finish reading my brochure. In the introduction, use a hook to grab the reader's attention.

Let's get started with some NoJo® brochure copy.

The outside of the brochure shows two infant seats. One has an old, plastic backing and it's beginning to crack. The other infant seat is covered with a made-to-fit mint green cotton coverlet. The picture shows the startling difference, asking the reader: "Which infant seat does your baby belong in?"

The inside left flap of the brochure condenses the NoJo Story:

"Two new mothers asked themselves that same question while visiting with each other one hot summer day. Both of their babies were fussy and uncomfortable.

"Both mothers commented that they couldn't find one store that sold soft and fluffy infant seat covers made out of material comfortable for baby's tender skin. So they began hand-crafting coverlets for their two babies, Noel and Joanna. Every mother who saw the fitted covers wanted one for her own baby, and they soon became the envy of the neighborhood."

The above history could be written in script with a photo of the two women and their babies. As you write your own copy, you can begin to see in your mind's eye the type of paper stock suitable for this piece. Imagine a wall-papered baby's nursery and select a paper that would blend; a light pastel with a glossy finish.

Notice the outline from week one was followed when writing this copy. The next section of the brochure discusses the quality of the product. I could use another photo of a woman at a sewing machine surrounded by beautiful fabrics in every color of the rainbow. The print and captions should be bold in order to get the reader's attention.

"THERE IS NOTHING LIKE OLD-FASHIONED FIRST-CLASS QUALITY. DOESN'T YOUR BABY DESERVE THAT? WITH THE NOJO® CUSTOM COVER YOU RECEIVE A HANDMADE PRODUCT, MADE WITH MACHINE WASHABLE, DESIGNER MATERIAL.

"WE OFFER A MONEY BACK GUARANTEE IF YOU ARE NOT COMPLETELY SATISFIED.

"WE KNOW HOW FUSSY MOTHERS CAN BE ABOUT WHAT THEY BUY FOR THEIR BABIES."

Notice I changed the outline around somewhat after I started drafting. Point two under "Cost versus Value" is emphasized in this section.

"WHY SHOULD YOUR BABY SIT IN A HARD-TO-CLEAN PLASTIC, STICKY PADDED SEAT WHEN HE OR SHE CAN BE CUDDLED IN A CUSTOM COVER AS COZY AS THE COMFORTER IN THEIR CRIB?

"When your NoJo® cover gets soiled, just put it in the washing machine on the delicate cycle. It's simpler to clean than the plastic pad.

The right inside flap of the brochure calls for action.

"There is a LIMITED SUPPLY of these beautiful, custom-made

NoJo® coverlets available. Quality work takes time and our designers never sacrifice quality for expediency.

"If you order yours today, we guarantee delivery within 10 days. Why not order two or three for yourself and a few for expectant mothers you know?"

"OUR PRICES ARE AFFORDABLE. ONE INFANT SEAT COVER COSTS $19.95. IF YOU ORDER SUBSTANTIAL QUANTI-TIES THERE IS A MAJOR PRICE REDUCTION. CALL US COL-LECT NOW FOR DETAILS."

An order blank on the bottom of the page, or an additional tear-off card should include: Name, address, city, state, zip, phone number (day-time), credit card number and expiration date, price, and breakdown of postage and handling.

The back of the brochure could show a small logo, the order blank, or tear out card.

I'm sure that the cost of their first brochure was minimal because they began the business with no start-up capital. Here are some tips to re-member as you write:

- All paragraphs or sections should begin with a topic sentence or a main point. When I talk about scarcity (limited supply), it is impor-tant that I stick with that point until I come to some kind of a conclusion.

- Each paragraph should be developed. If it is too short it will not con-vince the reader. Paragraph development allows you the space to give your product credibility.

- Organize your writing.

1. Examples: The mothers' story illustrates this.

2. Process: The mothers' story informs the reader about the stages of development the product went through from idea to sewing stage.

3. Compare and contrast: This organization is used on the front and inside of the brochure when comparing plastic to fabric.

4. Cause and effect: The reader sees how she could end up with a fussy baby using plastic, or a contented baby using high-quality covers.

Week Three

It is time to tweak and tone. This process reminds me of what artists do on the canvas when they add the finishing colors and touches to a painting. It really makes the work come to life but it takes care and discipline.

Writing expert Diana Hacker calls this stage of writing "global revi-sion." I call it chunking and linking because it sometimes involves making massive changes. Whole paragraphs might be eliminated. Sections of material on one page could end up in a completely different section. All the attention is on the larger elements of writing.

I find revisions stimulating but difficult. I have to walk away from my work for a few minutes or hours in order to become detached from the writing. When I go back to it, I try to view the work from the reader's viewpoint and not my own. I usually get a few people to assist me with this stage of writing. Ask your spouse or friend to read it from the customer's perspective. The following "Checklist for global revision" is excerpted from Hacker's *A Writer's Reference:*

Purpose and Audience

1. Does the draft accomplish its purpose-to-persuade, call to action, or a combination?
2. Is the draft appropriate for the audience? For the audience's knowledge of subject, level of interest, and attitudes?
3. Is the level of formality appropriate?
4. Is the reading level appropriate?

Focus and Organization

5. Do the introduction and conclusion focus clearly on the main point?
6. Can readers follow the overall structure?
7. Are ideas offered effectively?

Content

8. Is the supporting material persuasive?
9. Which ideas need further development?
10. Are the parts proportioned sensibly?
11. Where might material be deleted?

Paragraphs

12. Is each body paragraph unified, adequately developed, organized, and coherent?
13. Are any paragraphs too long or too short for easy reading?

After all the global revisions have been made, it is time for line editing. Line editing is done throughout the entire process of writing but the final spell checks, grammatical problems, and smaller deletions are completed at the end of the process.

If you used your own project during Speed Writing 101, then please complete your revisions and editing. If you worked on the NoJo® project, revise and rework the copy for the brochure.

Aren't you curious about what evolved from two mothers who started sewing infant seat coverlets out of their kitchen 20 years ago?

Today the NoJo® Company is the nation's leading designer and manufacturer of infant bedding and accessories. They occupy a 52,000 square foot warehouse-showroom. The next time you are shopping for a baby, look for the NoJo® name on baby comforters, diaper stack bags, pillows, canopies, sheets and pillowcases, and nursery wall hangings.

When you see a new mother holding her baby in a "side sling," think of the NoJo® name because Shirley Pepys, the co-founder of the company, and a doctor developed that product for their line. Once a Natural gets on a roll, there is no stopping her.

Part Three

TURN APPOINTMENTS INTO SALES

6 The Unaffected Interview: Simple Ways to Determine Employer-Customer Needs Fast

"Give what you have. To someone, it may be better than you dare to think."

HENRY WADSWORTH LONGFELLOW

Learn a lesson from nature and treat the approach point of the interview with as much care as a couple trying to conceive a baby. Great pains are taken to make sure conditions at a certain time of the month are suitable to increase the possibility of creating a human life. Once conception occurs, nature works fast during the first several hours. For the most part, the fate of your sale is predetermined during the first several minutes of your encounter with the customer. If you work fast, you may be able to give birth to a healthy sale in a lot less than nine months!

BE YOURSELF

The young adults who come to my programs worry about the impression they will make at the first interview. When they look too young, they feel they must lie about their age: "I am afraid the customers I call on will laugh at me because I look young enough to be their son or daughter. How can I gain their respect?"

"Earn it," is my standard reply.

"That's easy for you to say, Danielle. But what if they ask me how long I have been out selling?"

I give them my salesmom smile and say: "You just tell them you have been out here long enough to know the secret of success that very few people understand—SERVICE. Then look them straight in the eye

99

and tell them you are dying for a chance to prove you can deliver that service. Remember, there is no substitute for that kind of passion, and when a customer smells it, your age will become an advantage, not a hindrance."

YOU AND YOUR CUSTOMER ARE EQUALS

You must not fear the customer. The customer is another person, just like you. If you appear overeager and nervous at the interview, you will scare the customer. Remember that you are simply trying to exchange something you have that is valuable to the customer for something that is valuable to you. This is what business is all about and every salesperson must see himself as a business.

THE BUSINESS OF GETTING HIRED EVERY TIME

Natural salespeople treat each lead like a prospective employer. Every appointment is like a job interview that offers the opportunity of getting hired, or the disappointment of being turned down. Workers in our society need to view their vocation in the same manner as the natural salesperson. Young adults who think a degree in engineering is all they need to get the best jobs are foolish. One of the great Hollywood agents of our time, Henry Rogers, once asked a hopeful young actress he was interviewing how she felt about "door-to-door selling." She said: "I hate it. I don't understand how people could be so aggressive." Rogers told her she might as well go back home and get another job because actresses do more door-to-door selling than acting. He explained to her that every audition and every call-back is like selling to a customer. Those who have survived in the entertainment field have had to exemplify the same determination and belief in their product (their acting ability) as any salesperson who is out in the field calling on prospects.

THE EMPLOYMENT INTERVIEW THAT SELLS YOU

A natural salesperson I know and a giant in the automotive industry told me the story of how he got his first job. He wanted to work for a large dealership near his house, so one day as he was driving by, he decided to stop in and see what he could arrange. He recognized the manager walking around the showroom floor and approached him about a position. The manager was very nice and suggested he come back two days later at 10:00 A.M.

My friend was there promptly, but he had to wait until 10:45 to see the manager. As soon as he entered the manager's office, the manager said:

"Can't talk with you now, I am too busy. Besides, there is nothing open."

My friend was left standing in the manager's office and the manager went out. He took a seat. The manager returned and was angry at seeing my friend still there. Then he proceeded to rather sharply tell him so. My capable friend came right back at him with:

"Mr. Green, I had an appointment with you this morning at 10:00. I have been waiting 45 minutes to see you. I know that you have positions open from time to time, and I expect you to talk with me about a future, if not a present position. As a manager, your success depends on hiring good people. I am one of them."

The manager came back with, "Oh, I've heard that before."

My natural one said, "Yes, you may have heard that before, but you didn't hear it from me. I have ability and I can prove it to you. Business courtesy demands that I be given consideration, and I demand it as a gentleman from a gentleman."

Contrary to what you might think, my friend was asked politely to sit down, and had a very courteous interview. The manager said he would call him when an opening was available. Within three days my friend was hired.

A Harvard study reported these findings: If employees do 20% of what is required of them, (show up at work, punch the clock, and not make any waves) they know they will not get fired. The study shows there are very few "ninety-five percenters" in the work force. They are identified as those individuals who do 95% of what is required and not just the 20% effort necessary to keep a job. As a business owner who has hired and fired people for the past fifteen years, I must confess to you that every employer is constantly searching for a "ninety-five percenter." This is the attitude you must have as you approach a job interview.

Ten Good Rumors To Spread About Yourself In The Job Market

1. "He asks a lot of questions."

Whether you are entering the job market for the first time or changing careers, start an investigation. I call the investigation "informational interviews." If you are a senior in high school or college, visit people who work in your chosen profession. High school sophomores and juniors at the Hugh O'Brien Youth Camp attended a question and answer session with a panel of professionals. The panel consisted of a pediatrician, an engineer, an astronaut, a flight attendant, and myself.

One of the students commented on how glamourous it must be to travel all over the world and work on an airplane. She asked the flight attendant, "And what exactly do you do?"

"The best way to explain my job is to say I am a waitress, a flying waitress."

"What?" the astonished student said.

"It's true. I have to hustle and serve drinks and dinner in very close quarters in the same way as a waitress does in a jam-packed restaurant. Some of the passengers can get very grumpy."

The girl argued, "Yes, but you get to fly free to an exciting city."

The stewardess further enlightened her. "Most nights I arrive after ten o'clock and go directly to a hotel on a shuttle bus. I rarely see the city I am in because the next morning I leave on a 7:00 A.M. flight out to another place."

By now, our young investigator was a bit discouraged and asked, "Then what is so great about the job?"

"I meet some very interesting people. I like the work schedule of three days on and ten days off, and I get satisfaction out of serving weary travelers."

Every vocation, even those that appear glamorous, has its ups and downs. I used to think I wanted Joan Lunden's job on *Good Morning America,* until I found out she leaves for the office at 3:00 A.M., and does more homework than a college student.

It's a good idea to conduct informational interviews at cocktail parties, grocery stores, and with individuals who work in the field you are considering, before you go out on the first interview. Don't limit yourself to just conversation. Research the profession at the local library and record your findings. The other benefit of prequalifying yourself before the interview is once you are talking to an employer, you can discuss the position intelligently because you did your homework. Here is a good question to ask someone with whom you are conducting an informational interview:

"Tell me about your job. What activities are you responsible for each day? What do you like least and best about your work?"

This is called prospecting for a career. Don't be shy about calling successful people in a certain field and asking them questions. Preface the conversation by saying: "I am exploring future possibilities." People call me all the time about becoming a speaker. I always answer their questions either over the phone or in writing and then recommend they join *The National Speakers Association*. It is a terrific place to get an education about both becoming and staying successful in the speaking business.

Now that you have done your homework, you have a better understanding of a specific job. It is time to start rehearsing for a successful interview.

2. "She prepared in advance to be put on the spot."

I was in a Florida restaurant while a young woman at the next table was being interviewed for a position as a pharmaceutical representative by a very skillful examiner. Here is what I overheard:

"What would you do to get in to see the doctor—especially the ones in this territory who are very busy?"

Without missing a beat the interviewee replied:

"Well, the first thing I would do is try to get to know the doctor's nurse. I'd do some surveying with her. I'm presuming this is a new account, so the first thing I would ask her is how satisfied both she and the rest of the members of the staff are with Allergic Supplies, the current company they do business with. By the way, I just heard this morning their senior vice president has left that company. He was responsible for many of the big accounts that had been built up over the years. He originally started out in the field in the 1970s, calling on many of the young doctors who are now very prominent in my territory. This would be the perfect time to build that territory and talk to the doctors in this area about the tremendous price difference between the two products and that it does not affect the quality of what we manufacture."

I thought to myself, here's someone who acts like she works there already. She was asked several more questions which proved she had done her homework prior to the meeting.

Gathering pre-approach information makes sense. Many employees who are on their team may not know much about the history of the company or the founders. Investigate and research their advertising program. Study their brochures and all printed materials. Talk to people who prepared their advertising and find out their strengths, weaknesses, and company history. If you want the job, act like you do and go after it. Make it easy for the manager who interviews you to offer you a position.

Make a list of reasons why this employer should hire you. Tell the interviewer that you know you can serve the company well and offer original reasons why you can. You will be putting positive suggestions into the employer's mind the entire time you are being interviewed.

A few years ago, I flew to New York City to be interviewed by Harmon Publishing, the firm that publishes the *Homes Magazine.* The chairman of the board, president, and several officers were all present to interview me regarding the possibility of becoming their national spokesperson. I talked to their sales representatives across the United States for months before the interview, I asked many real estate agents about their satisfaction with advertising in the magazine, and I read everything I could get my hands on about the company.

By the time I arrived for the presentation, I had all my reasons why I would be their perfect spokesperson. I was excited about the fact that their magazine was a top advertising tool for the realtor. Every two weeks, *Homes Magazine* comes out in 210 cities from Fairbanks, Alaska, to The Virgin Islands. Their little red boxes are on street corners all over the United States, and over 40% of ad calls received from most North American real estate offices come from their publication. I knew I could sell all my real estate agents on advertising their properties in their fine magazine.

When the meeting started, it was obvious they had done their homework about me also. The chairman of the board said:

"It's hard to believe you sold all those houses while raising all those children."

It was a very positive experience because we knew we wanted to make the deal. There were no games, either. The chairman of the board got right to the point about halfway through the meeting:

"Danielle, we want to work with you. Do you want to work with us?"

"I sure want to find a way to work it out."

At that point, he got up and started walking out. He looked at the officers of his company and said:

"Let's make this work. And I know I will see you soon, Danielle."

3. "She's a producer, not a consumer."

Become known as a giver (producer), not a taker (consumer). During the aforementioned interview I wanted to get the Harmon people interested in what I could do for them as their spokesperson. My relationship with the real estate industry, my sales abilities, and my belief in their magazine made me the perfect choice to represent their publication. I came up with many different reasons why it would work before I got to the appointment. I knew that if I wanted to get anyone interested in me, I had to talk about what I could do for them. What I would give, not take, needed to be stressed. This is what making a good impression is all about.

4. "He's very unassuming."

We all know the cliché, "You never get a second chance to make a first impression." This is certainly true about the job interview. Choose clothing in which you feel comfortable and attractive. I like tailored, subtle but sophisticated, user-friendly clothes. Too much after shave or perfume is overwhelming. Be careful about wearing distracting jewelry.

Speak in a confident, relaxed, and dignified business voice. Avoid drinking too much coffee before you arrive. You could end up sounding too loud, a bit anxious, and uncomfortable. This should be a relaxed encounter. The person who is interviewing you is already relaxed, so if the air turns tense, you may be the culprit.

Remember, the goal is to fit into their organization, not stand out like a sore thumb.

5. "She has common sense and a good head on her shoulders."

My daughter Beth interviewed for a waitress job during the summer of her sophomore year in college. Before the interview, she was discouraged because she didn't have previous restaurant experience. Up to that point, she had only worked in a dress shop at a nearby mall.

She came back with the waitress uniform in her hand, chirping like a bird. "The manager asked me if I had any previous restaurant experience. I looked at him straight in the eye and said restaurant experience means a lot of people-contact and I've had plenty of that. In my previous job, I won the top award for serving customers who came to our shop. I know I will be transferring these same people skills over to your restaurant if you give me a chance and hire me."

That is Natural scripting—improv dialogue at its finest, combined with common sense.

6. "He doesn't believe everything he hears."

Often, classified ads make a job sound very appealing. The purpose of the ad is to get the phones to ring, just like selling any other product. Before you make an appointment, ask the receptionist a few questions. "I see in your ad that you are looking for a marketing representative. Does this involve travel, and approximately how much?"

Most of the time, the interviewers are not the people you will speak to on the phone. However, you can still ask the receptionist about the position to see if you want to pursue the position further.

7. "She knows where she is going."

Employers who are looking for professionals to fill positions with potential growth are curious about your future plans. Be prepared to be asked, "What are your career goals? For instance, where do you see yourself in five years?"

Prepare for this question prior to the interview. If you act dumbfounded it could cost you the job. On the other hand, if you act cocky it could cost you too. I hired a family friend who told me that she was going to be running my company in five years. At the time, I just had a string of bad luck interviewing people with very low self-esteem. When she came across like she ruled the world, I was refreshed and impressed.

The woman had not put in a hard day's work in her life. The first four months on the job she complained about every project she was asked to do. Thank goodness, I didn't have to fire her because she did it herself.

"I can't take this pressure. I thought selling would be more fun and less work. I think I'll try writing a book."

When you are asked the "This is your life" question, here is a simple, but bright retort:

"I hope to be in a growing environment similar to your company. I see this job as an opportunity to learn more about what customers are looking for in a good product. This experience can assist me with my desire to become a buyer within the next three to five years. I catch on fairly quickly and if I do a good job, I have faith that someone will notice my efforts."

Then ask the interviewer a few questions. Employers love to see that kind of initiative.

"What can the person you hire do to make this department more efficient?"

"Will the person selected have the opportunity to visit the representatives in the field?"

"Why did the previous person holding the position leave?" (You need to know that in order to protect yourself.) This gives you some insight into how they treat employees. If you find out that the person was promoted, that means good work will be recognized and there is a chance for promotion within the department for you in the future.

Be prepared to have that same question, "Why are you leaving your present job," asked of you.

8. "He's got class."

Don't act like a know-it-all. The employer says:

"Have you worked on a Toshiba XE1000?"

"Absolutely. I love it because it's a hard-drive. No muss or fuss."

You just got sent to the back of the class. That computer requires a DOS disk to boot.

It would have been far better to reply:

"I am self-taught on a word processor. I have a Panasonic Personal Word Processor W1500 and use it many times a day. I do have experience on the computer also. I catch on quickly."

People with class use good judgment and self-control during an interview. Don't smoke, drink (particularly if it is a luncheon interview), ask dumb questions. I've had people ask me: "How long do we get for lunch?"

"I have to pick up my child at the babysitter's house at five o'clock every day. Will working overtime ever be required?" Now I'm worried about her working during regular hours.

9. "She really makes a person feel good."

Flattery will get you everywhere—just make sure it is sincere and based on doing your homework.

"I understand that 80% of the widget market was captured by your division last year. Your advertising was everywhere. What else produced such incredible results for you? It really must make you feel proud."

"Your reputation out in the field, in the area of packaging, is truly envied. How many years of experience do you think it takes? Did you have any mentors?"

Bring the best out in the interviewer by interviewing *them* in a subtle fashion.

10. "He doesn't let any grass grow under his feet."

Take notes during the interview because you may need to refer to them on a call-back. Have your time-planner handy in case you get a positive response to this question:

"Would it be appropriate to call back tomorrow or the next day, to see if you have come close to a hiring decision?"

If they bring up salary before you do:

"What type of income were you looking for?"

I would be honest and say:

"My current salary is . . . I am hoping to get in the . . . range, if given the opportunity of obtaining this position."

If you bring salary up, do it close to the end when rapport is well-established:

"Can you give me an idea of what the salary range is for this position?"

Immediately following the interview, send the employer a *thank you note*. Here is a sample:

I appreciate the opportunity to discuss career possibilities with you. If selected, I would commit 100% of my capabilities to your service and consider it a privilege to be on your team. Thanks for talking to me today.

People do not follow up enough. Never take any appointment, phone call, or meeting for granted. Remember the "non-expectant" attitude discussed in Chapter 2. The Naturals cannot keep up with the jobs, opportunities, challenges, people, places, and events that come into their life.

THE CUSTOMER INTERVIEW

I get very upset when I watch incompetent salespeople. They are everywhere and it's about time we ban them from our industry. One day I walked into the hands of an ill-prepared, new salesperson. She was honest, but ignorant. Although every salesperson starts out "green," there are ways to prepare for a potential sale. There is no excuse for the way this woman acted and she cost her store over a $1,000 sale.

I was in the market for a new king-sized bed, mattress, down pillows and all the trimmings. I handed her the store's "White Sale" ad that I had clipped out of the newspaper that morning. She knew nothing about the ad or the special prices on the box springs and mattress. Finally, I suggested she ask another saleswoman who might know about the sale. She was told they did not have that merchandise at this location.

Then I asked her about down pillows. We walked over to the pillow bin and she didn't know a down from a duck feather. The two of us were fumbling around like idiots and she kept letting people interrupt her time with me. I staggered out of the place with two down pillows I found for myself. I was furious and exhausted.

The employment and the customer interview each have the same objective—to obtain the interest and attention of the listener. Naturals know that if a point of truthful contact is made during the initial approach between them and the customer, the sale is almost assured. A good salesperson leaves nothing to chance and accepts no excuses such as, "I'm a new salesperson and no one told me I was supposed to know that information."

Here is how I should have been approached and interviewed:

Saleswoman: "Thanks for stopping by. Are you in the market for some bedding or are you just looking?"

Remember that people who want to buy are eager for sales help. The person who buys fast is not a looker or a shopper with time to waste. They know what they want and they love someone who reacts as fast as they do.

Most of the time the stores cater to the lookers because they mistake the real buyer for the impatient intruder.

Danielle: "Yes. I need a king-size bed and mattress. I would like to know more about the ones that are on sale. I also need pillows and bedding."

Saleswoman: "The ad you saw for the mattress and box spring is only available at our Newport store, but I can call and have one held for you or perhaps we can ship it to your home."

She would then pause for a response. Then she would have walked me directly to the pillows and other bedding, knowing exactly where each item was located.

"What color is the room you are re-decorating?"

"Do you have a dust ruffle and a coverlet?"

"Tell me your favorite colors. We have a fine selection of the newest spring hues like peach, pink, and some nifty stripes. I'll show you some of the favorites and see what we can find for you."

This encounter feels good for both customer and salesperson when it is done correctly. The flawless interview is the right combination of asking questions, listening intently, and visually picturing in your mind's eye your product or service, and determining where the point of contact between your product and the buyer's need can fit together.

Point of Contact

The point of contact is when you gain the buyer's attention because you discover the customer's strongest motive for buying. It may be efficiency, cost, convenience, prestige, or comfort. You can only discover the customer's point of view by:

1. Setting up a comfortable environment, both physically and emotionally.

2. Scientifically asking questions and responding to those questions in an effective way that produces truthful answers.

3. Continually reassuring the customer that you are knowledgeable and capable, thus holding his or her attention.

The reason many sales are not consummated is because the salesperson never discovered the point of contact during the interview, or focused on the wrong one by trying to sell service when they should have sold price. Sometimes, the customer leads you to believe the point of contact is one thing when it really is another. Nothing you can do will be convincing enough because you didn't strike the right nerve.

Environmental Conditions—Physical and Emotional Space

1. *The Physical Space.* The customer makes his first impression of you, your line, and your company from outward appearances—yours and the physical one around you. It is only natural and reasonable that this customer should base her judgment of your ability and your company's character on what she observes firsthand.

Customers dislike careless and shifty salespeople, and they expect a company or store that hires salespeople to feel the same way. So, if the place is a mess, both you and your firm's reputation are headed for disaster. You cannot blame the customer for pre-judging because if they have been out in the world and exposed to first class salesmanship, they have become good judges of proper techniques.
Pre-Interview Physical Space Check:

- Empty all ash trays, wastebaskets, and so on.
- Check all bathrooms. Are they clean? Plenty of toilet paper?
- Are desks clear and free of old coffee cups, unanswered messages, and other disorderly clues?
- Are samples, merchandise, displays, and inventory clean, presented in the best possible light, and organized for easy access?
- What are the lighting conditions?
- Does the air smell fresh?
- Would some fresh plants, family photos around your desk, and framed testimonial letters add to your credibility?
- What can you do physically to add to the appeal of your store, showroom, or car?
- Can I provide privacy for my client? Interior designers, insurance people, realtors, computer salespersons, high-fashion salespeople, and big-ticket marketing people in public relations and advertising need a quiet and separate area to conduct an interview. If it is not your office, find some place fast.

2. *The Emotional Space*

Natural salespeople have their eyes wide open at all times. Your awareness level regarding the human condition will have a lot to do with establishing honest communication between you and the customer during the approach appointment. Be open-minded and do not pre-judge individuals based on outward appearances, but be smart enough to know how to read somebody who is in a bad mood, set in their ways, or of weak character.

At the time of introduction and approach, work on becoming "detached" from the customer. Synonyms for the word detached include objective, severed, fair, and neutral. This attitude is not a cold-hearted, uncaring approach to their problems, but a professional disengagement from their weaknesses, irritations, and fears.

In Chapter 12 review the Kennedy Twelve-Step Sales-Recovery Program. It will help you correct the weaknesses that prevent you from detaching from your customer. In this chapter, concentrate on being alert to the customer's disposition from the moment of first contact and approach.

Many salespeople are completely oblivious to the emotional tone or temperament of a customer and cause themselves undue heartache, wasted time and frustration. As a teacher and lover of the sales profession, it is my greatest desire to help thousands of salespeople raise their standards and improve their public image. Sales professionals have not received the respect from the public that they deserve. Too much emphasis is placed on how salespeople take advantage of the customer. People should keep in mind the treatment the salesperson receives from ill-tempered customers.

Customer Temperament and Character

1. *Easy-To-Love Customers:* Easy-to-love customers are like boy scouts—trustworthy, loyal, helpful, friendly, courteous, kind, obedient, cheerful, thrifty, brave, and reverent. I have many customers like this all over the world and they make me proud to be a salesperson.

2. *Easy-To-Hate:* Easy-to-hate customers are—untrustworthy, disloyal, unhelpful, rude, unkind, disobedient, irritable, miserly, cowardly, and disrespectful. Some Naturals do fine with these types because they stay detached. If you find yourself being eaten alive, you better disconnect and go find a few easy-to-love customers.

HOW TO SCORE A PERFECT "10" AT EVERY INTERVIEW

If salespersons could see an instant replay of every flawless interview that they have ever conducted either in person or by telephone, it would be obvious that these four questions were answered with a definite "YES."

1. Did I state the purpose of this communication?
2. Did I receive the customer's undivided interest and attention?

3. Did I repeat, as stated, the customer's specific, stated needs and criteria?

4. Did I tell the customer I appreciated his or her viewpoint?

Let's say you can determine the buyer's needs halfway through the interview. You ask a key question: "How much will your budget allow for this widget?"

The customer says: "I don't want to spend over $1,000."

You reply: "I really think you should consider stretching that figure up about $300."

Stop. That is way too soon to start handling objections. The only thing the salesperson needed to do at that point was to repeat the customer's concerns:

"You do not want to spend over $1,000."

Then acknowledge and appreciate her viewpoint:

"I can appreciate your wanting to stay within a certain budget."

You don't know yet how much she really can afford and how much she would be willing to pay for your product once she hears you deliver a dynamic presentation on the product's true worth. Too many salespeople cut off any further honest communication with the prospect because they do not listen or use the above four questions as their guide. Every interview can be divided into two distinct parts:

Form and Execution

Form includes eye contact, verbal and non-verbal language.

Execution involves the type of questions the salesperson uses during that interview to determine the customer's needs, and the style in which those questions are asked.

FORM

Imagine a couple that you have never met before sit down at your desk to buy your goods. You are a very attractive saleswoman who happens to believe that all the big financial decisions in life are made by the men. You are selling big ticket items, so during your conversations with the couple, starting at the approach, you make most of your eye contact with the male.

Suddenly, the woman interrupts the interview and says she just remembered they are supposed to pick up their son at three o'clock. The man looks puzzled, but he excuses himself and follows her out the door. You will never have a second chance to talk to them about your three-piece sectionals because she's headed to your competitor and her husband is right behind her.

Somewhere along the way, while you were giving him all the eye contact, the woman was thinking, "I don't want to be here. It doesn't matter if I am anyway because she barely glances my way."

Gentlemen, this rule applies to you, too. You may think you just need to address your questions to the man, but little do you realize the checkbook may be in her purse.

MASTER CONTROL OF THOSE SELLING EYES

Maintain strong eye contact with all parties during the interview. If only one person is involved, look at the customer straight in the eye every time you communicate what you have to say to him. Practice controlling your eye muscles by staring in the mirror at yourself. Stand back from the mirror and gaze at yourself, pretending that you see someone else. Walk closer to the mirror and stop when you can make clear eye contact with your image. Focus on the eyes in the mirror and see how long you can maintain strong contact without blinking. Your eye is just another muscle in your body, so work on strengthening it because the Naturals know how to maintain control of the selling scene with their eyes.

CUSTOMERS ARE LIKE TURTLES—GIVE THEM TIME TO MOVE OUT OF THEIR SHELLS

Be very sensitive to body language. In some Asian cultures, it is considered rude to touch someone you hardly know. Be polite and kind, but maintain your distance. If you do a great job with people, they may end up giving you a big hug every time they run into you.

MENTION THE MENTOR

If you have been highly recommended to this customer by a mentor, please remind the prospect of that at the beginning of the interview.

"Harold Williams told me I will be in big trouble if I don't give you my renowned first class treatment."

Sometimes the prospect forgets that you know Harold and you may use the "Mentor Dialogue," from Chapter 3 or say:

"Oh that's right. Harold called us several weeks ago and said such wonderful things about your work."

Just because you have a mentor rooting for you in the background, don't assume that the customer understands the importance of that mentor's name as much as you do.

THE CUSTOMER WILL JUDGE YOUR MENTAL CLARITY BY THE WAY YOU USE YOUR VOICE

Learn to modulate your voice correctly. Singers use their diaphragms to regulate the speed, pitch, resonance, and volume of their voices.

Speed: Pronounce your words with care and adapt the speed of the conversation to the nature of your discussion. Involved questions demand pauses and emphasis on certain words. If you talk faster than a customer, he may not understand you. Adjust to the customer's speed.

Pitch: Avoid a shrill pitch, even if the customer is a shrill-shrieker. Pitch shows intensity of feeling. Relax your vocal chords and take a few deep breaths if you feel yourself getting too high-strung. Always talk in a lower pitch than your prospect, but be sure you can be heard and do not mumble.

Resonance: The resonance of your voice shows the quality of the emotions. You can judge the customer on all of these factors, but remember the customer is also judging you.

Volume: This doesn't mean being loud. Volume shows strength and vitality.

Legend tells us that the Indian is a natural orator because he has been taught how to express himself by following the laws of nature. Good health is the basis of good language expression and clear thinking. No one who talks incoherently can become a good salesperson. When you speak, remember to accent the words you wish to emphasize just as you underscore them when you write. Here's an illustration: "I *know* someday you will *thank* me."

LISTEN LIKE A LOVER

Remember how you would hang on to every word your lover said when you were first dating? This is the kind of attention the customer deserves during the sales process. If you really listen to both the unspoken and spoken messages your customer gives you during the interview, your chances of making a sale that sticks are 50% greater.

TAKE NOTES LIKE AN "A" STUDENT

Use the Need Determinator form (see Figure 6-1 on page 115) and a legal pad to take notes while you interview your client. You can refer to the responses throughout the entire sales cycle. Your customers will be impressed with how well you remembered the details of the sales transaction.

EXECUTION

Use these questions to assure your customer that the qualifying time is valuable. If you feel self-conscious using a form in the beginning of the interview, please say this to the prospect: "I know how valuable your time is and I don't want to waste a moment. In order for me to do a more effective job for you, I want to take this opportunity to ask you a few brief questions to determine your needs, whether you end up enlisting my service or someone else's."

I call the last part of the above introductory dialogue the "Takeaway." When you can sincerely say to every new prospect "whether you enlist my service or not," or, "this is how I operate," it indicates to the

The Need Determinator

Name of customer: _____

Address: _____

City: _____ State: _____ Zip: _____

Work Phone: _____

Home Phone: _____

Is this the first time you will use this product? _____

What product or service are you presently using? _____

How many _____ do you generally use in a week, month, year? _____

How long have you been looking for this product or service? _____

Personal Information (if applicable):

Where are you both presently employed? _____

How many in your family? _____

Will the entire family use this service (membership)? _____

So far have you seen any _____ that you really like? _____

What prevented you from purchasing them? _____

How soon do you wish to purchase or take delivery of _____
_____ ?

What is the company you are presently using specifically doing for you? Not doing for you?

What would you like to see improved in this product or service? _____

What have you allocated in your budget for this project? _____

Will you be borrowing the money in order to make this investment? _____

Will you be converting any of your investments in order to complete this purchase? _____

Are you the decision-maker, or does this go to a committee? _____

What kind of information do you need from me to assist you in making a positive decision for my service or merchandise?

Figure 6-1

prospects that you can present an objective viewpoint concerning their needs.

Notice how the questions on the Need Determination form are arranged. The first several are very light and breezy questions, meant to be asked while rapport is being built; as you progress the questions are heavier and right to the point.

The goal of every interview is to discover your prospect's specific needs. Your ability to find out the absolute truth as soon as possible will determine your success in selling. Your attitude and feelings of comfort with yourself will come through with each new customer. I studied Edward R. Murrow in the 1950s when he was the first man on television to be invited into the living rooms of famous people to be interviewed. Others like Johnny Carson, Jay Leno, Oprah, Geraldo, Sally, Donahue, Regis and Cathy, Connie Chung, Larry King and more recently, Maria Shriver, have a "walk in like you own the place" style of interviewing.

I watched Maria Shriver ask a very personal question in an extremely tactful manner to a successful rock star who was raised in the ghetto by a single mother.

"In your neighborhood, the temptation to take drugs was all around you. How did you handle and overcome these temptations?"

He answered: "Yes, there were temptations and I was tempted many times. But my mother worked very hard for all eight of us children and I knew I would break her heart if I did something like that."

Her voice was warm and compassionate and her choice of words was very appropriate. The key word was "temptation." She didn't make the man feel like his desires were any different from anyone else's no matter where he was raised. Just because he was human, he might have been "tempted," in or out of a ghetto.

An unspoken question floating through the air at every interview is, "Are we compatible?" If the salesperson and the prospect are compatible, the trust will build between the two of them. Trust is created by building the relationship on a sound foundation of salesperson credibility and, to a lesser degree, common denominators. I never liked the idea of trying to become my customer's best buddy just so I could make a sale. A degree of compatibility on a personal level is nice, but not required. If it works out that you have children the same age, go to the same church, or both enjoy golf, then it makes for fast and easy conversation. However, becoming intimate with customers should not be your goal.

ESTABLISHING CREDENTIALS

Some salespeople give their business card both at the beginning and at the end of the interview for reinforcement. Often, business people from other cultures consider it a custom to exchange business cards during the first few minutes of introduction. If they do, follow their lead. At the end of your interview, it is critical that you do a complete presentation, displaying your credentials to your customer. Do this if you are selling a $50 piece of jewelry at a home-party, or if you are trying to land the Paramount Pictures advertising account.

The customer interview should be similar to the employment interview. Bring references, résumés, and a prospectus. Prepare an opening dialogue for this section of the interview after all the need-determination questions have been answered.

"No matter who you choose to represent you, always check out their credentials. I consider my credentials a passport to your business. May I present them for your approval?"

Suggestion: You may want to present your résumé, personal brochure, and testimonial letters inside of a dark blue folder with gold letters that resembles a passport. The title on the front cover could say, MY PASSPORT TO YOUR BUSINESS.

When you prepare this material, use the writing tips in Chapter 5 to assist you. Visit the public library and look up reference material on résumé preparation. Study other résumés and biographical sketches. My presentation piece has the Danielle Kennedy name and line logo across the front on a high quality brown tone stock paper. The inside has pockets on both sides that make room for a biographical sketch and a separate brochure outlining my credentials.

After I do an interview with a prospective client, an expensive white box is mailed to them. Inside the white box is a press package, video demonstration tape and biographical sketch. If you can do something similar before you arrive for the interview, and your presentation package is very impressive, your credibility goes up a notch before you even arrive.

LAST MINUTE REMINDERS FOR THE PERFECT INTERVIEW

1. If your merchandise is displayed during the interview, be sure to use it. Allow the prospect to touch it and explore its parts. If it is not available, please use the "Wait until you see" dialogue from Chapter 3 to whet his or her appetite.

2. Become comfortable with silence between you and the customer. Many of these questions will involve thoughtful pauses on the buyer's part. Don't rush, and give her time to think. The confident Natural doesn't need to be chattering every minute. That gets most prospects very irritated.

3. Don't be afraid to confess that you don't know the answer to a ques-

tion. "Do you know if Markborough homes offers the same landscape allowance as you do?"

You should know your competition's options backwards and forwards, but if you don't, simply say, "Let's find out right now." Then pick up the telephone and get the answer. If that is not possible, let the customer know when you can deliver an answer. It is better to be honest, than to act like a show-off.

4. Do not take anything for granted. Try not to assume that your customer knows certain details about the product you offer, or that you know what her budget is without asking specific questions. Cover all the bases. You could end up spending countless hours with a person who is not prepared to do business with you, or who does not need such a thorough explanation of one part of your service. You must discover the point of contact by asking the right questions and listening intently.

5. Do you want to be right or make your customer happy? Some salespeople would rather be right than happy. They go to the extreme to prove the customer wrong. Even when the customer is wrong, a good salesperson should make the customer still feel good.

"You scared me this morning, Mr. Buyer. I thought my banker gave me some wrong information yesterday afternoon at five o'clock. He told me our interest rate would be 10% on this purchase. So, when you reported a difference of opinion with me at our interview this morning, I went right over to his office and made him repeat it to me in person. It was entirely possible that you could have been right, but I am here to give you the most up-to-date information and I wanted to be sure I knew what I was talking about."

6. Likes attract likes. During the interview, notice people's speech accents, clothes, and mannerisms. They may end up looking and acting like you. I have found that salespeople ultimately attract people very similar to them. Build on that. My Midwestern accent has built a great deal of rapport for me over the years. "You sound like you are from the Midwest, too. Whereabouts?"

"Chicago."

"No kidding. Where did you go to high school?"

The next thing you know, I am no longer interviewing a stranger, but the cousin of a child that sat across from me in math 30 years ago. That type of common bond establishes trust. They think, "She's one of us. We can trust her."

Someone once asked Barbara Walters how she managed to get interviews with people that no one else could approach. She said she never gave up nicely bugging them. Dropping little notes, a quick phone call, or asking a mentor to put in a good word are all part of the process that brings a salesperson in front of the qualified customer.

7

How To Arouse Desire: The Natural
Rush of a Skillful Sales Presentation

"Desire creates the power."

Suppose you are studying the owner's manual for your new computer and you stumble upon a word you do not understand. You must stop and look up the word in the dictionary before you can continue applying the instructions. Just as you would consult a dictionary, salespeople provide similar information to customers that will give them a clear mental image of how the product or service will benefit them.

Through the course of the demonstration, you must use a variety of perceptions and explanations to arouse the customer's desire for your product. When prospects have a good understanding of your merchandise, they can apply your goods to their needs.

Read the following demonstration. Be aware of the different ways the salesperson awakens the customers' emotions and stimulates their intellect.

A Demonstration Case Study: Sold on Sailing.

Situation: A boat salesperson is about to demonstrate a 36-foot sailing sloop at a regional boat show. It is loaded with these options: generator, radar, loran, roller furling jib, cruising spinnaker, shower/head, refrigerator, gas stove, microwave, luxurious cabin, additional sleeping quarters for six, and a spacious, colorful salon. Price: $90,000.

Salesperson: Very reputable, knowledgeable—20-year veteran in boat sales.

Prospects: A couple in their mid-30s is considering purchasing their first boat. Their combined income is over $125,000 per year. The salesman ran a credit check after his interview with the customer two days ago. The salesman classifies these customers as "Be-backs" because the husband did a quick tour of the boat without his wife. Their names are Mary and Bud Landlubber. The salesman: Captain Mike.

Captain: Hi Bud. I see you brought your first mate with you today. Nice to see you. I'm Captain Mike. (Stretches out his hand to Mary for a handshake.)

Mary: (She returns the gesture) Hi Mike, I'm Mary Landlubber.

Mike is dressed in white casual pants, canary yellow golf shirt, and a pair of docksider loafers. The boating life has left him with a perpetual tan, a passion for the sea and a few extra wrinkles, which only add to his credibility.

Mike enthusiastically leads them up the stairs to the boat. After 20 years of selling, Mike instinctively knows how to mix his presentation with emotion, benefits, features, and facts. He loves boats, knows them inside and out, and is especially fond of this manufacturer and next year's model he is showcasing at this year's boat show.

Mike prefers to give the prospect a quick cook's tour and then go back and linger at special locations describing certain features. Often the husband and he will get very involved in detailed explanations of the technical aspects of the boat, while the wife looks around at living accommodations. Mike will keep a close eye on the wife while she roams, and will intermittently join her and point out special amenities.

Let's watch this seafaring Natural in action:

(Mike asks the couple to remove their shoes before boarding the boat. He jumps on board and leans out with stretched hand, bidding his buyers to come aboard.)

Mike: Hop on. Grab my hand, Mary. First, I want you to see the general layout, then we can go back and study features.

Mike starts demonstrating from the cockpit of the boat.

Mike: The naval architect designed this cockpit with the new open stern, which provides easy one-step access to the dingy. After you look at all the other new models at this show, I think you will find that this cockpit is the most spacious, with plenty of room for comfortable seating, as well as wheel steering for the helmsman. Bud, if you've ever been on a boat without wheel steering and a rudder taking up all kinds of room, you know it can get very cramped.

Bud: Especially when you have three kids on top of you like I did when we chartered that type to Catalina.

Mike: That's right. It makes a big difference. I wish we had her at sea right now and were sipping a glass of fine wine enjoying a magnificent sunset, but this is the best I can do, so sit down and see for yourself just how comfortable and spacious it feels.

He sits next to the steering wheel motioning for Bud to sit in the helmsman's place. Mary stretches out on one of the cockpit cushions.

There is a comfortable silence between the three of them. After about 30 seconds, Mike directs the couple up to the forward bow.

Mike: There are other features I will point out back here, but let's check out some other features first. Notice the life lines that go all the way around the boat. They are attached extremely well to the hull. This assures you, your family, and friends of their safety while under way. Keep in mind that the craftsmanship in this boat compares to sloops twice this price. (He hands Mary a brochure with the price. Bud got one yesterday.)

Bud: Why is this boat manufacturer so much cheaper than comparable boats?

Mike: I see you have been visiting other exhibits. Good. First of all, it's a popular boat and they sell a lot of them. They are manufactured on an assembly line and typically there is a waiting list of buyers. Because they manufacture so many, they are on top of the latest innovations and developments in boating. Their research and development staff is the best in the business.

The main reason they build a boat with such pride is because of the owner—Rudolph Regatta. Regatta fell in love with boating in his bathtub at the age of two. By four, he was stealing two by fours from the empty lot next to his house in Caper, NJ, so he could build his first rendition of a sailboat. He used his mother's old rags to make sails. By the time he was 18, he built his first boat, moved to California and worked on a boat assemblyline. By age 28, he was chief boat designer for one of the state's largest boat builders. At 30, he started his own company and the rest is sailboat history. Not bad for a boy who pretended his dirty bathtub was a lake until he turned 12 years old.

This company delivers a classy boat. I've sold many of them over the years to boat owners who have moved up or down to larger or smaller models from this same manufacturer. They resell well and hold their value.

Bud: How much anchor line does she have?

Mike: Six feet of chain and 400 feet of line. That's one of the best features of this boat. (As he opens the anchor well.) You see the anchor, chain, line, and electric windless are all stored here and closed up below deck when not in use. This way, your passengers have more room to stretch out while under way and there is nothing that can catch the sails or sheets while tacking. It has a nice clean appearance, don't you agree Bud?

Bud: Not bad.

Mike starts walking back towards the cockpit and the couple follows.

Mike: Let's take a look below. Mary, wait until you see how handy and well thought out the interior is. You'll appreciate the layout while preparing a meal in a quiet cove over at the islands. I imagine with two careers and three children you two get pretty busy. Sailing is one of the few hobbies that forces you to turn off the world and give your family and each other the undivided attention you all deserve. I've been a sailor ever since my children were babies. I credit our close relationship over the years to those times at sea we got to know each other in a way that has been possible because we can afford the luxury of boating.

Bud: Where can I keep this boat?

Mike: There should be slips available at our marina. I'll check and get all the details for you. While I'm at it, I will get you some information on joining the yacht club. The marina is a great place to socialize—there are some interesting events planned throughout the year.

Everyone is down below now.

Mary: (She moved into the forward cabin on her own.) I hope I don't get claustrophobia in here.

Mike: Come into the salon a minute, Mary. I want to show you why you won't have to worry about that.

Mary steps out and Mike moves into the forward cabin, opens the oversized hatch and turns on the reading lights along side of the queen-size berth. He goes back into the salon and instructs Mary to go back into the forward cabin.

Mike: Lie down and see how comfortable that V-berth is and imagine: The breeze is blowing through from above, it's shortly after sunrise, the seagulls are squawking overhead looking for breakfast, and the water is gurgling past your hull. You are taking a lazy stretch and trying to make important decisions for the day, such as deciding if you should gunkhole from port to port or sun bathe and swim in this private cove that only you and your family know exists.

Mary: (Giggling) I'm ready to live the good life, Captain.

Bud is watching Mike point out storage areas in the salon.

Bud: Let's find out what options you want or need because there is a whole grab bag of goodies you may or may not choose to select. Then I'll sharpen my pencil and do some figuring for you.

Mike leads the way and they all go on deck to work out some solutions.

There were many solid explanations and perceptions that Mike used during the demonstration. His explanations were succinct. He used personal intuition to adapt to his customers' understanding. When Bud needed more information about anchor lines, Mike had the knowledge on the tip of his tongue and relied on his intuition to know when to stop and move on to another feature. The important thing is not the amount of sales talk he indulges in, but the quality of that talk.

FOUR VITAL REASONS TO DEMONSTRATE

Naturals build their demonstration around four reasons and maintain their focus on those reasons during the entire demonstration sequence.

They do not waste precious time pointing out the wrong features to the right people or vice versa. Once the customer sees that he can use your product or service to save time, energy, and money, or that your offer is a good investment, his desire to buy will become more intense. Thus, the Natural salesperson can prove both intellectually and emotionally the value of the merchandise by putting sound ideas into the customer's head. The four reasons why Naturals demonstrate are:

1. To help the customer gain knowledge about their product. One time Bud chartered a boat with a rudder for steering instead of a wheel. The rudder took up all the space in the cockpit. Captain Mike showed them *why* his product worked better and Bud learned something.

   The true colors of every salesperson shine brightly during the demonstration. If he does not know what he is talking about, the presentation will lack substance and the customers may patiently go through the motions, but they will seek other sources of information before they buy.

2. To help the customer become a believer. Salespersons want to convert the customers to their way of thinking. Mike worked with Mary on her belief that she might feel claustrophobic in the forward cabin. He physically opened up the hatch and turned lights on and suggested she enjoy the spaciousness. In addition, he asked her to use her imagination.

3. To arouse desire in the customer. When desire is deeply aroused, the yearning for possession becomes overwhelming. If the customer has a desire to get away from the stress and strain of daily life, the salesperson must appeal to that desire through *suggestion*. Suggestion appeals to the customer's appetites for love, power, pride, and pleasure. Suggestion is a direct appeal to the senses and feelings. Captain Mike described sunsets, fine wine, and lazy days of sunbathing and swimming in out-of-the-way island coves, and that appealed to Mary and Bud's desire for pleasure.

   Salespeople arouse desire through *reasoning* when their product appeals to the intellectual side of the customer. The calculating and analytical mental powers of their customers require reasonable explanations, such as Mike showed on the bow when he explained the positive features of the anchor, lines, and storage. Good salespeople know how to mix and match the use of reasoning and suggestion during the demonstration. The salesperson can only do this authentically if he or she is aware of the buyer's emotional and intellectual "hot buttons" (pleasure, prestige, education, and other motives), which are discovered during an in-depth interview and by paying close attention to what the customer says throughout the entire sales process.

4. To induce the customer to action. If the salesperson has done a good job of courting the customer, he or she will be ready to say "I'll take it," when the Natural pops the question.

Bud asked about a boat slip. After Captain Mike made an especially arousing appeal to the good life of sailing, Bud wondered what the monthly payments would be. The customer is being induced into action and the salesperson must not delay with more sales talk. It's time to work up the numbers because the buyer is getting ready to take action and consider buying the boat.

KENNEDY'S 18 PRECEPTS FOR PROPER PRESENTATIONS

Assume the stage is set and your presentation materials, displays, or samples will be seen under excellent conditions. Previous interviews with the prospect went smoothly, so it's showtime. The Natural never takes anything for granted. Study my precepts and perfect them in order to increase your overall chances of increasing sales following a dynamic demonstration.

Precept 1: Design a blueprint and follow it.

When we remodeled our home, an architect designed a blueprint that outlined our specific improvements. This blueprint indicated the specifications a contractor had to follow to complete the project. Similarly, salespeople need to design a course of action that will be easy for the customer to follow during the demonstration. You can design your format after the customer interview. If you don't have time to do it in writing, do it mentally. Will you demonstrate from general to specific or specific to general? Captain Mike took the general approach with Mary and Bud by telling them he would usher them through the entire boat and then go back and discuss specifics. He stayed flexible enough to pause at certain locations when Bud or Mary asked specific questions.

When I sold real estate, I planned my routes to each home, purposely showed the finest home first or saved it until the last stop in the presentation, and followed a certain pattern of demonstrating each home and the individual floor plans.

Your plan instills confidence in the customer whether you are demonstrating a line of clothes or a list of services you provide. It also keeps you in charge of the demonstration because, without a format, the customer has the opportunity to take control in a territory that they know less about than you do.

Precept 2: Know exactly the type of information the customer desires and gear your presentation to those needs.

You will know this information because you discovered it during the interview and homework phases of your sales work. Perhaps, your customer is already sold by the time the demonstration begins. Do not get caught giving out information the customer doesn't need, or demonstrating features that are not significant.

A friend told me he bought a Mercedes-Benz from a salesperson who did not properly interview him or bother to find out the reasons he wanted the car in the first place. Those reasons included safety, and the look of the car that would impress business associates. The day he went out with the salesperson for the test drive, he annoyed him with detailed explanations of the mechanics and technical features of the car.

"Finally, I just told him I knew the car was technically superb and it was time he took me back to the office so I could buy the car."

If you don't emphasize the right reasons why the prospect wants your product, you could squelch the transaction.

Precept 3: Convert the customer to your viewpoint.

Captain Mike encouraged Mary and Bud to visit the competition. He felt his boat was far superior to the others. He had a strong conviction based on his own sincere beliefs. He presented a good argument when he discussed cost and quality of construction. He enjoyed telling the Rudolph Regatta story—one that appealed to the emotions of the average person who believes that hard work and following your dream pays off.

It's been said that the secret of selling isn't the product, but the salesperson. The salesperson must have two very strong beliefs:

1. A belief that his or her product is the best available in the marketplace.

2. A belief that those who purchase his or her product will be better off financially, intellectually, emotionally, spiritually, or physically after they buy it. Whether you are selling cereal or religion, you must communicate these beliefs from the bottom of your heart to the highest point of your intelligence. Prove it to your customer with your deep passion, knowledge, and expertise during the demonstration.

Precept 4: Involve the customer in the demonstration.

When I sold homes, I tried to place couples in a setting that closely matched what it would be like once they owned the place. Then I would give them some privacy and leave the room saying: "Imagine where you would place your own furniture in this room if you lived here."

A great example of customer involvement is the FAO Schwarz Toy Company. Everywhere you go, adults and children are playing games, winding up dolls, listening to stories, or watching videos.

Other types of customer involvement include cooking demonstrations, facials, and trial runs that influence the customer's buying temperature. Anytime you can give customers a positive experience about "what it would be like" if they owned your product or service, you are one step closer to making the sale.

Precept 5: Point out features and benefits the customers have not noticed.

When we purchased our home on a cliff above the ocean, we were pleasantly surprised during the second showing when the realtor pointed out to us the hidden wooden stairs leading to the beach.

"Only four homes along the coast in this section of town have access to the beach and this home is one of them," said the realtor.

Saving that information until the second demonstration created renewed excitement and clinched the sale.

When you demonstrate effectively, there is a climax of excitement building as each newly identified feature is pointed out. Don't waste time pointing out things that insult your prospect's intelligence. Avoid statements like, "This is the kitchen." When I was a new salesperson, I had a tendency to say things like that because I was nervous, and pauses in the conversation made me self-conscious. After I had put my foot in my mouth one too many times, I learned to choose my sales dialogue wisely.

Precept 6: Encourage the customer to ask questions.

Observe your customer carefully. When you see her yawn, start to lose interest, or get a blank look on her face, you may have lost her. The first time I sat and listened to a computer salesperson demonstrate for me, I found myself tuning out because he said something along the way I didn't understand, and instead of asking me if I understood what he was talking about, he just kept rambling.

Once the customer loses your train of thought, the rest of the presentation is a waste of time. Sometimes people are too embarrassed to say they do not understand what you are talking about. School children are often afraid to raise their hand and ask a question because they think everyone will assume they are stupid. Sometimes, adults do not outgrow such fears.

If you notice any signs of boredom, irritation, or misunderstanding, use the following statements and questions.

"If I explain something that seems confusing to you, don't hesitate to interrupt me and ask a question."

Intermittently, stop and ask: "How am I doing so far? Is there anything specific I have covered that needs further explanation?"

"Promise you will be honest with me. If I am going through this too fast or covering things you aren't concerned about, stop me. The most important thing is that you gain a clear understanding of how my product can save you time and money."

Precept 7: Enchant your customer with a "Tell and Sell" story during the presentation.

When a customer receives information about an owner or inventor of a product, it enhances the beauty and value. Captain Mike told the story of a young man who began building wooden boats at the age of eight and later became one of the premier boat builders in America.

I got the idea for the "Tell and Sell" dialogue one Christmas season when I heard a talented local artist in my community fascinate several people who were contemplating buying one of her beautiful paintings.

We were admiring a print of an original painting in her studio one day, while she mingled with customers. The artist is also a pilot and she photographed a crystal clear picture of Avalon Harbor on Catalina Island from her plane. Then she went back to her studio and recreated the perfect replica of that breathtaking moment.

She told us about her plane trip to Catalina, the 18 months she spent in front of her easel, and the precise detail the work required while using a palette knife and over 123 different shades of color.

She further explained that she was offering a "limited" number of the signed serigraphs over the next two weeks at a special pre-Christmas price. The combination of hearing the artist's own story and the opportunity to purchase NOW at a special price, motivated me and several others to reach for our checkbooks immediately. The "tell and sell" worked like a charm.

Precept 8: Use Product Eliminating Statements (PES) or Product Eliminating Questions (PEQ).

If you sell several brands of clothing or appliances, various insurance packages, or a large selection of homes and floor plans, try using some PEQs or PESs during the demonstration to narrow the choices down to a reasonable number.

PES: (When a home has little or no back yard) "I don't know if you enjoy doing yard work or not, but this home is definitely low maintenance."

You may get a response like: "I feel trapped in this small space. I love a big green lawn, not a small slab of concrete."

or "I hate yard work. We are never home anyway."

PEQ: (When the prospect is confused about which insurance policy to purchase) "Both the Land Life and Beauty Life policies provide excellent coverage, but the Beauty Life is a few cents more a month. I can tell you why if you are interested, or are you leaning toward the Land Life Policy at this time?"

Their response might be: "I've been told I may not be getting all the coverage I need with Land Life so please give me some more information."

PEQ: "All of these manufacturers build an outstanding product. Before we go any further, do you have a preference?"

Their reply: "We've used HardCore washers and dryers for 20 years and get good service. But maybe I am missing something that others are offering."

Here is where your knowledge of the newest changes in your marketplace can serve you well.

PES Salesperson: "You know, I have used their product for years myself, but Streamline is a fairly new manufacturer which offers the same well-built machine for about $200 less, and over the last couple of years we have received excellent feedback on this product. You may end up wanting to stick with your present brand, but let me demonstrate some of the features of Streamline."

Precept 9: Use pictures, drawings, and samples.

Color boards, carpet samples, illustrated drawings and sketches, photographs, and samples of your product give the customer a distinct, mental picture of your goods, or the quality of work that you are capable of producing.

I'll never forget the afternoon the children and I gave Andy, the door-to-door salesman, a round of applause and a $50 sale after he bedazzled us with a dramatic demonstration of his product.

He started with an endorsement dialogue: "Hi, Mrs. Kennedy. Your neighbors on the block, Betty, Vicki, and Jane, just purchased my 'Miracle Mix' and they all agreed it would be a good idea if I stopped by and demonstrated it for you, too." (He found out each name on the block by asking every woman who bought his product who the next door neighbor was and if they felt that person would be interested in learning about his cleaner.) Before I had a chance to open my mouth, my children were standing at the door listening, as Andy instructed someone to go to the refrigerator and get a bottle of catsup.

Then he poured a little catsup on his tie and white shirt and rubbed it in. He waited about a minute and took a bottle of Miracle Mix and a rag out of his case and rubbed out the stain in ten seconds flat. My children thought he was a magician.

Then he said: "Do you have grease stains anywhere?"

I could have kept this guy busy for a week, but the first place the whole family recited in unison was: "The garage floor." Andy's big dark eyes were beaming with enthusiasm as he commanded, "Direct me to greasy garage."

We all stood around as Andy poured a generous amount of his holy water all over the biggest stain we could find. He took a heavy-duty scrub brush, and with a circular motion, wiped out the stain in less than a minute. "You don't need much of my cleaner to see instant results."

We were all amazed and he could feel the excitement in the air. He went on, "How many children do you have, Mrs. Kennedy?"

"You are looking at all of them, Andy."

"What a tribe. You are going to love this cleaner because it does the job on clothes, floors, hub caps, drains, and other household wares. And by the way, I told your neighbors so I better tell you too, this is a one time opportunity. I won't be back in the neighborhood again."

Nobody can argue when the proof is right before your very eyes, so I bought a case of the supernatural potion for a clan of motivated elbow-greasers.

Precept 10: Break the silence about the competition.

It should be no surprise to you that people comparison shop. You do, so what makes you think your customer doesn't? Instead of skirting the issue, face it head on with a question like: "How does this compare to other models that you have been looking at?"

Or

"Are you interviewing several others before you make your decision? I am not nosy, just eager to show you how our machinery outperforms any of my competitors," or "I am familiar with all the other types. Let's do some comparing together."

I always remind builders that their salespeople should be completely versed on all the competing neighborhoods in their general vicinity. That means they know specific options such as upgraded tiles, carpeting, or landscape allowances that others offer, so they can use comparisons in their demonstrations.

Never knock the competition, but boost your own goods. Naturals are very scientific when they describe what their product offers the customer versus what the competition offers. There is no need to find fault, bicker, or take too much time discussing the competition with your prospect. If the competitor offers lower prices, then show the quality, value, and reasonable pricing of your product, and ignore the competition.

Precept 11: Recommend that the customer talk to your other satisfied customers.

Over the years, many people have asked me what I think of my competition and I always say, "I don't have time to think about them that much because I've got my mind on my own customers."

Once you confront the competition issue, change the subject by using a testimonial letter or a customer's name for reference. Look for the appropriate time during the demonstration to do this and choose a customer who has similar concerns and needs.

"You remind me of Harry. He owns a manufacturing company about the size of yours and he's been trying to trim his shipping costs, without sacrificing service, for several years. Here's what he says about the system I installed for him. Feel free to talk to him yourself."

Precept 12: Monitor your customer's moods.

Customers like working with a fellow human being, not a superficial robot. If you sense that you are pushing too hard, acting overly enthusiastic, or getting on their nerves, pipe down. As customers get further involved in your demonstration, you should be able to instinctively tell whether they are discouraged, uninterested, bored, or just plain exhausted.

One time I was demonstrating to a woman who seemed fairly friendly while I interviewed her in the office, but who kept getting more and more irritated during the demonstrations. Finally I said to her:

"I really want to do a good job for you, but I'm not sure if I am on the right track. Is there something on your mind I should know?"

She turned away from me quickly with tears filling her eyes and said, "Oh, it has nothing to do with you, Danny. But this is my sixth move in 12 years. I hate looking at houses."

I was so relieved that she confided in me because I was able to acknowledge her viewpoint, sympathize with all the upheavals she had been through and then, after taking time to really listen to her concerns, work on building her emotional tone up to the point of enthusiasm. Once she got emotional relief, I pointed out all the things my community could offer that other places in which they had lived never did. By the time we met her husband later that day, she was starting to look forward to the move.

Precept 13: Whenever possible, shut up and let the product speak for itself.

The salesman who sold me my five-pound, eight-ounce portable laptop left me alone to play with it in his showroom and I appreciated every minute of it. The day I bought my convertible sports car, the saleswoman stepped aside while I sat inside on the leather seats and quietly rejoiced that I was not sitting in a station wagon.

Precept 14: Sell possibilities to the unimaginative.

If you are selling a weight-loss program to a prospect, sell them on the possibility of being slim by a certain date. "Wait until your old classmates see you at the June reunion, wearing a slinky summer cocktail dress with plunging neckline. The old prom queen will be turning green with envy."

Once, I put a young couple with little imagination and a small budget, into a real fixer-upper home. It was the only thing they could afford and the possibilities were unlimited, but they kept complaining about how dull the place was. When we went back for the umpteenth time, we were all standing in the kitchen and the wife kept looking out the sliding door at a side yard that the last owner used as a dog run.

I started staring out there with her and said: "I'd love to get my hands on a big shovel, some fresh dirt, fertilizer, and talk to that guy at the local Green Fingernail Nursery who gives free advice on gardening when you buy his plants. You could turn this into a garden of beautiful plants and brightly colored flowers in no time. By the time I got those two back to my office, their imaginations had gone completely wild.

Precept 15: Don't get caught in the middle.

I met "Jane and Tarzan" when I was 18 years old and was selling women's dresses at a major department store. They came into my "Better Dress" section to shop for a dress for the wife to wear to her husband's office Christmas party. I knew there would be trouble when she quietly signalled me into the dressing room, while her husband madly inspected the racks of dresses.

In a low whisper she stated: "He's very conservative about what I wear. When I come out there in this nun's costume that he's picked out for me to wear to his stupid Christmas party, I am going to ask you how I look. Say something insulting."

I couldn't believe she was asking me to do that, so I said, "I can't get in the middle. I could lose my job."

Then she got arrogant and said, "Fine. I'm going to get the sexiest dress I can find and put it on, then you can watch the fireworks fly, honey."

I went behind the cash register, called my manager, and started acting busy. I had the feeling a couple of maniacs were on the loose. Five minutes later, she proved her point by strutting out of the dressing room in a revealing dress.

I glanced at the husband who was giving her the dirtiest look I have ever seen. Then he shouted, "Take that cheap excuse for a dress off before I rip it in half."

He turned around to see if anyone heard him and saw me staring at him. The next thing you know, he says to me:

"Go ahead, kid, tell her how ridiculous she looks."

Then she walks over and says: "Well, don't you think I look better in this outfit than I did in that convent collection Mr. Green-eyed Monster selected?"

By then, the store manager walked up to the man and asked them both to settle their differences somewhere else.

Under normal circumstances, when two people who are purchasing together start to disagree, say something like: "I cannot market my product to both of you unless you agree on all the terms. Why don't we list the points of disagreement? You both can agree to disagree during the discussion, and if you need time alone together, I will be glad to leave until you need my input again. It's important to me that you are both happy with the purchase."

Precept 16: Discuss affordability in your presentation.

Sometimes, salespeople assume that well-heeled customers pay no attention to price because it appears that money is no problem. Often, the more affluent people are, the more they watch where every dollar goes. A well-to-do client told me once:

"People think they can rip me off because I'm rich. They assume a few dollars down the drain doesn't bother old Mr. Richie. Well, I made my money by watching where it goes and I want to get my money's worth just like any other hard-working man."

Make it a point to talk about the affordability of your product, not just quality and good service.

Precept 17: Beware of customers who love everything about your product.

Have you ever presented to people who were simply too agreeable? They hang on every word you say and you keep thinking, "This is too good to be true."

It probably is, because people who do not object to anything sometimes can't afford what you are showing them in the first place. Or, they may be "people pleasers" who do not like to tell the truth about what is on their minds for fear they will hurt your feelings.

Why spend days with people who need to be entertained, or are afraid to confess what their true situation is? Try this dialogue instead. "It is important that we are all honest with each other. I need to know if this is within the price range for which you budgeted, and if you truly love this machine as much as you are indicating. Don't worry about hurting my feelings. I am here to help you, not myself."

Precept 18: Be patient and let the sales process take its course.

The bigger the item, the longer the decision time. If your product involves comparison shopping, let the buyers know at the end of your demonstration that you are patient and confident that your product will stand the test of time. It is better for them to comparison shop before they purchase from you instead of after the sale.

The best salespeople make every presentation as fresh and natural as their very first performance. One of the greatest Naturals on earth was the late Yul Brynner. He performed in the *King and I* over 4,000 times during a 32-year period. Mr. Brynner died of cancer, but no one would have guessed that during the last year of his life when he played his role as the King to packed Los Angeles audiences every night, and received chemotherapy treatments every morning. Through the exemplary life of Yul Brynner, we can all learn how to give the best we have to our audience—the customers we serve each day.

8

The Fundamental Science of Transforming Objections Into Opportunities

"Every sweet has its sour; every evil its good."

RALPH WALDO EMERSON

When I sold to my first customers I was not exactly sure how I had done it. They caught me completely off guard as I was driving them back to my office.

"We want it," they casually mentioned.

"You want what?" I innocently asked.

"We want you to sell us that home you just showed us."

"You have got to be kidding. Don't you want to think it over?"

I was hoping they would give me more time because I needed to practice filling out the sales agreement. But they were serious buyers, and much to my surprise I closed the sale that afternoon.

With all the talk I had heard from other salespeople about how difficult it was to overcome objections, I really wasn't sure how I got the order. It was only later, when I failed to make a sale with another customer, that I was able to put my finger on the exact point where I was weak in the presentation. Then I learned a valuable lesson about how I had not suitably, overcome an objection in order to make a sale.

An objection means you and the customer are not in agreement regarding some aspect of your product or service. The Natural doesn't have very many objections to overcome because she covers all the bases during the interview and demonstration. The reason the salesperson faced an objection is because she lacks the knowledge, conviction, interest, or understanding of her customer's need during the early part of the sales process. There is only one exception to this way of thinking—when you find yourself working with the "easy-to-hate" crowd who have no intention of buying, only barking.

134

But with normal "easy-to-love" folks, if the customer challenges you with objections early in the relationship and gives you something to overcome and you are able to do that, he will buy. Never fear objections because they will help you sell your product and give you the opportunity to prove your knowledge and expertise.

My first customers talked to me early in our relationship about their legitimate needs and raised plenty of discussion until they finally ran out of reasons why they shouldn't buy. Maybe it was beginner's luck, but I did my homework and prevented last-minute objections by confronting big issues right off the bat.

Never fear objections, and be grateful when you find a customer who is opening up and confessing his concerns. Your biggest problem is the prospect who seems too agreeable or who says nothing and then drops a bomb on you just when you think it's time to close the sale.

Let's go back to Captain Mike whom we introduced in last chapter's demonstration study and see what kind of objections he needed to overcome in order to help Mary and Bud buy that sailboat.

The Conclusion of "The Sold On Sailing" Case Study

Mary and Bud are sitting around Captain Mike's desk while he figures their monthly boat payment. Once he completes the worksheet, he passes it over to the couple and says:

"This figure of $659 a month seems to be right in line with what you told me during our first discussion a few days ago, Bud."

Mary and Bud seem very nervous. Toward the end of the demonstration, Mike notices Bud's enthusiasm waning, but he cannot figure out why.

Bud: "I am starting to think I should look at a few more boats before I make up my mind."

Mary: "Honey, we've been shopping for boats for a year. I thought you liked this line."

Mike believed he had covered all the benefits and features so he decided to come right out and ask Bud: "What do you think is stopping you from buying this boat?"

"I'm not sure I can handle sailing it all by myself."

Mike realizes for the first time that he never found out if Bud has any experience sailing. This could be a sensitive issue, so he approaches the subject delicately.

Mike: "I forgot to mention that we are offering free sailing lessons at the marina to the first five buyers who purchase this model at our boat show. I didn't even think to mention it earlier. The instructor is a real pro and I have attended his classes for refresher courses myself over the years. Once you complete that program, your confidence level will be high."

Bud looks relieved and says, "Frankly, I have been worried about handling a boat this big. I chartered a few smaller sailboats over to Catalina, but this is a bit overwhelming to me."

Mary: "Maybe the kids and I should take some lessons too."

Bud: "Not a bad idea. Say, Mike, let's get back to this financing. Where do you think I can get the best interest rate?"

Captain Mike overlooked an important question during the initial interview that could have cost him the sale: "How much sailing experience do you have?" The sales process was held up for only one reason— Bud was afraid to admit he did not know much about sailing.

Sometimes we take the obvious for granted. A legend in the car industry told me that it became common practice to take people out for a test drive because of the following incredible story.

It seems that a frustrated salesman, who worked with a prospect for well over a year, finally told his sales manager how puzzled he was that he hadn't sold the gentleman a car. One day the sales manager called on the customer and decided to come right out and ask him: "Why haven't you bought a car by now?"

The prospect replied: "Because I don't know how to drive one and I am afraid I will run into something."

Sometimes pride prevents the prospect from disclosing his fears. I am empathetic to this problem because I resisted purchasing computers, fax machines, and car phones because I thought I would spend hundreds of wasted hours trying to figure out how to operate the equipment. My electric typewriter served me well for 20 years and it took a great deal of patience and instruction for someone to show me that there was a more efficient way to write. No matter what anyone tried to tell me, I wanted to stick to my old ways until someone came around and took the time to prove me wrong.

FOUR WAYS TO ANTICIPATE AN OBJECTION

It is not always possible to overcome all the objections a buyer proposes, but it is possible to resolve most of them if you are extremely well-versed in your product. One of the biggest mistakes large companies make today is to put sales representatives in the field who are not familiar with the workings of every department back at the home office.

Since he is unfamiliar with the entire company picture, the salesperson tries to handle objections in the field with a lick and a promise. He makes commitments such as, "I can get you this in 30 days."

Then he goes back to headquarters and finds out the product is on back order for three months. When a salesperson makes little effort to familiarize himself with the workings of the other departments of his company, he is not equipped to overcome buyers' objections with up-to-the-minute knowledge.

When you know in advance a buyer's biggest objection is going to be, "You can't meet my deadline," it is critical that the sales representative be able to practice reciting, in advance, the reasons why the product is worth the wait.

"This toupee is the best selling head covering in our line right now. Believe me, you could go buy another piece today, but think of how embarrassed you will be when it blows off your head in a wind storm. The Magic Mylo Adhesive we use guarantees protection in any snow storm, hurricane, or wind storm. I spoke to our on-line designers this morning and they said this next batch of hair pieces will be the most natural-looking we've produced so far. Why not wait and get the best?"

Keep an objection journal. Begin a separate journal to keep track of objections. You can accumulate good ones in your day-to-day confrontations with customers. This list gives you the opportunity to formulate answers to future objections.

Examine every lost sale. I often write down things I should have said that may work with another customer. Objections can be valuable in making future sales.

Study human nature and temperaments. Certain types of objections seem to be compatible with certain personality styles. The conservative thinker may object to cost and affordability. Brush up on your financial answers to prepare for those circumstances. The technical type may ask operational or mechanical questions that require both you and a technician from your company to overcome. What happens if your customer is insecure and relies on a third-party expert to assist her with the decision-making? Is this person her accountant? Lawyer? Spouse? Mother? A whole executive committee at corporate headquarters? Anticipate the kinds of questions a representative of the buyer might pose.

Investigate proven methods of overcoming objections. Use your firm's sales manual and study proven ways to handle objections. Check other sources, too. Quickly adapt these sales talks to your own mode of conquering objections. My first mentor, Tom Hopkins, taught thousands of sales students some strong rebuttals to customer opposition. A Natural seeks solutions from every source she can find that are based on sound business principles and ethics.

Become a logical and clear sales communicator. When your knowledge of the product is comprehensive enough to give customers a clear understanding of your proposition, they are less likely to pose an objection. Then prospects can weigh all the positive points about your product against the negative points and overcome the negatives. Use my Problem-Cause-Effect-Cure Solution Selling Formula from Chapter 1 when you have a specific objection that continually stops the sale. This writing exercise will help you see things more clearly, and then you can prepare a stronger argument against your customer's objection.

SIX NATURAL INCLINATIONS OF A MOTIVATED BUYER

When customers get ready to make a buying decision, they follow a predictable pattern of behavior. Depending on the expense of the purchase, it can take anywhere from fifteen minutes to two years to act out these patterns.

Exploration. When the customer begins exploring for a product or service, she doesn't always recognize her specific needs. In the early stages of the sales process the salesperson is the informer, enabling the customer to explore possibilities. Do not become discouraged when she makes negative comments. When I market my video systems to companies during an all-day seminar, my initial conversations in the morning with the owners could be interpreted as hopeless by the uneducated observer. The owner says: "I will spend a fortune on your video system and then my sales staff will never bother to watch it." On that happy note, he walks away from my display table.

As a new salesperson, I could be discouraged from continuing my pursuit of the prospect, when, in fact, it was too early to worry if he was going to buy because he was still investigating other possibilities. While he explores, you must gain his confidence by allowing him to feel free to make any comments or objections he wants.

This delay gives you the opportunity to start driving home one, two, or three positive points about your product. When the prospect sees you answering three or four objections with positive answers, eventually he or she is convinced that you know what you are talking about and you actually enjoy handling his objections.

When customers allow you to see how they think, this gives you the chance to start overturning their objections. Once you convince customers that their objections are invalid, you can start explaining them away.

Captain Mike should have had the opportunity to discuss sailing school during the exploration stage, but he fastforwarded his presentation, past Bud's immediate concerns.

Slight withdrawal. Some prospects react enthusiastically from the outset about a new idea or product, but most refrain from early excitement. People carry with them their past life experience, basic personality traits, background, parental influence, and financial viewpoints. They may not be aware enough yet to accept a particular part of your sales talk that could influence them more effectively later. When I sense early withdrawal on the part of a video prospect, I remain positive, upbeat and confident because I realize it is the customer's own ignorance that forces him to say: "My people won't watch your video training."

Students not only watch the video, but put the methods into practice minutes after they turn off the television set. I feel happy that this prospect took the time to visit my display. If he was uninterested, he wouldn't have approached me. I might say something like this, as he stops talking and walks away: "Ask your sales staff who are here today how they feel about watching it, but not now. Wait until the end of the day when I am finished lecturing." Then I just smile and turn in the other direction. I know that if a sales manager is really interested in helping his people make more money, he will come around to my viewpoint sooner or later.

Let's say you sell "Detachable Wings" to executives who want to fly out their office windows at a moment's notice. When you made a first call, a few of the senior vice presidents let you fly out the window of their 19th story executive office and fly back in, causing great excitement among them. They all began chatting about the money they would save the company in airfare expense and how convenient it would be to get to work without going through traffic.

At the second interview, the management team seems slightly withdrawn. "We aren't really sure if we need these detachable wings right now. We are a growing company, but perhaps we should put our money to work investing in something more sensible."

More questions and interest. As long as you keep moving forward with an upbeat sales talk, knocking each objection flat on its face, the customer's interest is heightened and she will start to ask you more questions. A legitimate prospect enjoys challenging the salesperson's knowledge and dedication.

"Will these wings last five years without overhauls?"

"Did you mention we can get all the officers' wings at a 30% discount?"

I call these *verification questions.* Don't go into orbit with your own wings when the prospect shoots a few hot questions your way. I used to have to calm myself down when these great questions started coming at me. My mind was rushing ahead with thoughts like, "Yippee. You did it, kid. You sold them the wings." I learned from heartbreak not to jump the gun. Whenever I counted my commissions before they were cashed, I got bounced out of the bank. Just respond to further probing with cool, calm, collected, and confident answers.

Deliberate pondering and brain storming. Now the committee is having a pow-wow about the detachable wings. If you are in on it, remain quiet and listen. They may be getting jumpy because they are coming close to making a buying decision. In that case, you may hear meaningless comments and objections one minute and positive acknowledgments the next. Customers are walking contradictions when they reach this level.

"Isn't the lease on our corporate jet almost up?"

"I hope so. I don't want that thing sitting in the hangar eating up corporate funds, while we are all flying around like Peter Pan and the Lost Children."

"Do we need a pilot's license to fly?"

"That does it. I'm not buying these wings because tests make me a nervous wreck. After I passed the bar, I swore I'd never take another examination."

"What about your driver's test?"

"That's different. I take my 19-year-old son with me and he supplies the answers."

"Do we really need these wings, guys?"

You may be tempted to jump into this mess. Let the group work their way out of it themselves. If you have done an impeccable job demonstrating features and benefits, you will get another chance to clarify.

More doubt, questions, and anxiety. The only thing you do is remain positive and patient answering specific questions like: "You told us once, but tell us again—what happens if we break a wing?"

Keep listening closely in case things take a turn for the worse, as they did temporarily for Captain Mike when Bud indicated he was going to start looking at other boats.

Resolving and eliminating doubt. The customers have come full circle on their own through your expert guidance. The Natural now begins to "sense the sell." There is a feeling in the air that no stone has been left unturned. The customers are getting ready to allow you to make a final proposal of marriage to your product.

"If we put up the money for these wings and decide within a certain time frame that things aren't working out, can we get our money back?"

This objection might have been covered earlier when you said: "If, after 30 days you can't take off the ground, we will refund your money, no questions asked." But when customers are close to a buying decision, they need one last reassurance that no one is going to take advantage of them.

MEETING AND RESOLVING OBJECTIONS IN FIVE PARTS

The true objection must be overcome so that it will never be an issue again. The only reason objections keep surfacing is because the salesperson did not confront the objection completely and convince the customer satisfactorily. Use this criterion every time the customer puts up a barrier.

PART 1—Ignore the customer's self-talk.

There is a big difference between a comment and an objection. Prospects always talk aloud to themselves right before they decide to buy. Just let them ramble because they may make a remark that is insignificant. If the salesperson starts giving the comment some value by discussing it, it could turn into an objection instead of a comment.

Our family had both buyer's bliss and buyer's remorse when we sold the home my first five children lived in during their grade school years. It was a move near the ocean that we all dreamed of, but we worried about how it would affect our lives, each of us having different concerns.

My family members started talking to themselves out loud. I began calculating the new payment in my head, reviewing over and over how we could cut back to make it work. Then the kids started muttering about schools. My son Kevin worried about how he would get to gymnastics practice because the new home was further away from the gym. My husband commented on how nice it was that we had our present home just the way we wanted it and now we were moving so someone else could enjoy it.

Then the comments went from negative to positive. My son Daniel began to get excited because the home was so close to his favorite hangout. Then the girls were chatting about how much extra space everyone would have—more bathrooms, more bedrooms, and more privacy. I remembered that the home had a laundry room so I wouldn't have to do the laundry in the garage anymore.

Humans go through a metamorphosis at the time of purchase, especially big ticket items. They argue with themselves and carry on a debate about the pros and cons of the purchase. I've talked out loud to a salesperson in a dress shop right before buying a moderately expensive suit, with comments like: "Gosh, I love it, but how should I pay for it? I could put it on a Visa card, after all, I won't get the bill for another 45 days, so you might say I am paying nothing today for something I get to use right away. I could wear this suit for my friend's wedding."

I've observed some salespeople interrupt this line of logic with: "Yeah, what difference does one more item on your charge card make? You should see my bill. We are all in debt up to our ears." All that does is get the customer thinking negatively again. Be quiet and let them work this part of the issue out by themselves.

PART 2—Pay attention to the second-time-around comments.

When Captain Mike spoke to the boat buyers at the first interview, Bud mentioned that Mary might be concerned about seasickness. The second time the remark came up during the demonstration (remember Mary wondered if she would get claustrophobia in the forward sleeping quarters), Mike stopped everything he was doing and instructed Mary to come out into the salon because he was about to confront the sickness issue head-on. When the customer keeps bringing things up to the salesperson, remind yourself that no previous explanation has removed the obstacle. Listen up and then proceed.

PART 3—Repeat the objection for clarification and acknowledgment purposes.

"I understand that claustrophobia is a problem. Let's deal with that right now." Captain Mike opens up the hatch in the forward cabin and brings Mary in and has her get comfortable with the arrangement. Then he uses projection and suggestion to get her thinking about how to get her mind off of seasickness. He must pay attention to how Mary is reacting to his suggestions. Maybe she just has a minor problem on boats and her comment doesn't have the power to stop the sale. Or is it a more serious situation? The only way to find out is to analyze the situation.

PART 4—Analyze the worst case scenario.

If Mary was not satisfied with Captain Mike's explanation and she felt comfortable telling him anything that was on her mind, she may have continued with, "How much does the boat rock when the sea is rough?"

Captain Mike: "Do you always get seasick, Mary? Have you ever tried putting a patch behind your ear or taking seasickness medicine before you set sail?"

Or Mike might get more bold and say:

"How much do you enjoy sailing? Enough to get some seasickness prevention?"

When two or more people are making the buying decision, the salesperson has to analyze and clarify different types of objections for each member of the buying team. This can be tricky because something that one partner thinks is vitally important may have little or no meaning to the other. It is a good idea to get assistance from the partner who takes no issue with the objection.

"Bud, does it worry you that Mary gets seasick?"

"It only happens when she eats rich food or we venture out when we know the sea is going to be especially rough that day. Mary, I think we should pay close attention to weather conditions when you and the children come on the boat. On those days when there is a good wind and it might be too rough for you, I can always take a friend."

PART 5—Come to a conclusion together.

Captain Mike could now interject: "I want you to enjoy this beautiful boat for many years together as a family. I know Bud will make it possible for you to enjoy your time on the boat too, Mary. Perhaps you should talk to some good customers of mind, Dean and Diane Diehard. Diane worried a little bit about seasickness four years ago when they bought their Rudolph Regatta, and today she has a stomach of cast iron. Would it help to talk to them? They are usually over at the Yacht club on Saturdays and I know you wanted to stop in there and get some information on a slip. I want to see you two work this out."

The salesperson cannot always solve the buyer's problems. When you don't know an answer, admit it and tell the prospect that you know where you can find more information. If further investigating does not help, do not take their rejection of your offer personally. They may turn away from the purchase because, as a group, you came to the conclusion that the objection was too big to forget. Then something unpredicted happens, and two days later you get a call saying they have found a way to work around the obstacle and are ready to buy your product.

Once you get ready to write up the sale, there is often an important phase of the sales process that has to be settled—the game of negotiating to the point of agreement on price, terms, options, or delivery.

9 Natural Ways to Negotiate Applying Conciliatory Communication Methods

---

"We (Russia and U.S.) are beginning to see the light at the end of the tunnel, and that light comes from the bright sunshine of truth, faith, and friendship. Especially friendship."

FATHER THEODORE M. HESBURGH
(From his book: *God, Country, Notre Dame*)

When my children were babies, I carried a copy of Dr. Benjamin Spock's book on child care with me everywhere I went. When Spock said the best time to toilet-train was around the age of two years, four months, I paid attention and did it. Then along came "Bust-a-Bladder." In the beginning of our negotiations, I couldn't figure out what the big deal was, but he refused to use a potty chair. I'd take him to the chair at all the appropriate moments throughout the day, but he preferred to turn blue.

I kept repeating, "Do you have to go to the bathroom?"

"No."

Then I would tell him as nicely as I could, "Don't forget to tell me when you feel like going, okay?"

"Okay, mom."

As the days went by, I kept moving in tighter and tighter, practically following this child around with a bucket. The closer I got, the more stubborn he became. One day I decided to show him who had the power by giving him an ultimatum, which I later regretted.

"Look, either you start delivering the goods or you are not getting off this potty chair all day. Now don't get up until you've got something important to show me."

Hours went by and nothing appeared. I was serving him gallons of water, juice, and soda and I was stuck in the house with this little mule.

This started out as a game, but it turned into a battle. I couldn't figure out how he could hold in all that liquid for so long. But I figured, sooner or later, he's going to have to give in and go.

By night time, he decided to try some counter negotiation tactics. "Can I put my potty chair in front of the TV?"

"Will you go, if I do?"

"Maybe."

Maybe. I am thinking to myself, "Who does this brat think he is? By now he's got me right where he wants me, I have lost any power I might have had, and I move him in front of the television set. Then the rest of the family decides to get involved in the bargaining.

His sister says, "If you go like a good boy, I will take you to the park tomorrow."

Another chimes in with, "Just think, if you start going to the potty you won't have to wear dumb diapers anymore."

This episode went on until ten o'clock that evening. Just as I was about to tell him to get up and go to bed, my daughter yells from the living room: "Mom, hurry up. He's finally doing it."

In all my days, I have never seen such a rushing flow of water. I thought the whole family would need row boats just to find our way to the bedrooms. Poor Bust couldn't stop crying tears of relief. I kept telling him how proud I was of him and he kept saying, "I did it." That surprised me because I realized for the first time that he wanted to go just as much as we wanted him to go. I didn't realize just how afraid he was to let go. Bust taught me some valuable lessons about natural negotiation that have served me well both at home and in the marketplace.

IT'S ONLY A GAME

America's great negotiator Herb Cohen says, "Negotiation is just a game. You care about the outcome, but not that much." That is one of the reasons I never negotiate for my own speaking fees with a client. I am too emotionally attached and sensitive when it comes to representing myself. This close emotional attachment makes negotiating with my loved ones a bit of a problem, too. It's easy to take an unbiased position when we are representing somebody else's money, time, family, or career, but when it hits close to home, it is no longer a game—some serious business is at stake.

The more emotionally attached we become to an outcome, the tighter we move in to try to get our own way. Pretty soon we begin to lose our perspective. During my son's toilet-training days, I seriously began to question whether or not he would ever give up wearing diapers.

DECIDE IF YOU WANT TO PLAY

I think this is the most important step in negotiating. Why bother if it isn't worth the price you will pay emotionally and financially? Negotiating is a form of interdependent exchange. My buyer may *request* delivery by December first. I *respond* by saying I will check with the manufacturer. I check with the manufacturer and they claim the car cannot be delivered until February 1. My buyer *reacts* by saying she intends to look elsewhere.

Request, respond and *react* comprise the activities of negotiating. It is important to decide before we react whether or not it is worth it to jump in and play the game with this buyer. Do they really want this car? Are they trying to bluff by saying they intend to go elsewhere? Is there anything I can do about the delivery date? Would it be better in this case to tell her to shop some place else for a car?

I did not have to react so impulsively when my son refused to go on the potty chair. I trapped myself into thinking I had only two alternatives—either keep him on the potty chair all day or let him wear diapers for the rest of his life. Without researching what his particular needs and problems were, I assumed it would be a breeze to toilet-train him because the process was fairly smooth with his brothers and sisters. I knew very little about what was going on inside of my child's head and instead of bothering to find out, I reacted to his reaction in a knee-jerk fashion. This type of desperate behavior goes on every day in the sales field.

PREDICT PEOPLE'S BEHAVIOR AHEAD OF TIME

If I had taken time to study my son's reactions to earlier changes in his life, I would have understood his apprehension when a new routine was introduced. Before you go into negotiations with a client, it is important to have that same kind of information. In an earlier chapter I mentioned two types of buyers: the easy-to-love and the easy-to-hate. Most of the customers I have served in my career have been very easy to love. When it came time to negotiate, we all seemed to be on the same wave-length—All parties wanted to make the deal work. The Natural knows how to pick the right customers to negotiate with and then once the proceedings begin, they pick and choose the issues which are important enough to negotiate.

What about the 15% of the people in the world who cross your path that are easy-to-hate? Can you tell by looking at someone if he is going to be difficult to deal with? Our buyers judge us very early in the sales process, but we can't afford to operate that way. I can't tell you the number of times I used to say: "I can look a person straight in the eye and be able to tell what kind of an individual he or she is."

All that changed the day I met the Louses. They stopped into one of my open houses on a Sunday afternoon. They looked like the all-American family, with two children and a dog in the car. When they walked in, I couldn't get over how friendly they were. After they walked through the home I was monitoring, the husband said: "We like this place, Danielle. I am being transferred in from the East Coast and my company wants to be sure I find a nice home within the next 30 days. Who knows? We may buy this place. Can you assist us?"

These people seemed like dream prospects from out-of-state who needed a house yesterday. I assured them I was their girl and for the next several days put all my other business on hold and took them around to see at least 100 homes. Then I gave them tours of the recreation centers, malls, schools, and churches in the area. I took them to lunch on more than one occasion and babysat their children while they visited my local banker to talk financing.

Then strange things began to happen. They told me on Friday they were flying back to the East Coast that evening, but on Saturday I saw them from a distance at the local movie theater. He never told me the name of his company, only gave me the phone number. The following Monday morning, I called the number and had two quick shocks in a row: The company was the headquarters for a large national real estate franchise and when I asked his secretary if he was in, she told me he was on the West Coast "getting set up in housing."

I called someone who worked for the same company that was supposedly transferring him to my town. He was a good friend and I asked him to do some confidential snooping. He called me back and informed me that the man I was driving around town was the vice president of my friend's real estate company and had bought a property that weekend that was listed by them, acting as his own agent. By the way, it was one of the homes that I showed him earlier in the week.

How could I have prevented that from happening? If I had taken the time the day after the open house and called the number he gave me, that would have been my first clue. If he had not given me a number, I could have asked more detailed qualifying questions and not been so willing to base my judgment on first impressions. Instead, I found myself trying to negotiate with someone who had no intention of closing a sale with me. I began negotiating when I agreed to show them homes and introduce them to my area. All Naturals set the stage for negotiation before they become too involved with a prospective customer. They want to see everyone come out winners in any negotiation that is started, so they confer with people and establish ground rules and fair standards to live by during the course of future negotiation. Here are a few guidelines.

Establish objective criteria that seek solutions that satisfy all parties concerned. At the open house, I needed to ask Mr. Louse for a business card and verbally establish my position once he indicated he wanted to look at houses with me.

Here is the dialogue I began using after that hard lesson was learned: "Are you presently working with anyone else in the area? I see that you are employed by a real estate firm. Are you licensed? Don't you want to represent yourself in the transaction? How does your company feel about your purchasing from a competitor?"

Beware of the prospect who refuses to play fair. If I say tactfully, "I appreciate having the opportunity to work with you, but let's establish some ground rules right up front." And the prospect says:

"Salespeople are a dime a dozen. We are looking for the best deal we can get and we'll do whatever it takes to get it. You should be thrilled to get a crack at our business. If you are sharp enough, it will work out for you."

What does that tell you about future negotiations with this client? He's immature and wants everything to go his way. Do you really want to jump into the ring with him?

Eighty-five percent of the public will want to establish ground rules first because they want to be honest with you, too. My husband and I established ground rules with our builder after we hired him to remodel our home. We told him right up front what our budget was and we had to keep the work within that dollar amount. He wasn't offended, but said he would remind us of our original plan every time we diverted and began to weaken. Most people like to be able to foresee how the negotiations are going to go before they begin.

ASK NICELY, SAY THANK YOU

My husband negotiates for me in the speaking business. He says most of the meeting planners who call and request my services are wonderful to work with, but sometimes he is amazed at how unpleasantly some people begin a negotiation. One representative got our whole staff extremely upset when she began opening negotiations to have me come to her company to speak. She started out on the wrong foot with my seminar coordinator.

"Danielle came to our company in 1988 and many people on the staff requested her return, but do me a favor, tell her not to talk about her family too much."

My coordinator never heard anyone begin a negotiation with such remarks. When I heard about the comments, I called the representative up and asked why she said that.

"Well, I never heard you, but evidently you talk about your family a lot."

"That's right, but there is always a moral to the story—a teaching moral. If I can't talk about my family, I am not coming."

Then she backed down and said it was not a big thing and the overwhelming majority wanted me back again because they loved my presentations."

DON'T TAKE A HARD-AND-FAST POSITION

When you start negotiating, remind yourself that you want this agreement to work satisfactorily for everyone involved. If you take a position that says, "Either this goes my way or it's not going," you could end up very sorry. I have seen salespeople do their customers a terrible injustice by using this ploy.

"We aren't going to pay one nickel over $500,000 for that art work, Mr. and Mrs. Seller."

The customer wanted the piece more than the salesperson suspected, and when he lost it, he felt resentful because a position was taken that did not represent the buyer's viewpoint.

How do you deal with persons who try to force you to take a position? They are experts at backing people into a corner. Refuse to negotiate with them in this crude manner. Remain calm and mature no matter how they try to beat you down. Whenever I work with disagreeable people, I let them know up front I will not play their game.

They may say:

"Either you throw in 10 sets of workbooks with this video system, or I won't do business with you."

As soon as I hear, "Either you do this or else," I step in and stop the game. "I would love to work with you, but it doesn't sound like it could work right now." Notice I haven't said anything offensive. Because this type of customer is looking for trouble, you must weigh your words carefully and get them out of your way fast.

BE PREPARED TO WALK AWAY

Negotiating is a game, and if you don't care about the outcome that much, you can detach yourself from the situation and walk away. Detachment is only possible when you have other fish to fry in the business development and appointment circles. If an inflexible person is the only customer you have going for you, it may be difficult to negotiate objectively.

John Patrick Dolan, criminal attorney and expert negotiator, told me that there are three levels of objectivity that each of us brings to the negotiating table. The first level is, "I must have this." It makes it very difficult to give up when we feel this way.

The second level is, "I'd sure like to have this."

The third level is, "It would be great to have it, but if it doesn't work that is fine, too." Know ahead of time at which level of objectivity you are when you begin to play.

The older I get, the more I realize how important it is not to want something too badly. I find that the more alternatives I can come up with, the better off I am. When I care the least at the negotiating table, I have the most strength. Now that I know that nothing can force me to accept an unattractive offer, I don't feel that some decisions are as fatal as I used to think.

When I negotiate with a publisher or speakers' bureau, I know that if this engagement or book proposal doesn't work out, there will be other opportunities. I am sure of myself because I never stop developing new business and new projects, and some of them always turn out successfully. The universal law of sow and reap is on my side, along with wisdom and maturity. I no longer see any one avenue as the only way I can get my message across. I know that options are unlimited if I just take the time to research them.

KNOW THE COMPROMISES YOU ARE WILLING TO MAKE

Know in advance where you are willing to bend. The more you have at stake in this negotiation, the more you need to be prepared. Whether you are negotiating for an antique cedar chest or a corporate merger, you must collect the right kind of information ahead of time and be able to predict the other party's possible moves. After you do your homework, ask yourself what sacrifices you are willing to make to see the project through.

I had to negotiate with my husband and family when I decided to go back to school. Because Mike is my business partner, I needed to discuss the problems connected with my unavailability for *all* speaking engagements. We discussed some of the pitfalls, and then I decided to take only one class per semester and limit that selection to classes offered on Mondays. It would be easier to automatically block out one day a week and still not jeopardize our speaking business. This was a big compromise for me because I have a tendency to take on a full load in order to get things done quickly.

Next, I had to negotiate with him about babysitting. I would be driving to the city at dinnertime and he would have to be available to take care of our youngest daughter. He agreed, and then made his own requests. He wanted to go back to college on the weekends. Did I mind forsaking a common social life for awhile? He needed extra study time during the week, so could he take part or all of Fridays off, and would I cover for him at the office if necessary?

Both of us presented our cases well. I explained to Mike what my long-range plans were for the company and how my education would enhance our future. He expressed his desire to complete his education in the area of organizational behavior and management. Both of us were prepared for the sacrifices and discipline required, and we agreed to compromise for each other in order to lighten our loads as parents and entrepreneurs. We have faced many difficult days in the process, but we keep reminding each other of what is ahead and this helps renew the excitement and vision.

SEPARATE THE PERSON FROM THE PROBLEM

Big purchases and change go hand-in-hand. Because the customer's nerves are very sensitive at those times, the salesperson can expect to be a recipient of customer frustration. It's important to learn how to separate yourself from the person and his temporarily sensitive nature. I worked with a couple once who were under a great deal of stress and that relationship taught me a lot about people's feelings during negotiation.

She was expecting her sixth child in seven years and the whole family was crammed into a 1,500 square foot home that we were attempting to sell in order to move them into a bigger one. They had already purchased one that was under construction, and the wife was counting the days until it would be completed.

I sold their smaller home and when the appraisal came back from the bank it was $3,000 short of the sales price. I had to disclose this to the seller and then to the buyer in order to renegotiate the terms of the agreement. I called my sellers on a Saturday morning and the wife answered. When I told her the problem, she hit the roof. Up until that point, she trusted me implicitly, but when I told her about the appraisal she accused me of trying to price cut their sale in favor of the buyer. I tried to explain to her that I had not. She was very tired and somewhat irritable. Finally she hung up on me.

One hour later, her husband called, apologized and said she really didn't mean to attack me. I had to go over to their house that afternoon to discuss the sale. When I arrived, I knew she was embarrassed, so I started the conversation by saying: "I don't know how you can stand all this pressure, Diana. Let's see how we can work this out."

She gave me a hug and we sat down and negotiated the deal.

GET OFF THE DEFENSIVE

When the objections are flying and the negotiation is getting intense, do not become defensive. Welcome advice and criticism when it is given in good faith.

"Do I really get touchy when you bring up questions about the poor packaging? Actually, I feel embarrassed because I never thought it would leave the warehouse that way. Let's figure out ways to make this inconvenience up to you."

During my sales management days, I often had to intervene when the customer and a salesperson got uptight with each other. I discovered that at the root of the problem was a lack of knowledge on the part of my salesperson. When you know what you are doing and feel secure about any questions or problems that may arise, the customer cannot push your hot buttons. Customers know when you are bluffing, but you make it worse by becoming defensive. At that point, they would rather talk to someone else in the organization who is better versed on the product or service.

FACE-SAVING IS PEACEMAKING

Always keep the customer's dignity intact. Even if she asks a redundant question or is misinformed, keep your cool and respond accordingly. Some salespeople get very angry at customers with whom they must continually negotiate during a long selling cycle. I've listened to an irate salesman say: "Do you have any idea what it costs my company to keep sending technicians out here to get this software in operation? Our company would go broke if we didn't charge a service fee." All that does is fire the customer up and make her feel foolish.

ELIMINATE THE GOOD GUY/BAD GUY ROUTINE

When mature adults negotiate, everyone puts his cards on the table from the beginning. However, sometimes adults get mixed up with immature manipulators who try to play hide-and-seek with the salesperson. Anytime one or more of the decision makers is not present at the negotiating table, or they are present but want you to think they have limited authority, you could have trouble.

I have experienced this Good Guy/Bad Guy routine with husbands and wives or executives who claim they have limited authority.

"Gee, I'd love to buy it, but my wife won't let me."

This is a tactic many couples use to keep salespeople off their backs. They have an unspoken agreement that one is the bad guy and one is the good guy.

"I'm just a helpless victim. I would love to rush into this purchase, but my wife isn't one to tamper with."

Before you can proceed, you must find out whether or not the so-called good guy really wants the product, or just doesn't have the courage to say no. He may be using the other person as a way out. If you find that the good guy legitimately wants to get involved further, confront the bad guy. I handle this situation carefully.

"There is nothing worse than a salesperson pushing something down your throat. I do not intend to do that, but your spouse (partner) tells me this product would work well for you. Do you agree with him (her)?"

Then address the objections and see if there is a chance to negotiate a sale.

Ask the bad guy directly, "Do you have the final say in most of these types of decisions? Should I only speak to you regarding this issue? Your spouse indicated that he/she is ready to proceed once you have more information."

This puts the bad guy on the hot seat. If the so-called pushover really doesn't want the merchandise, the truth often comes out after you ask these questions. The bad guy often replies: "You know, it's funny how he imagines I have a problem with this purchase. But quite frankly, if he really wants it, he would get it. Sometimes he doesn't have the guts to say no, so he puts the blame on me."

If you are getting pressured by your sales manager because you haven't closed the deal, tell her what the problem is. Sometimes your supervisor may want to intervene with the following dialogue:

"If our product doesn't fit in to both of your lifestyles (each department or division of the company), perhaps just Mr. Good Guy will want to purchase it (or budget it for his department)."

This approach may bring the whole issue to a head. Good guy may retort with, "I wouldn't agree to anything like that," or "I think I will purchase this on my own."

My video system has been sold to both individual sales agents and broker/owners. Agents come to my product table at a seminar very enthusiastically telling me they will buy my system if their broker pays for half of the expense. They keep using the broker as an excuse to postpone the decision. We try to get the broker involved as soon as possible and if he is involved, I say: "Your agents really want this training library. Mary is thinking of buying the system herself if you decide against it."

If Mary is serious about the purchase, she chimes in with: "I won't share this with the office either. I'll keep it at my house. Don't you think it's a wise investment to get one the whole office can use?"

This comment puts the broker on the spot, but then I find out how serious both parties are about buying my videos. It isn't fair to the salesperson to waste valuable time with prospects who have no intention of doing business with him.

Here are some additional suggestions when you are negotiating with persons who have limited decision-making ability.

- Confront them and ask, "Who is the decision maker?"
  "Who is your boss?"
- Ask them for an endorsement.
  "When you discuss this with your partner (committee, spouse), you will recommend it, won't you?"
- Remember that if you all agree you want things to work out, things will work out.

ESTABLISH YOUR POWER BY RAISING THE LEVEL OF CONSEQUENCES

Remember the car salesperson in Chapter 1 who asked, "Are you going to buy the car today or not?" He used up all his power early in the negotiations by asking that foolish question. Just because a salesperson asks a question doesn't necessarily mean he is entitled to a reply—especially if the question is unreasonable. It was very unreasonable for that salesperson to put us on the spot before we could get a straight answer regarding the price of the car. Conciliatory communication starts out slow and nice, then builds. There is no reason to drop a bomb on somebody, because once you do, it is difficult to back down. I used to cringe when I negotiated with salespeople who used up all their power with the seller at the opening of their presentation of an offer. They started out saying:

"Your home may be fine for you, but my people hate blue carpet, small bathrooms, and two car garages. The only reason they are making an offer on your home is because they like the location. But it will cost them at least $10,000 to make improvements."

They believed this tactic of intimidating the seller would get the offer accepted. It worked so much better for me when I started out slowly, describing the buyer in the best possible light and communicating to the seller all the things my clients liked about their home. When people sell—their houses, cars, newest invention or work of art—they want to know the prospective buyer admires what they offer.

You can raise your level of power and do some strong persuading only after all the information the client needs is understood. Perhaps this very well-qualified buyer wants an answer to his offer within 48 hours because he has a time limit to consider. When negotiations seem to be going nowhere, then it's time to say:

"My clients are top executives. They love your home, but have moved several times before so they are smart enough not to get too attached in case things don't work out. We have selected two backups to write offers on tonight and tomorrow, if we can't come to an agreement with you."

You have the power and it's fine to use it when the timing is right, but never misuse it by moving to a higher level of consequences unless you mean business. The Natural's argument is always founded on a strong base of ethics, honesty, and diplomacy.

GRASP THE TWO TYPES OF NEGOTIATION

When our family went hunting for a car in Chapter 1, my son Joe made it difficult to negotiate. Every time the salesperson would tell us another feature like, "This car gets 50 miles to the gallon," Joe would jump up and down and say, "Did you hear that, Mom? Wow, isn't that terrific." I explained to him later that there were two types of negotiation—outside and inside.

Whenever you negotiate with customers or strangers, this is considered an outside negotiation. When a whole corporate team, senior management, or family have to negotiate with an outsider, they must negotiate first with each other to make certain they are all on the same team. If they are not in agreement before they go out and face clients, their lack of unity could considerably diminish their power with the outsiders.

UNDERSTAND YOUR SECRET NEGOTIATING VOICES

Herb Cohen tells a funny story on his audio program, *You Can Negotiate Anything,* about the two negotiators that live inside of him. One operates on the left side of his brain and one operates on the right side. The guy on the left is dressed in a black leather suit wearing whips and chains and talks like a German commander, constantly giving him orders to stick to the rules. The guy on the right is from Barbados, listens to music all the time, and is very cool and casual. Cohen says the ideal scene is to attempt to balance out the voices of both these negotiators. If one overrules, chaos will prevail. He exhorts us not to accept our own self-imposed oppression and to continually work on gaining greater control of our response. When we know ahead of time how we will respond, how the customer will respond and what concessions we are willing to make, the negotiation will be rewarding for all parties involved.

PRACTICE COMPASSION AND NEGOTIATE IN GOOD FAITH

My son taught me never to stereotype people. Sometimes what we assume about others is incorrect. I thought Bust was being stubborn because he wouldn't start using the potty-chair at the age that his brothers and sisters did. It was insensitive of me to box him in and use the most powerful consequences I could without asking him nicely if he was ready to get rid of the diapers, or how he felt about this change in his life. Don't get stuck with your narrow viewpoint. Show compassion when people are struggling over buying a car, furniture, or a vacation. Let them air their emotions, make comments, present objections and feel comfortable about whatever is on their minds. Before you know it, all parties will be agreeing that it is time to close the sale.

10

Closing Customers Naturally: The Art of Preventing Customer Postponement

---

"The prospect is persuaded more by the depth of your conviction than he is by the height of your logic."
CAVETT ROBERT

Some sales are quite simple to close—the buyer has an urgent need and desire to fill it immediately. If a trusted friend recommends a salesperson who can facilitate that need, the sale is imminent. A few years ago I was told by my attorney to purchase some disability insurance as soon as possible. Because I travel so much and my entire livelihood is dependent upon my ability to deliver a speech, he was concerned what would happen if I suddenly became sick or disabled. I trust my attorney implicitly so when he offered to contact a friend of his who sold this type of insurance, I agreed wholeheartedly.

My schedule is very tight so the man called me on the phone, introduced himself, asked me some questions and informed me I would need a medical exam. He would handle the scheduling and other details with my secretary. He was very accommodating, but I never actually met him until the day he delivered the policy. When he brought it over we stood in my entry hall and chatted briefly. I thanked him for the service and then he did something very awkward—he attempted to close another sale without determining if I had a need, nor did he make an effort to demonstrate any type of benefits, handle objections, or negotiate. Here's what happened.

Just when I thought he was getting ready to leave, he looked at me and said:

"By the way, I talked to your attorney and told him I went ahead and drew up a $1 million life insurance policy for you. The premium on it is $1,000 a month, but you will have it paid off in twelve years."

157

I was completely taken back and couldn't say a word. He must have taken this as a positive sign so he continued.

"Now if this doesn't work, I also have a term policy in my brief case for the same amount, but it's only $190.00 a month. However, this rate keeps escalating and you will have to pay higher premiums on it the older you get. I would definitely go with the whole life policy if I were you."

I had all the insurance I wanted and had no intention of buying more, especially after purchasing some very expensive disability insurance. I looked at him and said: "I'll talk to my husband and get back to you." I suppose I could have educated him on his foolishness but he was so matter-of-fact about it, I was convinced he would not understand the error of his ways. He called the next day and wanted to know my decision. I told him we weren't interested.

PREMATURE CLOSING FEELS UNNATURAL AND AWKWARD

This insurance salesman was like the student who shows up at the final exam completely unprepared but attempts to sit through the test. He struggles through the multiple choice questions using the "When In Doubt Pick Letter C" method of selecting answers, hoping the luck-of-the-draw will come to his aid. He bluffs his way through the essay portion of the test, realizing that he has no idea what he is writing about. He walks out of the testing room feeling like an impostor—pretending he is a student.

Under normal circumstances, closing the sale should not be difficult if everything is handled properly during the sales process. It only becomes difficult when some portion of the sales presentation was handled incorrectly. Remember how Captain Mike forgot to probe deeply enough during the interview and missed the clues about Bud's apprehension toward sailing? Sometimes the closing sequence can be stalled or forsaken because the salesperson never overcomes a poor first impression or the sales demonstration does not go smoothly or is not thorough enough to meet the customer's standards of satisfaction.

Whenever a sale is lost, enter the circumstances of the event in your sales journal and analyze what could have gone wrong by taking apart the entire process in your memory. There are many reasons the sale may not have worked out. Asking too early as the insurance salesman did is one reason, but asking too late could be another problem. The Natural understands the importance of asking various degrees of closing questions throughout the entire sales process.

RAISING THE BUYER'S TEMPERATURE WITH CLOSING QUESTIONS

The Natural knows that one of his goals in selling is to raise the prospect's buying temperature. During the interview the customer's reading is normal, but when it is time to close, his desire should be feverish. This symptom is made possible because closing questions delivered on a gradient that the customer can acknowledge or accept are posed many times during the sales process. The Natural doesn't stop asking after the first try. Here are the results of a survey taken on closing attempts at the University of Notre Dame.

46% asked for the order once and then quit.

24% asked for the order twice.

12% asked for the order four times.

The study also revealed that 60% of the affirmative responses came on about the fifth attempt.

Never make the actual closing of the sale a big ceremony. The closing began with a very low grade question during the time of the interview when you might have asked the prospect:

"Have you seen any detachable wings that you really like?"

Then the temperature of the questions begins to rise and gets hotter the more you arouse the buyer's desire and the more you get into agreement with him on certain points of contact. Every time he agrees, you can take the questions to a higher level.

"Would you sell the corporate jet if you buy these wings?"

THE TEN QUESTION PRE-CLOSE CRITIQUE

Here is a readiness questionnaire that can help you judge whether it's time to close the sale or further develop a certain part of the sales process, such as handling objections or negotiating, that may have been neglected in your presentation. You can judge yourself and other salespeople by keeping this list of questions handy during the sales process .

- Did I do my homework and completely prepare for this sale?
- Was my approach strong, confident, respectful, and positive?
- Did I make direct appeals to what I knew were the buyer's specific interests?
- Did I adapt my natural sales dialogues to the particular buyer's moods and temperament?
- Was my sales dialogue natural, logical, reasonable, and persuasive?

- Did I demonstrate my product or service in the best possible light?
- Did I anticipate and confront all objections and turn them into a selling point?
- Did I prove the value of my product?
- Did I begin asking closing questions as soon as I got feedback and validation from my customer?
- Do I realize that the purpose of the visit with the customer is to close the sale for the benefit of all parties?

PREPARATION OF YOUR CLOSING TOOLS

All your closing materials should be at your finger tips, eliminating any sense of awkwardness. Pencils should be sharpened, pens handy, and contracts prepared or in the proper place. If you are selling merchandise, be sure you can deliver the goods if that is what was promised. Take your time and be prepared to stop and give the customer clarification when needed.

How is the lighting in the room? Is privacy guaranteed? Interruptions can break the closing mood and excitement. Make it as easy as possible for the customer to buy your product. Remove all obstacles that could delay or stop the sale. When a customer buys a car, house, computer, or copy machine and it's used during the closing sequence for involvement, be sure everything is in working order. Don't take anything for granted. There is nothing worse than sitting with a customer who has a high buying temperature and watching it drop dramatically because everything you touch starts malfunctioning or falling apart.

DON'T GET TOO EXCITED

Keep your voice down and stay calm. If you get too excited the buyer may wonder if this is the first sale you have had for awhile. I interviewed a literary agent who went overboard trying to do business with me. It was such a drastically different attitude from what I had experienced with other agents who were very busy and who could barely answer my phone calls, that I seriously wondered whether this agent had any other clients. I did some research and discovered the person only worked part time, because she was very well-off financially, and was very sporadic about her commitment to the publishing business.

CLOSING THE CUSTOMER IS FOR HIS/HER OWN GOOD

The Naturals believe their product is the best there is and they thrive on making converts. However, they don't force the customer—they just keep asking and sometimes this requires working within the framework of a long sales cycle with tougher customers. The goal is to induce the customer to make a closing decision with no guilt present on the part of the salesperson. You are helping him make a decision that will benefit him for life. This is only possible when you feel you have something very valuable to offer to the public.

I watched the nuns work from this position of passion when they taught English and other subjects. Sometimes they would pile on the homework and have to tell us why they were so strict. "Someday you will thank me for making you toe the line. When other adults around you can't read or write, you will be happy you put in this time."

Thanks to the good sisters my most successful closing script is called *The Someday You Are Going To Thank Me* dialogue. I have used it to inspire the customer to buy clothes, furniture, houses, and now educational materials.

The customer says: "What do you think, Danielle? Be honest. Do you really think we are doing the right thing?"

Danielle: "Someday you are going to thank me. Once you take my product home and make it your own you will be very happy you made this decision. I would not be saying this if, in good conscience, I didn't believe this was right for you. Keep in mind bad news travels fast in my business and if I steered you in the wrong direction, you wouldn't think twice about spreading bad rumors. I want your friends to work with me too. I know that if I don't treat you right, that won't happen. I am so sure that this system and your company are totally compatible that I know you will thank me and tell everybody else about how they can get involved."

CLOSING THE CUSTOMER IS FOR YOUR OWN GOOD

All the time, energy, and enthusiasm you have used on your prospect is wasted if you do not make the sale. Every time you do not complete the sales process, your business is in danger. Naturals *must* close and get the order because they have deeply aroused the buyer's desire for their product and there is no looking back. However, it will become impossible to close the customer unless her desire has been awakened. The insurance salesman who attempted to sell me a million-dollar policy might as well have been talking to a corpse.

SEE THE CUSTOMER'S VIEWPOINT

Put yourself in the prospect's shoes and try to imagine the questions that are going through his mind right before he signs on the dotted line. "Do I really need to buy this?"

"Is this product as good as the competition?"

"Should I wait?"

"Will they stand behind their product?"

"What will my friends think?"

Anticipate these concerns and then create a sales presentation that reduces your customer's anxiety. Recently we bought some expensive recording equipment so I could make my audio programs at home. All the previous questions went through our minds. Should we wait and continue to pay expensive editing fees in a professional studio? Will the quality of work be as good? What will my friends with whom I have done recording business think about this? Can the company really afford this expense right now? The salesperson who closed the sale focused on the excellence of the equipment. He was a master technician and used his knowledge to convince us that in the long run his product would give us better programs, at a great savings, in a convenient recording location—our office or home.

SPOTLIGHT THE BIGGEST NEED

Every Natural knows that he must work the closing around the need that is pressing on the customer the most. The recording salesman kept listening to me say how concerned I was about the quality of the recording on his equipment in comparison to what is used in a studio. He helped me discover that his equipment was exactly the same and his credibility was strong. He had been in this business his whole life and had worked with some greats in the speaking and music business. Everywhere I walked I saw photos, letters, and memorabilia from his successful career. During the course of my sales presentations I concentrate on what the customer brings up over and over. "I love your system but how can I get my staff to use it?"

I will spend most of my time discussing how to implement the program and keep the staff motivated to continue to use it. So rather than spend too much time talking about how the whole curriculum will increase office productivity—a workbook on that subject has been developed giving specific guidelines to follow—I know that my time is better spent on this customer's biggest objection.

CONFRONT PROBLEMS BEFORE ATTEMPTING TO CLOSE THE SALE

Mercedes-Benz automobiles' biggest problem may be price. The salesperson must prove value and worth in order to overcome the buyer's concern that the price is so much more than the competition's. If the value of that car is not clearly understood and an attempt is made to close, the salesperson will hear, "We need a little more time to think this over." Then they will go back to the BMW dealer and compare again because, in their minds, they still don't believe they will be getting more for their money.

NO SURPRISES, PLEASE

"I don't think I mentioned that the price doesn't include air-conditioning."

"You still have to buy the legs. It only includes the table."

This is the best way I know to throw a wet blanket over the end of a closing presentation. Do not ask the customer to sign on the dotted line until every fact is out on the table. I have been involved with car salespeople, decorators, contractors, architects, hotel managers, and others who keep secrets until the end. In one instance, I was quoted a price, agreed to it, the goods were installed, and three months later I received the bill in a different amount than I had been quoted. The cover letter said: "The cost of these materials went up and the labor took longer than estimated. I never received a phone call apologizing or explaining what happened. I suppose I could have ripped the shades off the windows and sent them back, but instead I just stared at the bill and felt like once again I had been taken advantage of by a so-called professional.

INVOLVE THE CUSTOMER IN THE CLOSE

"Test these wings, Joe."

"What is your favorite color carpet, Jean?"

"Where is the first place you will go on this motorcycle, Bernie?"

When I sold houses I often stayed at the home to close the sale. "Let's sit out on the deck and go over this purchase agreement together. I've got one copy and here's one for you."

If you sell stoves and ranges, get the customer cooking.

If you sell bikes, get them riding.

If you sell copying machines, get them operating one.

Bookstores are filled with people thumbing through the merchandise. Music stores blast the latest tunes over the speakers while customers listen and buy.

Whatever it is you sell, put it to work for you with the customer.

A GREEN LIGHT MEANS "GO"

I've taught my children the same song for 25 years when they reached the appropriate age to cross at traffic lights. It's a perfect closing tune, too:

"The green light says go. The red says stop. A yellow light in between. We look to the left and to the right and then we cross on the green."

The customer gives us feedback and sometimes we must use caution (yellow light) before we proceed, but other times customers give us both verbal and nonverbal signals to move ahead—green lights—and that means move fast. Captain Mike got a green light when Bud asked him how much the monthly payment on the boat would be. The forward-moving signals come in the form of questions and statements.

"Can I pay for this video on the payment plan?"

"How soon can I get delivery?"

"Do you have a money-back guarantee?"

"Are the introductory prices still in effect?"

The customers make positive statements that give you the go-ahead.

"We've been looking for someone with your knowledge for a long time."

"The price is well within our budget, surprisingly enough."

"I am so glad you have these in stock."

Besides questions and affirmative statements buyers may ask you to fill some requirements before they are in a position to purchase.

"I have to have the system before Christmas."

"We need training in order to operate this machinery."

"We will probably buy one of your videos and see how we like it."

Non-verbal expressions are buying signals also.

- The buyer leans forward
- You notice excitement in the face and eyes
- They agree and nod frequently
- Some of my customers have hugged me and said: "I love it. I absolutely love it."

Whether they are subtle or bold with their acknowledgments, it's time "to look to the left and to the right and start crossing on the green."

THE SEVENTEEN BEST CLOSING DIALOGUES I KNOW

Tom Hopkins taught me this when we were negotiating my first speaking engagements with his company. I hadn't agreed yet, but he knew I was excited so he used the famous *Trial Close.*

"Which month should we plan on your delivering your first sales seminar, July or August?"

This closing solution is only appropriate after the customer has given you plenty of agreement that you are both on the same closing path. Many salespeople try this approach too soon. I walked into an art gallery one evening and the saleswoman talked to me about an artist for about five minutes and started using the Trial Close with a painting that cost $32,000. I just listened, but it was rather funny.

"A $2,000 deposit will reserve this piece for you. He may not be doing any painting for the next few months because he's starting some sculpting. Think about at least reserving this one because his things move fast."

The woman didn't even know my name at that point. I was casually appreciating an artist's work and she started finalizing the deal.

Some customers need help putting the whole picture together before they say "Let's do it." This is called the *Sum-It-All-Up Close.*

My friend Ruth King who manages a hotel in St. Joe, Michigan, works with corporations, assisting them with their sales meetings and yearly events. Recently she told me how she landed a big account by using the Sum-It-All-Up close.

"Mr. Smith, we can provide you with a completely equipped conference room that seats up to 300 people. In addition, we can give you four small rooms that accommodate the workshops you have planned. Our staff will provide a delicious lunch with three menus you can choose from at a cost of less than $6 per person. I will also make sure every participant gets writing materials and plenty of ice water. Should I go ahead and reserve our facility for your group on August 6th?"

I've used this method for years and it always gives my buyers a positive picture of my proposal. Learning International conducted some sales research and found that 75% of the salespeople who used the summation method of closing combined with a direct closing question were successful at getting the business. The next close comes near the end of the presentation when you are 95% assured of the outcome. It's called the *Assumptive Close,* and believe it or not it is the most natural of all the closing solutions; but it takes the most experience and self-confidence. Watch the bottled water representative who comes into your home or office and notice how he assumes and then acts on behalf of his product for your own good. You may have three full bottles of water but he just notices the one empty one. Without saying a word he walks in with the full bottle and walks out with the empty one.

When you go see your doctor with a sore throat, he takes a look at the problem and then may say "I'll give you a shot of penicillin."

How would you feel if he turned around before he walked out of the room and said to you, "What do you think? Should I give you a shot?" You would seriously question this so-called expert. When the closing scene is sizzling, the excitement is flowing through everyone's veins, just get the agreement out and start to write.

When I am selling a video system, the buyer gets a free homework package of my books and tapes. When I use the Assumptive Close with an enthusiastic customer, I write up the sales slip and call for an exchange of autographs.

"I need your autograph and phone number on this line and while you are doing that I will give you mine inside of your new book."

Sometimes they respond with the request before I get a chance. I will say: "I need your autograph on this line."

"Only if I can have yours in my book, Danielle."

Talk about natural!

I Own This Product Myself is a close that has always impressed me both as a customer and a salesperson. It works because your credibility skyrockets when the customer knows you own the same product or service that you are recommending. Imagine that you are talking to a car salesperson who says:

"I have teenagers too, and I can honestly speak from experience. I just bought our family this same car about six months ago and we all love it. I am getting 40 miles to the gallon and it drives very smoothly."

When you talk to a buyer honestly you are no longer just a salesperson trying to make a commission, but a fellow consumer who has invested in the same product.

My customers were dying to move into the same neighborhood I lived in when I sold homes because they knew and figured I was on top of property values and no agent in her right mind would put her housing dollar in a bad location. My only problem was, once I sold all the houses in my neighborhood to my customers, I had to start wearing disguises in the grocery store.

Be careful how you use the next solution—*The Friday Night Special Close.* In order to get the buyers to act immediately, entice them with a special discount, gift, lower prices on quantities, a credit plan, or some added feature.

We offer our homework package of books and tapes for $199 at the seminars. They normally sell for $305 by mail. I tell my audience of student/customers that they must act today in order to get that price. It includes five items and sometimes the buyers test me and say, "Well, I already have one of the tape albums or the book so you can deduct the retail price of that from the special homework package price."

That arrangement takes away from the impact of the special. If I start making up all sorts of side deals with buyers standing at the counter, it could have a negative influence on others waiting in line to buy my materials. When you offer a concession, be sure you stick to the plan, otherwise the buyer might start wondering if the product is worth it or how much lower they can negotiate with you. If you want to offer several options, write it up before you open your store, booth or counter for business. If you decide to do one special, make your offer a legitimate one, and don't allow yourself to get backed into a corner.

Use *The Single-Issue Close* when the customer brings up a problem. Recently I used a trial close on a customer to whom I was selling a time planner. "Which do you prefer, the black or the burgundy velcro cover?"

The woman said: "I really wanted it in leather."

It doesn't come in leather, so I began to use the *Single-Issue Close:*

Danielle: "As I understand it, the time planner suits your needs?

Customer: "Yes, the size and layout are perfect.

Danielle: "Do you feel the price is reasonable?

Customer: "No problem.

Danielle: "So the only issue is the leather?

Customer: "I love leather.

Danielle: "When I first developed this planner I agreed with you, but my customers started complaining about the scratches on the leather, the fact that it had no secret pockets to store little pieces of scratch paper, and the general appearance of it after a few months of use. Everyone began turning it in for a velcro planner. The velcro holds up well, is stain-resistant and looks smart. Leather is a wonderful product, but we found that it didn't belong on the cover of a time planner. Keep in mind it would have to be a more expensive product if it was made out of leather."

Always be patient with the customer and use your experience and knowledge to help you with the single issue close.

Because some customers shopping for clothing get very confused, a smart Natural knows how to use *The-Narrow-It-Down Close.*

I worked in Dayton's Department Store in Minneapolis while I was in college, and one time a woman came in to buy a winter coat. She must have tried on fifty coats. Finally I said to her:

"You seemed confused. This happens to me, too, when I have so many choices. Let's narrow it down to our favorite choices."

She agreed, and we concentrated on the coats that were attractive on her. This approach works with just about anything—different types of insurance policies, service contracts, homes (and all their components such as flooring, countertops, bathrooms, and appliances) and cars.

The Pros and Cons Close is an essential solution in complex situations where there are many considerations for the buyer to contemplate. Just write two lists: On one side of a piece of paper you write "Pros"; on the other side write "Cons."

Let's use the detachable wings for our example. Near the end of the presentation, all of the executives are beginning to argue among themselves and it's time for you to step in.

"I know this is a complex situation. Let's list the reasons for and against this purchase so we can get a clearer picture of how effective this change can be."

The Natural does everything in her head and gets customer involvement. Start with the pros so that by the time you come to the cons the flow is upbeat.

Pros

- Unlimited travel possibilities
- Over the long haul, the expense is minimal compared to airline flight prices that are rising daily
- Safer once you learn the hang of it
- Complete implementation program offered to all personnel from our trained staff
- Convenient—just fly out the window
- Innovative—you'll be the talk of the industry
- Better service offered to your customers because you eliminate travel problems

Ask the buyers to bring up the first objection:
"Now tell me some negatives."

You will be amazed how few negatives are cited once you bring everything out in the open.

Cons

- Messes up the hair in flight
- Poor weather conditions

Have faith in your product and rely on your knowledge. Objections do come up in the closing process too, so be prepared. Many times the salesperson tries to resist the worries that the customer has all the way up to the closing sequence. Put them on paper and analyze. After you have countered each objection on the cons side, wrap it all up with another trial close.

"It looks like the pros far exceed the cons. Some of the negatives you brought up will be far from your thinking in three months when you see the increased productivity and happy spirits of your fast-flying personnel.

"Since these wings must be special ordered, shall I put a rush on this or will the standard four-week delivery suffice?"

The Dollar Is It Close is a must for people who are very concerned about the bottom line. I used this with investors who told me, "Don't call me unless the numbers are right."

Then I would select investments that worked for their financial portfolio. I put all the numbers together on a work sheet so that I couldn't be taken off guard.

In the case of the detachable wings, bottom-line might be a big issue. Try options like this.

"What value should we assign to better decisions made faster, Mr. Executives? Could the better decisions increase your company profit by $1 million a year?"

Do your calculations ahead of time. Remember, almost anything can have a dollar value placed on it. Always put conservative values on certain issues because inflated figures won't be believed or acted upon. Compute your figures in two ways.

1. On a yearly or monthly basis: "Your airline bills are presently running $100,000 a month for the executive team. I've studied the seasonal pattern of the trips. If we just fly to cold areas by commercial airlines from November to April, you can show a possible savings of $35,000 a month."

   On a long-term basis:
2. These wings will last a minimum of 10 years. That's a savings of $1.5 billion over that period of time."

Use round numbers to help the prospects grasp the total picture. With detail-oriented buyers, pull out your pocket calculator and get as detailed as necessary.

The Gosh I Hope We've Got It Close creates a sense of scarcity and customers respond to that when the product is truly worthwhile and popular. We all remember the "Cabbage Patch" doll. The public went crazy and the dolls became very scarce and hard to find within the first week of their arrival in stores all over the country. When customers couldn't find these dolls in their cities they would get on a plane and look in other cities until they found one. I kept track of this sales coup and one night I watched a man on television tell the story of his fight for one of these dolls.

"I stood in line for 2½ hours in Fort Worth, Texas, to get my little girl one of these dolls."

The announcer asked him how his daughter had heard about the doll and why he bothered to respond to her difficult request.

"She saw it advertised on TV and she decided that it was the only thing she wanted for Christmas."

When the supply is low, the buyer is motivated. If the prices are about to go up, you owe it to the prospect to use *The Gosh I Hope We've Got It Close.* The approach is that they should buy now while they still can. When we remodeled our home, the carpet representative from the mill told me that I should order the goods before December 6th because the cost per yard was increasing another $1.50. She computed the extra cost and told me what my savings would be. Since every product can be obtained if the buyer is willing and able to pay enough, fear of scarcity translates into fear of having to pay a higher price. Even on ordinary commodities like gasoline, this can become a real problem when the buyer cannot conceive of an acceptable alternative.

How do you use this close without resorting to the old-time high pressure tactics that are so likely to make the buyer angry? Be scrupulously honest. As long as you do, you will continue to build the long-term relationships with buyers that are the source of a lasting business.

"I don't want to sound like I'm crying wolf, but I'm really concerned about a strike. The best thing to do is buy the materials right away and get them out of the warehouse in case a strike shuts the plant down."

"The artist is not going to be doing this type of work for the next year while he is on sabbatical. There are only two pieces left."

"At the rate her May calendar is filling up, I would try to select a date immediately with your committee and call back so that I can at least put a hold on that date for you for the next 10 days."

Besides being based on the truth, everyone loves to know that their choice is in demand.

Use the *Why-Wait-Close* to give the customer some long-term perspective. Very few things besides computers, calculators, and telephones have gotten cheaper over the years. Mickey Rooney said when he was a kid he bought a chocolate soda for 5¢. Today, depending on where you go, it costs almost $3. Ask the customer at the closing sequence:

"Is it really smart to wait? Think about items you purchased 10 years ago (be specific). What would it cost to replace your car, home, or art collection today? (Include a personal story.)

Sometimes when people seem to be stalling during the decision time, they may be worried about something. Worry shows up when confidence is missing. When buyers feel self-confident they usually buy immediately. Self-confidence to buy comes from many factors—the salesperson's knowledge and ability to determine the customer's needs early in the discussions, past experiences with a product or sales representative, financial capability, the ability to see a bright future.

The Natural cannot read a crystal ball when the buyer wonders:

"Will diesel gasoline be available in five years?"

"Will convertibles go out of style?"

"Will the prices in this neighborhood go up?"

Only the past and the present is a sure thing. Use the *Confidence Close* when you have done a thorough job of explaining things to a worrier, but he wants you to read the stars.

"All we can do is look at this product's track record. We've studied these figures very closely, and it has come through beautifully for us in the past. Remember, every decision anyone makes is a hostage to fate. Isn't that what keeps life fairly interesting? When I bought this I didn't know what the future would bring either. If I had delayed, I could never have taken advantage of this opportunity. All of us must examine the facts and make the best possible choices, and then proceed. Don't you agree?"

The first-time car, house, insurance, computer, designer clothes, or other big-ticket item buyer is nervous and you can help him or her with the *Confidence Close.* Show your buyer plenty of testimonial letters from satisfied customers and include true stories of cautious buyers that you helped cross over the buying bridge.

When everyone is ready to buy your product and no one wants to make the first move, take over and use the *Let's Just Do It Close.*

Start filling out the purchase order and ask reflexive questions.

"What is your home address?

"Telephone number?

"When would you like the wings delivered?

"A $2,000 deposit is required. Do you want to write a check or put that on a credit card?"

There is no need to say "Do you want to buy these wings?" I found that between the time I started writing out the form until I completed it, the indecisive client usually had reconciled himself to the purchase if everything else was handled professionally. Your personal belief and confidence in the product has a great deal to do with how effectively this close can work.

Sometimes a customer may stop and ask: "Do you really think we are doing the right thing?"

At that point, I find my *Someday You are Going To Thank Me Close* very appropriate and effective.

"I not only know you are doing the right thing, someday you will thank me. Just imagine how relieved you will be every time you fly over the airport in your town and see all those passengers waiting in line trying to board an overcrowded plane. You can fly low and give them the peace sign and take off like a rocket."

Notice how I spotlight a certain point that I think will strike a nerve. My buyers hate airports and with the detachable wings they can kiss those days good bye. I keep reminding them of it even during the *Someday You Are Going To Thank Me Close.*

The Frozen-Chosen Close was used to sell hand made buckskin boots to advanced ice skaters.

"These boots are only for those skaters, like yourself, who have been out there on the ice performing for several years. The beginner would not appreciate the comfort or durability of the boot as well as the flexibility allowed for high jumps and low sit-spins."

I used this close and have passed it on to students in many industries. Some may think it sounds a bit snobby but if used in the proper circumstances, prospects should end up feeling entitled to the product because they've earned the right to buy the product or service. A good example is the American Express Gold or Platinum Cards or the Advantage Air Miles offered at American Airlines and other companies that have mileage programs. "I think you are entitled to this service, but I need you to fill out some information for me. Can you provide me with the names of three people who are willing to recommend you to our program?"

Colleges, graduate schools, and exclusive country clubs all use the Frozen-Chosen dialogue to close. It depends on what motivates people. Some want knowledge, prestige, or maybe safety. (An example of the latter is the buyer who has to be approved by the board of directors to move into a guarded-gate community.)

The Naturals in insurance sales use this approach with customers for certain health policies. "You will need to pass a strenuous physical exam before I can guarantee you this package. It's been earmarked for the non-smoker who is very fit physically. You seem like an excellent candidate."

The buyer really wants the policy now.

The Shall We Dance? Close is my favorite. In the beginning of my sales career I never had the courage just to just come right out and ask at the right time. I beat around the bush in my own way because I was afraid of rejection. Sales educator Larry Wilson says, "Fear of failure and fear of rejection are the most significant barriers to success and fulfillment in selling."

The closing moves remind me of my experiences at the Friday afternoon "mixers" back in my high school days. I went to an all-girls high school and the students from a nearby boys' high school came over for a dance on Friday at 3:00 P.M. I love to dance and could hardly keep my feet still when the records startèd blaring, but I hated to ask the boys to dance. I finally realized that they were all glued to the side of the gym walls, and unless I started something, I'd really embarrass myself by dancing alone.

The first time was the most difficult. Once I broke the ice, everybody began to dance. Then the boys started to ask me to dance. I told each guy that asked, "I'd love to, but I promised Pete this one, so how about the next fast song?" Later I began having the same problems in selling. Once I started asking, everybody got into the swing of things and on many occasions buyers were backed up waiting to ask me if they could buy.

Here is how to use the *Shall We Dance? Close.*

"You are giving me every indication that you are just crazy about these wings. What have you got to lose? With your assistance I would like to write this order up. Shall we dance?"

The Celebration and Appreciation Close is enjoyable. You did it. Recheck all your paperwork and make sure you filled out the forms correctly.

Now confirm everything by saying, "You did the right thing. I get very excited every time someone gets involved with my wings because I know how much you will enjoy them. And thank you so much for doing business with me."

Don't forget to ask for referrals.

"Do you know of anyone who might want to buy a pair of wings?"

More after-sale habits will be discussed in Chapter 11.

HOW TO MANAGE THE BUYER WHO SAYS NO OR MAYBE

Jimmy Durante ended his television shows on Sunday nights like this. He walked to the door and put his coat and hat on, paused, looked around at the camera and said: "Did you ever have a feeling like you wanted to stay?"

Then he'd start taking his coat and hat off and look at the camera again saying, "Did you ever have a feeling like you wanted to go?"

Some buyers can be like that. No matter what a salesperson did, they were up in the air about buying the product. When some customers don't have the courage to admit why they are hesitant use the *Stop Closing Close* to get to the truth of the matter.

I worked with a couple who I knew couldn't purchase a home until they sold their present home. Finally, one Saturday I got a call from them telling me they had sold their home and wanted to come down and buy the one I had shown them. They had seen everything on the market and explained that they were "ready to buy because we have to be out of our home in 60 days." We made an appointment for four o'clock that afternoon.

I spent the entire morning singing "Someday you are going to thank me" thinking I was close to a sale. But they spent the entire morning looking at homes that were under construction. Because builders were giving away the store during that cycle, they were charmed by the developers who promised a trip to Hawaii for two if they bought a home from them.

I met them at the scheduled time and used all the right words and moves but something odd was happening. He kept going to the bathroom and she kept tapping her finger on my desk. Before I started writing anything up, my instincts directed me to the following *Stop Closing* words.

"I want both of you to know that I am first and foremost a person, not a salesperson. I understand what people do and how they feel because I am one. I sense that you are struggling with an issue regarding the purchase of this home. I want you to know that I think it would be great if you moved into this place, but if you decide against it, it won't be the end of the world for any of us. But before I go any further, I am compelled to ask you something—do you need to give me an update on your situation?"

Do not say anything further until the prospective buyers answer your question. I waited for what seemed like eternity, and then the wife said, "Frankly, Danny we put a deposit down on a new home earlier this afternoon and we were going to compare the two homes. We had every intention of buying from you, but a billboard on the freeway directed our attention to this other location. We can't pass up all the options they are going to offer us."

I thanked them for telling me the truth and then asked them what those options were. Then we worked a Pros and Cons sheet between the two homes and the other home won out.

It's never easy to lose a sale when you spend months or maybe years working on a big order. Use the *Stop-Closing* solution to end everybody's misery. Buyers are human and are capable of doing unpredictable things when it comes to money. Be understanding and compassionate. Sometimes that means you have to bite your tongue. There are some specific suggestions to handle sales recovery in Chapter 12. Remember not to become attached to any one prospect. If you are business developing daily, these disappointments won't be as devastating.

Be polite and gracious and keep your ethics intact. Don't resort to being dishonest or making promises you can't keep out of desperation. These things come back to haunt salespeople. If you feel there is a chance to make one more presentation to the customer, by all means follow your instinct. Maybe a third party testimony or a deeper explanation of an overlooked point could turn it around. If it doesn't, know when to give up.

Another reason the buyers may be saying no is, the buyer wants to take a closer look at competing products. "Danielle, we want to see what the Victor Video Training System is like before we invest in anyone's program."

While I would never knock anyone else's product, I would review the strong points of my program one more time and emphasize the features that I know Victor and some of my other competitors do not offer.

"I understand you want to comparison shop and it seems only right, but keep in mind that I am the only sales educator who has a video on the family, health, and overcoming stress. In this day and age you have to make more than just professional how-to's available for your staff."

I want to make it easy for my prospect to call me back at a future date and purchase my product.

Another reason you lost a sale could be that you overlooked or did not do something. Take a close look at the lost sale so you can avoid making the same mistake next time.

— Did you arouse interest early?

— Did you spend some time thinking through the questions you asked your prospect?

— How did the demonstration go?

— Did you ask for the order too early or late?

— Did you summarize at the end?

— Did you do the same things wrong at previous lost sales? Is there a certain negative pattern you have gotten into?

Another problem could be that you gave up too soon. When we put together the Kennedy Clinic, one of the weaknesses of my telemarketers was that they gave up too soon. I had salespeople from different companies tell me that they only received one call regarding the program. People give up to avoid

— wounded pride

— irate prospects they previously talked with

— any further threats to the ego.

People come in all shapes, sizes, and moods and you simply cannot take their reactions personally. I have eaten my words over the years with prospects. Some customers have been very ornery to deal with and then suddenly they call back or walk over to my booth at a convention two days later and say, "I'll take your whole system."

Please review the following case study and answer the questions that follow. You will recognize many closes and solutions that were presented in this chapter.

A CLOSING CASE STUDY

During the past year Dixie Robb has been calling on a very large national sales company in hopes of selling several of the offices the Danielle Kennedy Video Sales Library. The company has purchased other competing systems but not the Kennedy System. This firm dominates the industry, and Dixie would love to land her product in their branch offices nationwide. She has called on the senior vice president, Ted Trainer, four times over the last few months and is about to make a fifth attempt.

Since her last visit to see Ted, Dixie's company has come out with a new series of programs on recovering from a sales slump. She knows these tapes are unique and decides to make this her reason for calling on Ted today.

Dixie: Hello, Ted. It's nice to see you.

Ted: (In a friendly voice) Good to see you too, Dixie. But if you are going to try and sell me some video tapes I might as well tell you right now, it's not in this quarter's budget.

Dixie: I am sorry to hear that, Ted, because Danielle has just produced a new series of programs that is going to revolutionize the sales industry. (She takes out a beautifully packaged five-pack series of tapes called the Kennedy Sales Slump Recovery Series.) The sales slump is the biggest problem salespeople face and no one can address the topic more credibly than the Mother of Sales Development herself—Danielle Kennedy. And there is no educational series on the market today that handles the problem. This program will get your burned-out salespeople back in action fast. We are forecasting that within 12 months, sales managers will notice a 25% increase in market share because their staff will have the tools to counteract a critical slump and outside negative forces that immobilize their productivity.

Ted: Sounds appealing.

Dixie: (Handing the video series to Ted) Because of our company's research and development department, as well as the expertise of Danielle Kennedy, who studies the market trends continually, the most up-to-date case studies and solutions are presented on her programs. Don't you think our packaging is first class too?

Ted: You people do a nice job.

Dixie: Her sales slump series gets very specific. She gives activities each day that ensure the salesperson will be making money within a given period of time. A great deal of research went into this plan. Now that Ms. Kennedy has her own recording studio and graphics art staff, we've been able to hold down our prices to a very competitive level. What do you think?

Ted: (Looking at the brochure and program) I like it, but as I said before . . .

Dixie: (Breaking in and focusing on the budget problem) Ted, I can appreciate your budget problems, but I am in a position to ship you as few as one or two systems at group discount prices and put you on a three-month payment plan, so you can get your sales staff on the recovery program immediately and see how your weaker members can start producing again.

Ted: (Showing more interest) Well, I would like to try it, but I just can't see how we can do it today.

Dixie: That's too bad Ted because I am running this line of videos on a very special introductory price. The individual programs retail at $89.95, but we are introducing this series at $49.95 each, and I would still offer you a group discount. (Dixie feels as if she may have him wanting the goods, but she thinks he will try to put it off for awhile.)

Ted: That is a very good price, but I'm just ...

Dixie: (Interrupting Ted) And we will throw in a Homework Package if you get the whole system. That is Danielle's complete library of audio tapes and textbooks, worth over $400. That saves you an additional 25%. (Dixie really wants this account because it will give Danielle a major foothold in a large international company plus future profitability. Under normal circumstances she wouldn't have included the Homework Package.)

Ted: (In a subdued voice) My people really love her work and this sure sounds like something I should take advantage of.

How Would You Handle The Close?

1. Do you think this sale will close?
2. What would you do after Ted's last comment?
3. What appeared to be the biggest obstacle to closing this sale?
4. Did Ted give any closing signals? Identify them.
5. What did you like and what did you dislike about Dixie's closing style and methods?

Part Four

SERVICE

11 The Lingering Style: Unforgettable Personal Promotion and Five-Star Customer Service

> *"It is just the little touches after the average man would quit that make the master's fame."*
>
> ORISON SWETT MARDEN

The Natural creates a new member of his powerful sales force every time he or she closes another satisfied customer. I built a 100% referral system over a four-year period with little or no after-the-sale gift and remembrance budget by delivering outstanding service during the time of the original sale. NOTHING REPLACES THE SERVICE YOU DELIVER TO THE CUSTOMER. If you take care of people, they will take care of you.

One of the most dedicated members of my auxiliary sales force was a man I like to call "Wonderful Jack." He bought from me and then, over the next 12 months, instructed 10 of his friends to go do the same thing. The slickest advertising campaign in the world couldn't generate that kind of business.

One day Jack called me and said, "Remember when I first met you I mentioned I had diabetes? I recently had a diabetic attack and I have lost the vision in both of my eyes. It is necessary for me to review all my assets and investments and make sure my family has a strong financial foundation, in case I cannot go back to work.

"I realize that I have too much cash tied up in the wrong places. You always say people need more real estate so I want to buy property now and get some appreciation growing that can be tapped for my children's college education at a later date.

"Do me a favor, Danny. Go to your office and pick up a blank sales contract and bring it over to my house. I will have a deposit check waiting for you when you get here. Show me where to sign and then pretend my eyes are your eyes and find me a good investment property."

What did I do to deserve that kind of response from a customer? When I worked with Jack and his family I did not drive a fancy car or have extra money to spend on personalized gifts. All I had was my desire and energy to give him service beyond the call of duty. When he received such service, he gave me his trust and powerful support.

If you don't have a big budget for self-promotion and after-sale gift programs at this point in your career, concentrate on communicating frequently with your customers. You will impress them every time you pay them a visit, write a personal note, or make telephone contact. It doesn't take a big splash to dazzle people. Most of us just want a little communication that keeps us informed and assured that someone cares about our welfare.

To the ordinary salesperson, closing and finalizing the sale is the completion of servicing the customer's needs, but for the Natural, it is only the beginning of a new business development series of events. Ted Levitt, editor of the *Harvard Business Review,* says: "The sale merely consummates the courtship. Then the marriage begins. How good the marriage is depends on how well the relationship is managed by the seller."

Follow-up with communication that has a positive effect with the customer. Some examples follow:

—Initiate a call to the customer to say "thank you" and find out if he or she is pleased with your product.

—Accept full responsibility for problems that may have developed. Don't pass the buck and say, "Shipping should have known better."

—Tell the customer what you can do for him rather than what you cannot do for him. A friend gave us an expensive cappuccino machine for a wedding gift that leaked. When we took it back to the store to find out if we were doing something wrong or to get a new one, the salesperson said: "Oh, I remember selling this, but I have no idea how it works. Our floor manager is out to lunch. Do you just want to leave it here and pick it up later?" The saddest part of this story is that saleswoman's post-sale methods are common practice in today's business world.

THE KINDERGARTEN FOLLOW-UP CLOSE

I learned a simple but effective method of follow-up communication from my daughter's two kindergarten teachers. Every Friday she came home with the "Kindergarten Kronicle." This was a sheet of colored paper divided into sections such as: nursery rhymes, math, science, or special projects. The top of the Kronicle always had an eyecatching statement like

"What a week!" Under a category like science the teachers wrote the following summary:

- We finished our five senses unit.
- We studied hearing and did the "sounds of music" experiment.

The page was filled with specific activities the children were engaged in throughout the week.

When I read the weekly report every Friday, I was reassured that these teachers were doing an outstanding job. Those teachers are a couple of Naturals who know how to keep the parents happy. If you are working on long-range projects with customers, write your own version of "The Kindergarten Kronicle" to keep those you serve informed.

FELICITOUS FOLLOW-UP RECOMMENDATIONS

Ask yourself one question before you begin any follow-up effort with the customer—How can I be sure I will get the job done? If you know from the start that you will not remember to send a note or make personal visits on a regular basis, then sign up for a follow-up program that does the work for you. I always handled my own follow-up work with the customer because, to me, there isn't a better source of new business development than a satisfied customer.

Here are some follow-up pointers that only you can make work with your group of supporters.

- When a customer is pleased with your service, ask for a testimonial letter immediately (See Chapter 3's Endorsement Dialogue). Use quotes from these letters in your printed advertising and brochures.
- Write old customers personal, hand-written notes frequently.

   "I was just sitting at my desk and your name popped into my head. Are you still having a great time flying all over the country on my detachable wings? If you need any extra wing cleaner, I can stop by with a case any time. Hope Jim and the rest of senior management are having a great year."

   If you run into an old customer anywhere, follow up with a note: "Great seeing you at the UDC Christmas Party. You must be running marathons these days. How do you keep so fit? I will call you in the early part of the new year for a quick lunch or a run!"

- Don't sacrifice the personal touch for electronic convenience.

   A friend of mine who is national sales manager for a window-covering manufacturer recently made this comment:

   "There is no longer 'the personal touch' present in business communications. I haven't actually talked to a member of my sales staff for weeks. I've listened to their voice mail or received their message by facsimile. The sad part about it is that that is how we are communicating with our customers." I don't count leaving messages on voice mail or answering machines as legitimate follow-up. If you are having trouble getting through, leave a message on the machine that you want to talk to them directly or intend to stop by in person at a designated time.

- Follow-up calls are business development calls. When you initiate a call or a visit to an old customer, you will discover she has been waiting for you to call so she can give you more business. "By the way, Danielle, Jenny Craig International is one of my clients and they saw your video on health the other day and want to talk to you about making a purchase."

  Thus, it makes no sense at all not to call or write notes frequently to past clients. You no longer have to prove yourself. Just show up!

- Organize your follow-up system. I used a card file and once a month I worked on contacting names under one letter of the alphabet. I spent the next two weeks working that group by foot or phone. Keep the past customers in a filing system separate from current prospects. You may want to keep records of them in the trunk of your car as well as your desk, in case you are out in the field and want to make a quick visit.

  Certain salespeople prefer to pay for an outside client follow-up service to ensure birthday and anniversary cards are sent. The ideal scene is a combination of both. I like to use the spontaneous check method throughout the year. Out of the blue one of my customers might receive a card that has a message on it that reminds me of them. Often that card has arrived when my customer needed a quick pick-me-up. That type of thoughtfulness stays with people a lot longer than a predictable birthday card.

- Follow up by following your intuition. I drop everything when my intuition reminds me to call an old client. I remember one time I was driving down the freeway and I started thinking about an older couple to whom I sold a two-bedroom home a few years back. Something told me to pull off the road, look their number up in my address book and call them immediately. As soon as the woman answered I knew something was wrong.

  She said: "Don died over the holidays and he just loved you so much that before he passed away he warned me not to put this house up for sale with anybody else but you. I was thinking about calling you the other day because I can't stay here alone anymore. My daughter wants me to move in with her this summer. Can you drop by and get things started for me?"

KEEP THOSE CARDS AND OUTRAGEOUS GIFTS COMING

My dad received more client gifts during Christmas week than any other person I have ever known. People valued his business and showed their appreciation with Wisconsin cheese baskets, leather-bound almanacs with his name engraved in gold on the cover, clocks, books, and special jellies and preserves. He loved every minute he spent opening the gifts and explaining to mother and me who they were from.

His favorite gift came from a man Dad did business with for over 25 years. The customer made him a "This Is Your Life" scrapbook that included photos, memos, and newspaper articles about my father. He kept that scrapbook on the living room coffee table until the day he died.

Gifts like that take time and love to put together and you can't put a price tag on their value. You don't have to spend a fortune to show people that you care. If you are high on creativity but low on funds, you can come up with some interesting mementos for your customers.

My budget was minimal when I passed out Christmas presents my first year in sales, but I made the most of what I had. I found a woman who hand-carved Christmas ornaments in my neighborhood. She designed each ornament in the shape of a house with a welcome mat at the front door. Then I had separate ornaments made for each of my customers with their name inscribed on the welcome mat. When they hang my ornament on their Christmas tree each year, I hope they still remember me.

As your business begins to grow, it becomes important to make allowances in your budget for gifts and promotional items. There are many companies and catalogues that can provide you with great gift ideas. They will send these items anywhere in the country. Here are just a few suggestions I have found in my research:

Golf accessories that include ballmarker money clips or golf cart clocks, The Ultra-Thin Calculator Business Card Case, calendars, clocks, data banks, memo minders, key rings, luggage tags, picture frames, briefcases, pen and pencil sets, leather coasters, software programs, desk planners, attache cases, and executive overnight bags.

I know a Natural who uses a gift service that prepares customized baskets of unique gifts for any occasion throughout the year. She has sent me a Valentine's Day basket filled with all my favorite candies, a pocket mirror and lipstick set, a heart-shaped picture frame and perfume. Those are fun to open because each gift is individually wrapped inside the basket.

I believe that Christmas is the most important time of the year to keep in touch with customers. Birthdays, anniversaries, and special holidays like Valentine's Day or Mother's Day are fine too, but sometimes you can overdo a good thing. I preferred the Christmas season to say thank you and then kept in touch by note, personal visit, or phone calls throughout the year.

Spur-of-the-moment surprises also work wonders. I enjoyed delivering a carton full of groceries on moving day to my customer's home. Items I included were milk, cereal, fruit, and bread. After I handed them the staples, I told them not to bother cooking that first night because a reservation was made for them at the best Italian restaurant in town, compliments of me.

It is very important to tie in a gift with the customer's need. They appreciate something that they would normally not be able to give themselves but would love to own. Chapter 4 lists 12 months of gifts and promotional ideas you can implement when the time is right for your budget and your credibility.

CONSISTENCY COUNTS

Customers like consistency. My dad always knew he would receive the Wisconsin cheese basket from a certain manufacturing company. He counted on the birthday card from the salesman he worked with in the Southwest. He was no longer their customer but a cherished friend.

Remember the local butcher who ordered your mother's turkey for 25 years. How about the dentist who put braces on all 3 children's teeth? Now he is wiring up your granddaughter's mouth. Your insurance man may be white at the temples today, but when you two first met he had just come back from his honeymoon.

NOTEWORTHY NEWSLETTERS

Newsletters are becoming increasingly popular in service businesses where after-the-sale follow-up and education is important. I found them very effective because I could keep my customers informed of current changes on a regular basis. Don't start the project unless you can meet deadlines and make it interesting each month or quarter. Apply the writing tips you learned in Chapter 5 and follow these additional suggestions:

- Give yourself a monthly drop-dead date to complete your next newsletter. Put it on the calendar.
- Newsletter writers run out of news fast. Be sure you understand what you are getting into before you make a commitment you may not be able to fulfill.
- Newsletters should contain practical information, not advertising.
- Research newsletters from a minimum of five other industries to get ideas about format.

The *Kiplinger Letter* was my model when I began writing a newsletter for homeowners. I subscribed to it for many years and found it very enlightening. I had a small budget and couldn't afford to hire a graphic artist to design my logo and format, so I went to a local junior college and visited the advertising department. I explained to one of the teachers what I needed, and she agreed to have her class submit some designs to me as one of their projects for the semester. Schools are happy to use the business community as their laboratory of study. Many of the students are very gifted and want the opportunity to display their talents.

POST-SALE PROBLEM SOLVERS

Danielle Kennedy Productions offers a money-back guarantee on all products. Sometimes after people buy a time-planner or a video tape, they take it home and realize it is not what they wanted or they need some creative suggestions on how to use the material. My staff knows that a customer complaint should never lead to conflict or the loss of business if they handle the problem correctly. Our company philosophy regarding complaints is: "View the problem as an opportunity."

No matter how good your product or customer service department is, complaints and problems will come up. Aim to please the unpleasable with these suggestions.

- Let customers vent their feelings. Encourage them to get their anger and frustration out in the open.
- Don't argue with a customer.
- Never say: "You do not have a problem." If the customer is upset, whether the problem is perceived or real, acknowledge her viewpoint.
- Share your point of view. As politely as you can, begin to explain what you think happened.
- Don't delay taking action to remedy the situation. I was furious when the cappuccino saleswoman put me on hold with her attitude.

• Imagine you are the one with the complaint. How do you want to be handled at such frustrating times?

THE BONUS OF ADD-ON SELLING

I met my insurance salesperson 20 years ago outside of church. He specialized in selling casualty and life insurance to individuals. I asked him if he would stop at the house because our family was growing and life-insurance protection was needed.

After he listened to our needs, he did a thorough job explaining his programs that best suited our situation and we went ahead and bought a policy that offered a built-in savings program, too. Then he taught me a lesson in natural selling that I later applied to my own career—he kept on selling after the sale.

"Danielle, how much life insurance protection do you have?"

I had a $5,000 policy.

"If I were you I would consider getting some more protection. There is a term policy that I would like you to take a look at. It doesn't have a savings program on it, so the premium is inexpensive. You don't need a savings program policy because the one you both just bought covers those needs. Take a look at this rate chart and see how low the premium is for an additional $50,000 worth of term insurance, especially for you."

We were surprised we could afford the premium and went ahead and added it to our insurance protection.

Add-on selling is a fact of life in today's economy. You don't get a printer when you buy the computer. The new home doesn't include the granite counter tops or the marble flooring. The suit looks snappier with a new tie and expensive dress shirt. Naturals know that customer satisfaction will increase if they present additional options to their customers.

Follow these add-on selling rules.

• Prepare ahead of time. Have a list of options and prices handy. Create sales talk that suits this type of presentation.

"For an additional $9.95 you will receive the 16 Business Forms that Danielle talks about in Chapter 24 of the book you just purchased. You can use these practical forms to track prospect calls or document important information that you may be forced to find months from now. Most of our customers purchase the forms when they buy the book because they both work together to help you make more sales."

• Don't make suggestions too early. I watched a saleswoman aggravate a woman right after she sold her a very expensive evening gown.

"You must have these Louis Lure Shoes to go with this ravishing Peyton Petite."

This increased the woman's buying remorse and she canceled the Peyton Petite sale and left the store.

- Use the thoughtful and positive approach.

    Do not ask customers if they "need" shoes or ties. Instead say: "We just got some beautiful holiday pumps in that would look smashing with that dress. Take a peek and see what you think."

THE THREE BASIC PRINCIPLES OF PERSONAL PROMOTION

The lingering style of the Natural results from doing a good job during the sales process, delivering customer service with speed and honesty, and initiating planned follow-up programs that produce bonus business. In addition, when your budget allows you to spend more money, begin to orchestrate personal promotion campaigns that will keep you on the minds of your customers every time your product or service comes up. The foundation of personal promotion is based on these three principles.

1. Your name is your best advertisement.

2. Your face is your logo.

3. Your reputation is your trademark.

These three factors are more important than how much you are able to impress the public with your grand-slam promotional events. If you keep your integrity and reputation intact every time you close another satisfied customer, the personal promotion ideas I am about to present will merely enhance your solid reputation.

KENNEDY'S ADVANCED PUBLIC RELATIONS METHODS

Natural selling is similar to political campaigning. The public relations pointers that I am about to give are regularly implemented by any candidate running for an office. Don't try campaigning for business unless you have a budget proposal. As your career begins to grow, add any of the activities I suggest when the need arises. For instance, a photograph that you are presently using on stationery or cards may have been taken by an amateur when you were short on funds earlier in your career. This photograph change may seem like a little thing, but customers may get the idea that you are a vain 60-year-old peddler using a 16-year-old prom picture.

Some of you may be reluctant to plaster your photo everywhere or feel self-conscious about making a big splash in your community in order to get attention. I can appreciate your feelings because I was raised in the Midwest, where most of us were taught to play down our talents and remain "humble." It is hard for me to believe that I overcame "call reluctance," since my biggest fear growing up was that somebody might call me a "show off."

My customers are responsible for starting me on the personal promotion campaign trail. When I began to win top sales awards, my company contacted the newspaper and reporters interviewed me for a story. My customers would cut out the newspaper article, send it to me and include a note that said, "We are so proud of you. We brag to all our friends about our wonderful salesperson. I have shown this story to all my neighbors. Keep up the good work."

I realized that self-promotion's purpose is to establish personal credibility. It gives you the opportunity to spread more good rumors about yourself and keep up the momentum. Do not confuse personal promotion with showing off or acting overbearing. If you have proven your worth every step of the way during your career, there is nothing wrong with letting people know that you can do a good job. You owe it to the public to let them know you are out there because you can save them the heartache of choosing disreputable people to handle their business affairs.

The Kennedy Method is a Four-Step Process:

Step One: Size up your first-step
What is your present situation?

— Are your basic materials still effective? Photos, stationery, business cards, brochures.

— Can you afford to hire a personal public relations representative? It may be worth it but be sure you are clear about step number two.

— What are you trying to do? Create more market penetration? Better Positioning?

A few years back I began to feel like The Flying Nun. I am referring to Sally Field's role in the television sitcom. I read that Sally tried for years to break out of the image that the entertainment industry had of her. She couldn't get any other decent parts on television or in the movies because producers stereotyped her as the flying nun or Gidget, another role she played during the early days of her career.

Finally Sally got the opportunity to play the role of *Sybil*, a television drama about a young woman who had multiple personalities. She did such a magnificent job in that role that she landed her Academy Award-winning role in the movie *Norma Rae*. This progress took years, and she claims she had to completely reposition herself and distance herself from people who tended to box her into a certain image.

I can identify with Sally because once I became well known as a speaker in the real estate industry, I was also trapped. I needed to let the rest of the business world know that I had accomplished many other things besides selling homes.

Step Two: Create objectives. It is time to list the goals and needs you discovered when you sized up your situation.

One item on my objective list was to write a general sales book. If you are trying to reposition or expand your business, you may write: "Develop more ancillary products." The detachable wings sellers may need to offer free flying lessons to interested prospects to expand their customer potential.

Step Three: Devise the plan and be specific. A point on my plan said, "Enroll in a writing program. Get a Master of Arts degree in writing and develop the sales book while attending graduate school."

Your plan might specifically say, "Go to flight school and get a Peter Pan Pilot's License. Who else can sell and give flight instruction at the same time?"

Step Four: Initiation and proaction. Now you must implement this program. Much depends on how much money you have to work with or whom you know that can assist you in developing certain written materials you may need. The following suggestions are based on the same type of advice a public relations firms offers. Prospect by phones or by mail. I have done it, and once you get started it is just like any other type of selling activity. Talking to a newspaper reporter or a TV producer is really no different than door-knocking a business or a home. Remember to use the friendly "phone-home" voice and "walk in like you own the place," strategy.

Here is a public-relations checklist you can customize for your own use.

— Develop new materials, such as stationery, logo, brochures, press package, product, and services. You should use one or more depending on your budget or access to talented helpers.

— Compile a list of targeted media contacts and send each one an updated press kit. My list includes: major women's magazines, business publications, airline and travel publications, major broadcast outlets, regional/local print and broadcast. (Local libraries can help you locate this information.)

— Write a half-page personal profile about yourself. Pretend you are a reporter writing a press release about the most interesting character you have ever met—you.

— Have publicity photos taken. Be sure you select a professional who puts you at ease in front of the camera.

— Reprint articles you have authored which can be sent to media.

— Generate stories about you, your industry, or related topics. As soon as stories are completed, contact reporters by phone and determine their interest in running this type of feature. If the interest is there, a media kit should be sent out immediately. A follow-up phone call should be made and further interviews would be set up with you.

— Prepare a column that deals with your product or service. This column can be circulated locally or nationally.

— Write a magazine article. Publications regularly accept authored articles for publication.

— National broadcasts. This is not easy to do, but if you have an interesting slant which is newsworthy, contact producers to determine their interest. Contact local newspapers and television or radio stations and generate reasons why you would be an excellent guest on a show or person to be interviewed.

Personal promotion, public relations, after-the-sale follow-up, and customer service are all terms for prospecting and generating more business. Naturals seize every opportunity to show just how valuable their products and services are to the public. A Natural's behavior is based on personal habits of living that develop Supernatural character and willpower.

12

Overcoming Sales Slumps: Recovery, Renewal, and the Return of Your Natural High

"Where there is hatred,
Let me sow love,
Where there is injury,
pardon,
Where there is doubt,
faith . . ."

ST. FRANCIS OF ASSISI

Every time you work your way out of a sales slump, you practice the virtue of forgiveness—forgiveness of self and others who have betrayed or ignored you. A sales slump develops when a salesperson stops prospecting and becomes lazy which leads to guilt and fear of failure. It creates an imaginary life of its own that lashes out and attempts to defeat your inner voice and spirit, filling it with self-doubt and negativity.

I always know when I am in a slump because it kills the passionate kid inside of me who is full of good ideas, energy, and a positive outlook about people, places and things, in spite of setbacks or misfortune. The central focus of this chapter is devoted to the healing and recovery process that follows a sales slump. An important part of this rehabilitation is reacquainting yourself with your inner child from the past—the energetic and playful one that rebounds from setbacks and disappointments. This part of you is critically needed to cope with the built-in roller coastering inherent in the selling life.

193

RESILIENCY

For the last 25 years I have been surrounded by resilient and energetic children. They have taken me on a perpetual roller coaster ride up and down some scary places like the corridors of hospitals, a result of their risk-taking and flamboyant behavior on skateboards, surfboards, trampolines and high bars. Their ability to pick themselves up, dust themselves off, and continue on, just as if nothing had ever happened never ceases to amaze me. But I must admit, in the midst of observing each of their temporary defeats, their behavior had a bearing on keeping my own irrepressible spirit alive during my bouts with destiny.

THE ULTIMATE REBOUNDER

When my son Daniel was 13 years old he started surfboarding the waves of the southern California ocean. Before and after school each day, he donned his wet suit and paddled out to encounter his favorite companions—three- to six-foot waves. I never realized how committed to surfing Daniel was until one fateful afternoon when the lifeguard station called my husband at work and told him that Dan had been in a "bad surfing accident."

It seems that one minute Dan was freewheeling and riding high on the crest of a wave and the next minute he was thrown off and reeling under it. Only this time when he surfaced to the top of the water, the point of his board was speeding directly to the center of his face. The corner of his right eye made contact with the point, bringing the board to a sudden stop. Daniel's eye was blinded with blood while his body somersaulted uncontrollably deep within the aftermath of the lost wave.

To this day I cannot imagine how he made his way to the shore. When the lifeguard first noticed Daniel he was almost on the sand, crawling on his knees with one hand covering his eye. Mike rushed him to the emergency room and then they were sent to a plastic surgeon's office. His eye was saved, but he received 26 stitches that began at the inside corner of his eye and ended at the bridge of his nose.

It was the only time I wasn't around to comfort a child during an emergency because that afternoon I was on an airplane flying back from a speaking engagement. By the time Mike and Daniel picked me up at the airport, Dan's eye was stitched up and sealed with a bandage.

On the way home from the airport, he told me the whole story of his accident. I cried and told him how sorry I was that I was not at home when he needed me to be by his side.

He said, "That's okay, Mom. You don't know how to surf anyway. Guess what? The doctor said I can go back in the water in seven days."

I thought I was hearing things. How could he do this to his mother? I never wanted him to go near water, even a bathtub, for the rest of his life.

For the next week he kept pressing me to let him get back on his surfboard. One day, after I had repeated "no" to him for the 100th time that week, I gave in and he left me teary-eyed and speechless, as I watched him head to the beach.

"Mom, you taught us never to give up." Then he handed me a bribe—a framed poem that he bought "because it reminded me of you."

Mother To Son
by Langston Hughes

Well, son, I'll tell you:
Life for me ain't been no crystal stair.
It's had tacks in it,
And splinters,
And boards torn up,
And places with no carpet on the floor—
Bare.
But all the time
I'se been a-climbin' on,
And reachin' landin's,
And turnin' corners,
And sometimes goin' in the dark
Where there ain't been no light.
So, boy, don't you turn back.
Don't you set down on the steps
'Cause you finds it's kinder hard.
Don't you fall now—
For I'se still goin', honey,
I'se still climbin',
And life for me ain't been no crystal stair.

The handsome water rat is over twenty-one years old now and ranked among the top thirty amateur surfers in the nation.

Dan taught me a valuable lesson that I immediately applied to recovering from sales slumps: WASTE NO TIME FEELING SORRY FOR YOURSELF. START OVER IMMEDIATELY.

TWO TYPES OF SERIOUS SLUMPING

There are two types of sales slumps: Type A—The "Real Slump," and Type B—The "Contrived Slump." The Real Slump is a manifestation of conditions beyond the salesperson's immediate control. Some factors that contribute to the Real Slump are a downturn in the economy, poor health or temporary physical handicaps, extended personal or family problems, or exhaustion and overwork.

The Contrived Slump involves such things as a bad attitude, a negative sales environment, lack of consistent business development, poor self-discipline, and low-level product affinity.

The Real Sales Slump

The Natural triples his business development efforts in a poor economy. If it takes 100 phone calls to get one good, solid lead under normal conditions, count on making 200 or 300 phone calls when times get tough. Perhaps the prepared entrepreneur or storeowner sees a slow Christmas season coming, plans ahead by offering after-Christmas sale prices in the fall to stimulate buying activity. She begins her Christmas hours early in the pre-season which increases the chance for sales. She makes it affordable and convenient for the customer and adjusts her profit-share accordingly.

The slump caused by the economy is the easiest to cope with, if you are willing to roll your sleeves up and go to work without complaining or fighting the facts of your current business life. I see far too many salespeople acting like helpless victims, complaining to each other about the difficulty of the situation, and refusing to change their work habits to keep up with present circumstances. Their idea of selling is order-taking. This type of activity is merely a response to a customer who is waving money in our face. It requires no people skills or proactive business development. A dog can be trained to fetch an order blank and a check from a customer's hand and deliver it to the person standing at a cash register. In some cases the dog moves faster than some salespeople I know. When challenging times hit, a Natural takes the following precautionary measures.

- Go over the books and find out if your pricing is competitive. Be prepared to reduce your profit margin in order to present a very attractive package to the consumer. "You can't afford not to buy now at these prices."
- Entice the buyer with perks and benefits. When the new housing market flattens in southern California, builders make an all-out ef-

fort to attract buyers by offering substantial savings on their existing homes. They offer buyers new cars, landscape allowances, interior design bonuses, trips to exotic vacation spots, and appealing financing packages.

- Examine ways you can make it easier for the customer to get involved in your product. As a sales educator, I have noticed that many salespeople cut back on training materials when a down-turn affects them. I do everything in my power to offer affordable homework during those times because I know that is when they need to study the most. The ideas I offer to my customers will decrease their financial pressures and get them back in business fast. Because our company believes we can help people live more productive lives during any economic situation, we strive to offer opportunities such as the special video-of-the-month at prices they cannot resist with flexible payment plans.

  Treat your customer the same way you would a family member who is struggling to do his best but experiencing some temporary difficulties. Make the necessary sacrifices but still stay in business and profitable.

- Adjust your budget but do not make noticeable advertising cutbacks. Now is the time to get the word out that you have something special to offer that the customer will not have the opportunity to take advantage of at a later date. Cutting back on effective advertising is as harmful as ceasing your business development efforts. Keep track of advertising effectiveness and be prepared to make adjustments but do not move away from the public eye. Dig in and let the marketplace know you can serve them.

- Create and present exciting marketing plans to attract the consumer.

  One Christmas when times were tough, a major discount store created an ad campaign and price cuts on designer children's clothing. "Don't waste money on toys you end up paying for on credit for the next 12 months. Buy quality children's school clothes that last all year long at pre-Christmas special sale prices."

- Contact every past satisfied customer you have and ask for his or her assistance in a positive, upbeat manner. "I have got a problem. There has never been a better time to buy detachable wings. Help me get the word out. Do you know of anyone who may need to pick herself up, dust herself off, and take flight?"

  Even if he or she cannot think of anyone at the moment, your call puts the idea in his or her head and gets the wheels turning.

- Band together with other salespeople or business owners and brainstorm ways you can increase everybody's productivity. When I owned a sales company, I created the "Open House Weekend" concept with many other brokerage firms in my area. I contacted my competitors and suggested we all band together and buy a double-page ad in the weekend papers announcing our open houses, triple each office's number of houses held open for the public to preview both during the week and on weekends, and cooperate with each other by directing traffic at every open house to other properties advertised. It got all of us through some slow months and now the concept has been adopted by real estate companies nationwide.

Real slumps that are caused by personal problems, poor health, or exhaustion and burn-out require a certain recovery time. Follow the Kennedy Twelve-Step Plan and be patient. Hard work has proven to be therapeutic for me. After my divorce and the shocking death of my friend, it was the selling life that helped me recover more quickly. My customers helped me regain my self-confidence and feel better about myself.

The Contrived Sales Slump

Since I first began selling I have noticed how the attitude of a salesperson can make or break a company. Why do sales managers keep an "attitude without gratitude" around? Do they realize what terrible damage they can do? The following story is true and it happened at an outlet of a national store that I will never frequent again.

Several years ago I needed to buy some mini-cassettes for my pocket tape recorder. I was in a hurry to catch a plane, but when I arrived at the store I was forced to slow down. A salesperson had posted a sign on the door: "Please come back in fifteen minutes."

I looked in the window and saw a man behind the counter poring over paperwork and answering the phone. I decided to tap on the window to see if I could talk him into opening the door. They advertised their nine-to-five business hours and according to my watch, it was one o'clock in the afternoon.

He kept ignoring me and I kept knocking. Finally he yelled, "Can't you see I am closed?"

I said, "But it is in the middle of the business day. I need some items before I catch my plane in one hour."

He walked halfway to the door and said, "Look lady, I am snowed with paperwork and phone calls. I need to catch up. Try some place else."

Every sales manager should insist that her sales team do some self-examination at least once a year, in order to prevent personal and company recessions. When you suspect your sales slumping involves a problem between your ears, ask yourself these *8 Deadly Questions:*

1. Am I keeping bad company? I call bad company the "quicksand

crowd." You can find one of these rumor-control mongers hanging around coffee or copy machines, ready to criticize even the most heroic efforts of their fellow salespeople or management staff.

Refuse to get into a negative discussion with these fear-filled people.

Quicksander: "Did you see this stupid memo?"

The Natural: "Not yet."

QS: "We are all losing half our territories to that new rep."

N: "Find out who wrote the memo and confront him."

This comment always shuts up the complainer because he does not have the courage to speak up about his problems.

2. Am I lazy? Every lazy person is full of fear. She hates to give up her personal comfort to do something she finds distasteful. She expects all activities to be fun and if she finds out she has to do something that requires effort, she whines. These pleasure-seekers hate the word "process." This problem is very common in our society and stems from a lack of maturity, self-discipline, and willpower. It starts in the home when children are not given the opportunity to figure out their own problems or face consequences for certain behavior.

Remember that those things that you resist, always persist. You can make yourself physically ill by avoiding activities you know must get accomplished. Naturals do tasks early in the day so they can enjoy the rest of the day.

Here are a few examples of relief-filled activities:

—Calling a customer and reporting bad news.

"I feel terrible about this too, but I just found out the couch will not be ready for Christmas delivery."

Deliver the news like a person who cares and the customer cannot hold it against you. If you try to avoid people and keep them in the dark, they will end up causing all kinds of trouble.

—Return all messages promptly. Letters and phone calls will haunt you unless you handle them immediately.

—Keep promises you make. I hired somebody once who was very talented, but I lost sight of that talent because he never finished anything he started. In time, procrastinators lose all their credibility with the customer.

3. Do I avoid risk? Put yourself in green and growing situations at all ages. Adult development is a fact of life now because we are living longer than our grandparents did. Read the book *Age Wave*. It reassured me that I was on the right track by going back to school. Achievement in one area of a person's life does not give her the right to stop growing. Sometimes material success takes people out of the real world of risking and learning.

I have met many interesting people through the National Speakers Association, but my favorite members are not just speakers but people who do not take their abilities so seriously that they have stopped exploring other parts of their life. How interesting could a speaker be who never does anything but speak? What would they talk about?

4. Am I waiting around for things to get better? If you knew you had six months left to live, would you sell until your last dying breath? Would you be treating your loved ones the same way you do right now? What would you do differently?

I see people waiting for the strangest things—watches, retirement, vacations, better working conditions, better houses, and spouses. An adult loves to wait—a child hates to wait. An adult needs a shock to bring her back into the present moment.

A magazine interviewed the survivors of a major airline crash a few years back. Their comments were revealing:

"I rarely complain anymore. The simplest things in life, like the smell of a fresh cup of coffee, thrill me."

"I started telling my family 'I love you' every day."

Why aren't we grateful? One of the most memorable moments in my speaking career happened in Soweto, South Africa, lecturing to students who matriculated through high school. For these young people who grew up in a one-room shack with eight brothers and sisters, very little food, poor living conditions, and an average school drop-out age of eight years old, their graduation from high school was little short of a miracle.

I gave them my "Keep it up. You got this far, so keep on going talk." I never received so much appreciation for my efforts. At the end of my speech, their applause was deafening. Then they began to sing in unison, like birds, filling the air with familiar sounds of soul music. I couldn't help myself, I just had to start dancing. Then they started dancing for over an hour. I didn't want to stop celebrating the precious, present moment with the happiest, most grateful people I have ever met in my life.

5. Am I giving in to mood swings? I was very moody when I started selling. The moods resulted from false expectations. I thought it would be easy to make a sale, and when it took longer than I thought, I got down on myself. I expected my friends to do business with me. I expected my family not to ask me questions like: "Did you sell anything today?"

False expectations, along with poor nutrition, can cause mood swings. Let everyone in your world know what you sell, but do not expect your friends to do much business with you until you prove yourself to the stranger first. Wake up every morning and say, "Anything is possible today. Am I ready for it?"

6. Am I comparing myself to others? The selling environment is highly competitive. If you are new on the sales force and you mind everybody else's business, you could be headed for trouble. When I was a sales manager I watched new salespeople psyche themselves out by comparing their efforts to those of the seasoned salesperson. Perhaps the veteran

brought in an order that appeared to be an easy sale to the new member of the sales force. They did not understand that the Natural has credibility established and is receiving the rewards of hard work and long hours that were put in earlier in his career.

There is plenty of business to go around, but first concentrate on earning the right to receive it.

7. Do I talk too much? Sometimes the biggest distractions in the world are the people who work with us. I remember one morning going into the office very early in order to get some calls out of the way so I could spend a solid afternoon business developing. I loved to go in the office early because it was quiet and I could get many things completed before normal business hours. I was just starting to bask in the quiet when a full-blown conversationalist walked in. Her opening remarks broke my concentration for the rest of the day.

"I had a terrible night. I got home late so there was no dinner prepared. That put my husband and kids in a rotten mood. Then they started complaining because there was no bologna in the refrigerator for tomorrow's lunches."

She kept rattling on and I started wondering if there was any bologna at my house. I dropped everything I was doing and called the family.

"Do we have any bologna, Joe?"

"Heck no. You better go get some."

"Okay."

Like a fool in a trance, I went out and bought bologna, brought it home and was told that there was no bread to make bologna sandwiches.

"What good is this without bread, Mom. Just give us lunch money. We can't wait around for bread."

8. Who is responsible for my motivation to sell? Motivation is rooted in reality. My motivation started with the desire to buy a family freezer. Once I earned enough money to buy the thing and fill it up, all I did was stare at the food inside of the freezer because I was too tired to prepare a meal and my motivation had changed.

"Somebody take me out to dinner," I cried. When basic needs are satisfied then we get extravagant reasons for wanting to make money. Motivation comes from within and nobody can motivate you but you. Sometimes we get ourselves stuck in a sales slump because we lose sight of the reasons that excited us to work hard in the first place. Our customers are part of that motivation, but the well-rounded Natural takes a periodic inventory of her strengths to determine what needs are not being met in her life in general. She senses, when she begins to feel lopsided or out of balance, that it is time to reevaluate her priorities. The money goals begin to center around parts of herself that have become stagnant while she was working to accommodate basic needs. Now that she has experienced financial success, it is time to do a self-evaluation in areas of her life that have been neglected.

Whether you have been experiencing a Real or a Contrived Sales slump, or just intend to focus your targets on certain neglected parts of yourself, the next two exercises will rejuvenate your energy and keep your motivation high.

TAKE AN INVENTORY OF YOUR STRENGTHS

The following is a list of strengths and assets people may possess. Take a separate piece of paper and record all of the strengths you believe you have.

SPORTS AND OUTDOOR ACTIVITIES: Active participation in outdoor activities and organized sports, camping, hiking, and so on. Regular exercise program.

HOBBIES AND CRAFTS: All hobbies, crafts, and related interests including any instruction or training in such crafts as weaving, pottery, and jewelry making. Any other interest to which you give time.

EXPRESSIVE ARTS: Any type of dancing, writing, sketching, painting, sculpture, modeling with clay. Ability to improvise music or play a musical instrument, definite rhythmic ability, and so forth.

HEALTH: Good health represents a strength. List any measure for maintaining or improving your health, including seeking adequate medical treatment when needed or yearly medical checkups.

EDUCATION, TRAINING, AND RELATED AREAS: All education beyond grade school, including high school, college, advanced study, specialty schools, on-the-job training, seminars, or special courses you have taken. Any high grades, any scholastic, and related honors.

WORK, VOCATION, JOB, OR POSITION: Include years of experience in a particular line of work (sales, management) as well as having successfully held different positions or received awards. Owning or managing your own firm. Job satisfaction including enjoying your work, good relations with co-workers or feelings of satisfaction with customers or staff.

SPECIAL APTITUDES OR RESOURCES: Having hunches or making guesses which usually turn out right. Following through on these hunches. Having a "green thumb." Mechanical ability. Sales ability. Mathematical ability. Skill with hands in constructing and repairing things.

STRENGTHS THROUGH FAMILY AND OTHERS: Having a spouse who gives love, affection, understanding and is interested in things you are doing and gives support. Relationships with children or parents which are sources of satisfaction or strength. Close relationship with other relatives and close friends as a source of strength.

INTELLECTUAL STRENGTHS: Applying reasoning ability to problem solving. Intellectual curiosity. Thinking out ideas and expressing them out loud or in writing. Being able to accept new ideas. Doing original or creative thinking. Having the ability to learn and enjoy learning.

AESTHETIC STRENGTHS: Recognizing and enjoying beauty in nature, the arts, or people. Using aesthetic sense to enhance home and physical environment.

ORGANIZATIONAL STRENGTHS: Developing and planning sensible short-range goals. Carrying out orders as well as giving them. Experience in organizing enterprises, projects, clubs, social, political, or other. Leadership positions in key voluntary and fund-raising projects.

IMAGINATIVE AND CREATIVE STRENGTHS: Using creativity and imagination for new and different ideas in relation to home, family or vocation. Working on developing and extending your imaginative and creative abilities.

RELATIONSHIP STRENGTHS: Ability to meet people easily, make them feel comfortable. Ability to talk freely to strangers. Good relations with neighbors. Treating people with consideration, politeness, and respect. Being aware of the needs and feelings of others. Being able to really listen to what others have to say. Helping others to be aware of their strengths and abilities as well as their shortcomings or problems. Relating to people as individuals regardless of so-called barriers. Giving people the feeling that you understand them.

SPIRITUAL STRENGTHS: Feeling close to God, a supreme force, or nature. Living what you believe. Being humble. Recognizing the dignity and brotherhood of all people.

EMOTIONAL STRENGTHS: Ability to give as well as to receive affection and love. Being able to feel a wide range of emotions. Being able to do or express things on the spur of the moment. Ability to put yourself in the other person's shoes; to feel what he/she feels. Understanding the role of your feelings and emotions in everyday living.

OTHER STRENGTHS: Making the best of your appearance by means of good grooming and a discriminating choice of clothes.

Humor: As a source of strength—being able to laugh at yourself and to take kidding at your own expense.

Liking adventure: Pioneering, exploring new horizons, or trying new ways. Ability to stick your neck out, to risk yourself with people and situations.

Perseverance: Having a strong drive to get things done and doing them. Ability to manage finances, evidenced by investments and savings.

Linguistic Skills: Knowledge of languages or of different people's cultures through travel, study, or reading.

SIX SECRET LETTERS

As you review your inventory of strengths, it will remind you of certain events and experiences. You will find yourself wanting to resume some activity that brought you pleasure and satisfaction earlier in your life. When I completed my list, I realized how much I missed taking dance class. I needed to lose some weight at the time and bring my cholesterol level down, so I began a three-times-a-week dance class and covered two categories on my inventory sheet—health and expressive arts.

Once you have tackled your inventory sheet, the following exercise will move quickly for you. You are now aware of the different aspects of your life that you wish to improve. You can best do that by taking the time to write six secret letters to yourself.

As an only child, I learned to develop a great imagination. I talked to imaginary friends and wrote in secret diaries to keep myself entertained. As an adult, this turned out to be very constructive for me. Secret letter-writing brought relief and a sense of excitement into my life when I needed it most. I realize now that it started my long-range goal setting. I prefer simple letters even today because it activates my imagination, in a way that charts and cold, calculated reports never will.

Through the years, all my wish letters have come true. I do it once a year and take them out to reread two or three times through the year. They are very helpful when I start to lose my sense of direction. It gives me the same kind of a thrill that some people receive when they read their horoscope. Instead of reading the stars, or paying other people to read into my future, I formulate my own plans through personal intuition, as well as my deepest desires and motivations. Letter-writing tips:

- Make a date with yourself to do this activity. Early morning or late evening when the house is quiet is the best time.
- Don't tell anybody about what you write.
- Write your letters in the second person just like a fortune cookie or a horoscope is written. This gives the letter a sound of authority. Let your other self—your inner trainer—write you a letter about your future.
- Be descriptive. Create vision and use your imagination. This will jump-start your motivation and you will take action.
- Include role models that excite you.
- Write six separate letters to cover the most important areas in our life: Spiritual, Physical, Mental, Family, Work, and Social.

Here are some samples to help you get started:

Spiritual

Dear Danielle:
Opportunity will open up this year for you to get away quietly for three days to your favorite retreat center to pray, meditate, and examine your daily life. Begin to plan the time and make responsible arrangements for your family's care while you are gone. This quiet time will energize you and refocus your commitment to serve others.

Your peaceful and calm friend, Danielle

Physical

Dear D:
Cut out that picture of Jane Fonda in a bathing suit and place it on your refrigerator. You will resemble that body soon. Choose dancing for your exercise because the music and movement recreates your childhood spirit of play. Select a book to educate yourself about food. In eight months you will be able to slip into a size four dress. Congratulations ahead of time. How did you ever get so slim after having all those children, my dear?

Your skinny friend, Danielle

Mental

Dear D:
You only have 30 more credits, less than two years, and you will have your college degree. This is the year to go back to school so go sign up immediately. Imagine how proud your family will be when they see mother wearing a cap and gown on her graduation day.

Your smart self, Danielle

Family

Dear D:
During the next 12 months you will take time to be alone with each of your children during certain times of every week. They are getting older and need more one-on-one time. If you think you communicate well with them now, wait until this time next year!

Your other mother, Danielle

Dear D:
You are going to go on a wonderful golf outing with your husband.

Surprise him and take some golf lessons first. Get a list of the top resorts and surprise him with a just-for-two weekend.

Your romantic friend, Danielle

Work

Dear D:
In twelve months you will be working full time in teaching and telephone sales. The next six months of classes will involve weekend and evening time away from family. Make no social commitments and cancel all extracurricular activities. Your financial position will remain the same during this difficult time if you do not incur additional expenses. This time next year you will be money and career ahead.

Your tough self, Danielle

Social

Dear Danielle:
Follow your intuition and eliminate that routine social engagement that is boring you to tears. Replace that time slot with a variety of fun with old friends you've been neglecting for years.

Your best friend, Danielle

THE KENNEDY TWELVE-STEP SALES SLUMP RECOVERY PROGRAM

Are you ready to protect yourself from those awful sales slumps? If you can make the commitment, begin this 12-step program immediately. The inspiration for this plan came from Alcoholics Anonymous and its founder Bill W.

Step One: Detach yourself from all customers and resume a heavy business development schedule immediately.

I worked my way into sales slumps because I counted too heavily on one or two customers coming through for me. When you spend all your waking hours hounding one or two people, hoping against hope, and acting like they are the last breathing prospects on the face of this earth, you are headed for a slump.

—Reread Chapters 3 and 4 on business developing by phone and foot
—Practice your two favorite phone and foot scripts

—Make an appointment with yourself to business develop

—Fill in the time, dates, and places on your time planner

—Begin keeping these business development appointments with yourself within the next 24 hours.

Step Two: Confront all unresolved problems and incomplete cycles of activity.

There was a woman who ran the Los Angeles Marathon, came in last, passed out at the finish line, and almost died from dehydration. Four months later she was interviewed on a national morning talk show. The host asked her why she kept running.

"I just wanted to finish," she said.

Humans can get carried away when it comes to completing activities we start. It doesn't feel good when we live in a world of unanswered phone calls, broken promises, and half-completed projects.

A good way to dig your way out of a sales slump is to start by cleaning up your physical surroundings both at home and office. Cleaning out the cobwebs, throwing away junk, or goods you never use anymore is therapeutic. It has nothing to do with being too picky. It does have a lot to do with clearing your environment of all objects from the past that no longer serve a purpose. This clutter is getting you down and taking away necessary energy.

Jeff Mayer, author of an excellent book on self-management entitled *If You Haven't Got The Time To Do It Right, When Will You Find The Time To Do It Over?*, says: "Stop cold, drop everything, and get organized. The issue isn't whether a desk is clean or messy. That's a smoke screen. The real issue is time and money: the quality of your work and the length of time to complete it. With an organized desk . . . fewer things will slip through the cracks. You can stay on top of all your unfinished work, locate papers and files within seconds, and become more productive."

This applies to both the home and the office, and everything you use in between including your car. Here are some guidelines to get you started. The clutter is getting you down. When you finish this assignment you are going to feel energized from completing so many physical cycles of activity.

The Home Zone:

Pretend it's moving day. Order a dumpster on a Saturday and get the whole family to help. When the job is done, plan a fun event or outing.

1. Buy plenty of garbage bags for trash or to package up items that can be donated to charity.
2. Sort all stuff into five categories: Clean, Sell, Donate, Trash, or Store.
3. Decide where to begin. This is tricky. Don't begin sorting one basket

or drawer full of trinkets when you can hardly walk through the room.

4. Work from large to small messes.

5. Do it all: Garage, closets, desks, drawers. Every family member handles his or her own space.

6. Elect a supervisor to sign the room off. Choose the pickiest member of the family to do this. Otherwise, the job for some of the kids may turn out to be rearranging junk into neat piles. The supervisor makes sure everything is thrown away.

Family Files

1. Either the husband, wife, or both of you can do this job. It doesn't have to be on the same day as clean-up.

2. Create Files: Correspondence, Tax, Reading, Action, Insurance premiums, Warranties, Photos to be put in albums, Family documents, Wills, Licenses, Passports, School information, Immunizations, Report cards, Pet records, Unpaid bills, Paid bills from A to Z.

3. Build three stacks and use the TPO method—"touch paper once." As you organize your desk, files, and drawers, pick up a piece of paper and make a decision. Do I dump this? Try these four stacks for TPO efficiency: a. To do, b. To file, c. To read, and d. To dump.

The Office Zone:

Go in early or stay late and reorganize and dump useless materials. Other people will distract you so do this in private if possible. Spread a big plastic bag or newspaper on the floor next to your desk. Take out one drawer at a time and dump it on the newspaper.

Use the same TPO method for all papers and objects you pick up. Act on all items immediately.

Place the most important green spectrum project on your desk in a file folder. Have it waiting there for you every morning.

Clean out your car. Use the same methods as indicated. Start with your trunk. Keep emergency child-care and first aid kits in your trunk. Keep some toys, books, and emergency supplies. How about an extra set of exercise clothes and shoes so you can sneak it in when the opportunity arises?

Step Three: Admit your mistakes.

Take responsibility for every problem you have placed on yourself. Be brutally honest and tell your customers if you have made an error. Naturals never lie because they know that nobody ever gets away with it. Sooner or later the lies land on your doorstep. I admire people who tell the truth, no matter how ugly it gets. My family and staff all know that they can come to me with any problem or trouble, as long as they are telling me the truth. I expect this of myself and those that I love. It is the only thing I have ever wanted in all my relationships. When truth isn't possible with people, I usually cut the tie because it is only an illusion.

Step Four. Forgive yourself.

My best friend killed herself in the middle of one of her worst sales slumps. The week before she died four of her buyers canceled their sales agreements with her and she took it personally. She blamed herself continually for problems that were not of her making.

Her suicide taught me to ease up on my own negative self-talk. Take me seriously when I tell you to quit dwelling on all the reasons you blew it with the last customer or made a mess out of your life back in the sixties. More misery is self-generated by individuals who won't let themselves off the hook for mistakes of the past. Never forget to love and forgive the best friend you have—YOU.

Step Five: Associate with sane, green, and growing Naturals.

Avoid the quicksand crowd and other friendly enemies. Some anonymous wise guy once said that a man is known by the company he avoids. Ask yourself:

- Am I altering plans for the day just to keep someone off my back?
- Am I taking time for a long lunch with a gossip-monger instead of brown bagging it in the office so I could go home early?
- Am I made to feel guilty by a certain group because I don't participate in every celebration that comes along?
- Are long moments spent on the phone with people I really resent but to whom I simply can't say goodbye?
- Do I find myself constantly caught in the middle trying to choose between my family and a certain friend?

If you answered yes to any of these questions, you are hanging out with a member of the quicksand clan. Use the word "commitment" frequently when dealing with these people. Remember the quicksanders cannot confront people directly. If they talk behind somebody else's back to you, don't kid yourself, they are doing the same thing to you when you aren't around.

A Natural who represents a sportswear line told me:

"I fired all my negative friends. I have many positive people in my life and we do not gossip. We try to figure out why we act and live the way we do and then create ideas to help each other grow and change. I feel much more at peace since I changed my friends."

Step Six: Say NO frequently.

Cut down on all activities that take you away from building a solid sales career and living a sane existence. Breakfast meetings, receptions, going-away parties, long lunches and dinners are not essential parts of the selling life. I never lost out on my career because I didn't attend certain functions. Avoid activities that extend your work day to your family and personal time. Do not make bold statements such as: "I wouldn't be caught dead at another one of those drunken retirement parties." Just quietly avoid these dates. If you are pushed for an answer say: "I am sorry but I have an important commitment."

Step Seven: Start eating right.

Salespeople pick up terrible nutritional habits by eating on the run. I was guilty of being a junk food addict in my early selling days. All that did was contribute to my mood swings. Sugar on an empty stomach takes you up and then down the emotional tone scale in a matter of minutes.

Food Tips:

—Eat plenty of fresh fruits and vegetables

—Eat whole wheat breads, grains, cereals, and pasta

—Cut down on sauces. Ask for spaghetti sauce and salad dressing on the side.

—Read labels. How much fat content does the item have? Remember that for every gram of fat indicated, you multiply that number by nine calories.

—Drink at least eight glasses of water a day.

—Eat when you are hungry. Do not snack on foods all day.

—Schedule your heaviest meal as close to six o'clock in the evening as possible. Do not go to bed on a full stomach.

—Moderate your coffee intake. It increases your appetite and makes you very nervous.

—Practice control over alcohol.

Ask yourself questions like: Why am I eating this?

What am I eating?

Sales slumps and unconscious eating habits go hand-in-hand.

Step Eight: Follow a disciplined exercise program.

I exercise four times a week for approximately 45 minutes. I started running when my 19-year-old daughter was three years old. I gained and lost 50 pounds before, during, and after childbirth. It was never easy for me, but I committed to exercise just as I committed to eating a meal when I was hungry. Exercise must be part of your survival or you will never do it.

Naturals use exercise to dance, bike, or run off frustration when they find themselves in situations that they cannot control. Disloyal, easy-to-hate prospects, or frustrating days of incomplete cycles of activity are mentally manageable when you take time to exercise your body.

Get a complete physical exam before you begin a program. When you get your heart rate up you are lifting your spirits as well. Chemicals called endorphins are produced in your brain and rush through your bloodstream when you work out. This type of natural high helps prevent the contrived sales slump that develops from a bad attitude and a depressed mind.

Use a measuring tape, not a scale, to monitor your weight loss progress. If you are having difficulty losing weight on your own, there are many positive commercial programs to assist you.

Step Nine: If you have a family, act like you do.

Naturals do not sacrifice family life for professional life. They accomplish everything they want to and use "back-burner" thinking. Here is how it works—force yourself to stop thinking about work. It is very hard for Naturals to do this at first because they are so passionate about their customers. But if you do not start practicing the habit, you will head right for a sales slump out of sheer exhaustion and lack of a personal life. Eventually you will hate your job.

One of my international computer sales stars is a working mother who sells up a storm. She conquered an out-of-balance lifestyle with my back-burner method of thinking. She told me she wrestled with her inability to put work on the back-burner at the end of each day. "For a long time I couldn't shift gears when I came home. I felt torn between my kids, kitchen, mail, and my briefcase. I was half listening to my husband and children. Now in order to keep my sanity, I force myself to put all job affairs aside until the children are asleep. With practice I have become very good at turning one thing off and another thing on. I am a master of compartmentalization. At first I felt awkward. When I arrived home each night I craved the personal time with family but was still wound up on work. Sometimes I just dropped everything and sat in a rocker with my baby and we would hug like crazy."

It has been difficult for me to learn this, but you have to put your foot down. At the office, my secretary screens my calls. At home I flick off the switch on my telephone. I'm not the President of the United States. Nothing is so important that it can't wait a few hours longer.

Another Natural salesman and dad told me he feels less stress since becoming a parent, thanks to his ability to compartmentalize. He says his overall workload has doubled but his stress level has been cut. Before he had his son, he would bring home work problems and worry needlessly. Now he focuses on his child and realizes that there is nothing he can do about these things until the next day.

Step Ten: Fight to stay an original.

Marsha Sinetar comments in her helpful book *Do What You Love And The Money Will Follow:* "To the extent that we accept our own greatness, the mission and charter of our own life, we want to work against anything either external (in society or through the actions and efforts of others) or internal (our own 'enemies within') that would hold us back."

It isn't easy remaining true to yourself and accepting your own unique greatness. On the one hand society admires people who are very much themselves—Woody Allen, Katherine Hepburn, or Stephen King (to name a few), but it isn't easy to be who you are. We are all tempted to conform to what society dictates as cool and acceptable. I have been criticized for many things that make me uniquely who I am.

I was told I would never make it as a salesperson, speaker, or a writer because I wasn't "upscale-market" enough. I guess that meant I was too simple-minded for the group. These comments made me doubt myself but only for a little while. The older I get the more I want to emphasize what makes me different from everybody else.

Stand up for yourself and be real. I tell new speakers that the only reason they copy each other's material is because they are afraid to be who they are. It is easier to present a cheap imitation to a crowd than a vulnerable and authentic version of the self. It ensures acceptance because someone else has used the content and been received well, so the copy cat assumes she can duplicate the other person's experience with the group. The content didn't have anything to do with the success of that speech. What earmarked it for greatness was the style, vulnerability, and willingness to love the audience that the speaker carried in her heart.

Step Eleven: Keep laughing. We are all going to die, anyway.

There is no medicine in the world that cures our ills like a good belly laugh. I am entertained constantly because I live with a bunch of comedians. When things look so bleak that I can hardly lift my head, someone in my home always makes me laugh.

My good friend John Rice, the other half of the "Rice Brothers" speaking act, was in a bad accident when a 75-year-old woman ran a red light. She put John in a body cast for over six months. The first time I talked to him after the accident he told me "how lucky" he was to be alive. He said, I am going to write a book called: *Breakfast in bed . . . and lunch . . . and dinner . . .*

John had to be turned over every few hours because he broke his neck. All he could do was lie still and look straight ahead. I asked him what I could send him that would make him feel better.

"Funny videos."

Step Twelve: Be grateful, count your blessings, practice faith.

Faith promotes peace and contentment. I was born into a family of believers, not religious fanatics, and I am thankful for that. My grandparents and other members of my family believe in something outside of ourselves that makes this world a miraculous place to live. They taught me to believe in a God that I could trust. Their faith was based on the belief that we are all God's children and we must respect everyone, no matter which church they attend. They showed me how a faith that is passionately practiced could provide the way, even in the dark, when I am not sure where I am or where to go. I learned by their example to trust my faith to provide peace in a world where anxiety and stress prevail.

My family has given me priceless gifts which I now feel compelled to pass on to you—an enthusiasm and appreciation for life, a divine faith, and the "sell-to-survive" instinct. Here is to the next one hundred years of Natural Selling and Natural Living.

Be sure to write for more information on Danielle Kennedy's
books, cassette tapes and video programs.

Danielle Kennedy Productions
219 S. El Camino Real
San Clemente, CA 92672
714-498-8033

D A N I E L L E

K E N N E D Y

READING LIST

Sales

Tom Hopkins, *How to Master the Art of Selling* (New York: Warner, 1980)

F. P. Buck Rogers, *The IBM Way* (New York: 1986, Harper & Row)

Danielle Kennedy, *How to List and Sell Real Estate in the 90s* (New Jersey: 1990, Prentice-Hall)

Thomas J. Stanley, *Marketing to the Affluent* (Illinois: 1988, Dow Jones-Irwin)

Charles B. Roth and Roy Alexander, *Secrets of Closing Sales* (New Jersey: 1983, Prentice-Hall)

Jeff Slutsky, *Street Smart Marketing* (New York: 1989, John Wiley)

Sherrill Y. Estes, *Sell Like a Pro* (New York: 1988, Berkley Books)

James F. Bender, *How to Sell Well* (New York: 1961, McGraw-Hill)

Business Books

Dr. Stephen R. Covey, *The Seven Habits of Highly Effective People* (New York: 1989, Simon and Schuster)

Roy Rowan, *The Intuitive Manager* (New York: 1986, Berkley Books)

Morgan McCall, Jr., Michael M. Lombardo, Ann M. Morrison, *The Lessons of Experience* (Massachusetts: 1988, Lexington Books)

William Davidow and Bro Uttal, *Total Customer Service* (New York: 1989, Harper and Row)

George R. Walther, *Power Talking* (New York: 1991, Putnam)

Nancy Anderson, *Work With Passion* (New York: 1984, Carroll and Graf)

Jan Carlzon, *Moments of Truth* (New York: 1987, Harper and Row)

Rosabeth Moss Kanter, *The Change Masters* (New York: 1983, Touchstone)

Tom Peters, *Thriving on Chaos* (New York: 1987, Knopf)

Marsha Sinetar, *Do What You Love and the Money Will Follow* (New York: 1987, Dell)

Warren Bennis, *On Becoming a Leader* (New York: 1989, Addison-Wesley)

Denis Waitley, *The Psychology of Winning* (Illinois: 1978, Nightingale-Conant)

General Interest and Inspiration

Napoleon Hill, *Think and Grow Rich* (New York: 1960, Fawcett Crest)

Theodore M. Hesburgh, *God, Country, Notre Dame* (New York: 1990, Doubleday)

M. Scott Peck, *The Road Less Travelled* (New York: 1978, Touchstone)

M. Scott Peck, *People of the Lie* (New York: 1983, Touchstone)

Shad Helmstetter, *What to Say When You Talk to Yourself* (New York: 1988, William Morrow)

John Bradshaw, *Healing the Shame That Binds You* (Florida: 1988, Health Communications)

Robert and Jane Handly, *The Life Plus Program for Getting Unstuck* (New York: 1989, Rawson)

Melody Beattie, *Codependent No More* (New York: 1987, Harper/Hazelden)

Judith Briles, *The Confidence Factor* (New York: 1990, Master Media)

Time, Self-Management, and Concentration

Ken Dychtwald, *Age Wave* (California: 1989, Tarcher)

W. Timothy Gallwey, *The Inner Game of Tennis* (New York: 1974, Bantam)

Jeffrey Mayer, *If You Haven't Got The Time To Do It Right, When Will You Find The Time To Do It Over?* (New York: 1990, Simon and Schuster)

Writing for Sales

The Right Word (Boston: 1983, Houghton Mifflin)

Richard Bayan, *Words That Sell* (New York: 1984, Asher-Gallant Press)

The Random House Thesaurus (New York: 1984, Random House)

Diana Hacker, *A Writer's Reference* (Boston: 1989, St. Martin's Press)

Health

Robert Haas, *Eat To Win* (New York: 1983, Signet)

Robert Haas and Cher, *Forever Fit* (New York: 1991, Bantam Books)

Covert Bailey, *Fit or Fat* (New York: 1977, Houghton Mifflin)

Audio Programs

John Dolan, *Negotiating,* (Colorado: 1991, Career Track)

Herb Cohen, *You Can Negotiate Anything* (Audio Renaissance, 1990)

Danielle Kennedy, *Selling—The Danielle Kennedy Way* (18 audio programs including the meditation tape for overcoming sales slumps: Danielle Kennedy Productions, San Clemente, California 714-498-8033)

Index